Overcoming the Overwhelming

A 40-Day Journey toward Rediscovering Faith in God

Revised Edition

By
C. D. Hildebrand

xulon PRESS

Definitions of Greek words, unless stated otherwise, are derived from Strongs Concordance.

The author has chosen not to use gender-specific pronouns unless specifically indicated, as she finds writing and reading "he/she" and "him/her" to be tedious. Please assume that any truth applies to both genders even though he, him, his, or mankind are used.

A free study & discussion guide for this book is available for download at: http://graceandfaithministries.org/overcoming-the-overwhelming.

www.xulonpress.com

*This book is dedicated
to my dearly beloved husband, David,
who is my closest companion
in life and ministry,
Our beautiful children,
Christina, Joella, and Timothy
who are our most precious treasures,
Their dear spouses, Eric, Ben, and Amanda
for whom we are so thankful,
and our ten amazing grandchildren,
Emma, Levi, Joel, Grace, Nathan, Amy,
Anne, Joshua, Alice, and Samuel
who bring us immeasurable joy
and who are the sprinkles on the icing
of the cake of our life.*

Table of Contents

Overcoming the Overwhelming

A 40-Day Journey toward Rediscovering Faith in God

Foreword

$\mathcal{T}$hese brave souls were the first to read the manuscript for this book. Their insights greatly contributed to the final product you hold in your hands. Read what they have to say about <u>Overcoming the Overwhelming</u>.

"I recall a trip I took one day as a young 20-something to Pier 39 in San Francisco. Exploring with a friend, we enjoyed watching the sea lions, breathing the ocean air, and eating Boudin sourdough bread and Ghirardelli chocolates. Walking along, we encountered a street performer getting ready to start his show. This man's specialty was freeing himself from a straitjacket with several chains and locks. Once the crowd made sure there was no possible way to get free, he'd narrate, with much humor, his escape. Quite certain he would never be free, I was surprised and delighted each time a chain came off him! How did that happen?

Once only the straight jacket remained, so he called me up from the crowd to verify how bound he still was. Let me tell you, he was snug! Sure, he could move some and talk plenty, but he couldn't do much beyond entertain the crowd with the jacket on. However, as I returned to the crowd, with a few quick motions, he freed himself! I'm not exactly sure how.

My mom's writing is kinda like that street performer. She is on a mission to bring Biblical freedom to those who love

Jesus. With her teacher voice, she exposes beautiful truths from the Bible. With each one, another chain falls. If you have overwhelming situations you are facing, take a look at this book and see how much God loves you! You will find yourself surprised and delighted each time a 'chain' falls right off of you. I am already planning on rereading chapters 9 and 33. What day will you find encouraging?"

Joella Haley
Wife to Ben, Mother to Joel, Nathan, Annie, Alice, and Sam
Beloved Daughter and Friend

"What I love about Cathy's writing style is that as you read, you get the impression you're traveling with someone who's been there. She doesn't write from a lofty theoretical perch, but rather as one who's quest for grace and truth has led her to something very special, something the whole world needs to hear!

In <u>Overcoming the Overwhelming,</u> you are invited to experience a 40-day journey of hope and illumination. With theological integrity and down-to-earth humility, Cathy uncovers many of the questions that have left us searching for clearer answers in discovering more of the personification of grace Himself, the Lord Jesus Christ. I am honored to recommend this book to you!"

Jeremy White
Lead Pastor at Valley Church in Vacaville, California
Author of <u>The Gospel Uncut: Learning to Rest in the Grace of God</u>
Co-Author of <u>40 Days of Renewal: A Journey Toward Freedom</u>
Husband, Father of three boys, and Friend

"I have known Cathy and David for more than five years through Facebook. The very first Facebook group page I became a part of was Grace and Faith Ministries, which

Cathy created and for which she is the administrator. I was still then very new to the revelation of the pure grace message, and the interactions and discussions of issues about Christian life and ministry helped me so much in my growth in the grace and knowledge of the Lord Jesus Christ. Since there was no one who shared and mentored me in the gospel of grace, God used Cathy and the members of the group to strengthen my understanding of the gospel of grace. Cathy and David became my personal friends. They also trusted me in the reprint and distribution of her first book, Are We Preaching Another Gospel?, in the Philippines, which is helping many believers, ministers, and pastors in their understanding of the gospel of grace.

Cathy's second book Overcoming the Overwhelming is another excellent book. It lays the scriptural foundation for triumphant and victorious Christian living through faith, not through human performance; by grace, not by the law; and by the Spirit, not by the flesh. While it is a natural reality that the believers will face challenges in life, God has provided His children the supernatural and divine enablement to overcome the overwhelming, as the title of the book says. The book touches topics and issues very relevant to Christian life and ministry. It is not so theological that it becomes irrelevant to practical Christian living, and yet the book remains very Biblical.

I am honored and privileged to be among those who have read this manuscript before its official publication. I highly recommend this book; it is worth your time and investment. Congratulations, Cathy, for a project well done."

Leopoldo B. Solis
Founding Senior Pastor, The Full Measure of Jesus Christ Christian Ministries
Co-Founder, Regional Bishop and Member of the Council of Bishops, Light Center
Professor, Grace Academy and Philippine International College

Speaker-Lecturer in Camps, Conferences, Seminar-Workshops, and Leadership Symposia
Author, The Reality of Our Rest in Christ
Husband, Father, and Grandfather
Beloved Brother and Friend in Christ

"Liberating and exhilarating, insightful, and sincere; this Biblically sound teaching clears away the dulling smoke and mirrors of an overwhelming, and burdensome Christianity, and in clear and simple terms reveals the truth of Jesus' Gospel that actually sets us genuinely free."

Donald Harris
Pastor and Teacher
Husband, Father, and Grandfather
Beloved Life-long Friend

"Thank God Almighty for inspiring my cousin, Cathy's, newest book, Overcoming the Overwhelming. Statisticians assert you can never prove anything, but through God's holy and true word, she proves that by grace through faith we have the power to overcome any and every anxiety, calamity, challenge, hardship, heartbreak, fiery dart, wearisome job, or troubled relationship.

Before reading a word of her manuscript, I wrote down a list of scriptures and even old gospel song lyrics that I hoped and expected to read given the title. Cathy not only filled my "wish list" with scriptures that sing to our hearts, minds, and even to the Holy Spirit within us, but also exceeded my hopes by sharing personal situations, experiences, and circumstances so that readers could truly identify and realize the power of the truth of overcoming by grace through faith that believers outright own—paid in full on the cross!

Her selection of scriptures and words of hope quicken our courage and endurance to overcome, to know absolutely that Christ truly makes a way for us not only to persevere but to overcome. She does a beautiful job weaving this tapestry of truth: Believers are overcomers through the blood of Christ on Calvary's cross. He is risen, alive, and sits on the right hand of God. The Overcomer, our Savior, our Healer, the Lover of our souls, reigns within each believer, within the residence of our eternal soul.

If you want the peace that passes all understanding and an overwhelming joy that cannot be overcome, read this book, and rejoice and be glad!"

Nancy Morin
Copy Editor
Wife, Mother, and Public Educator
Cousin, Friend, and Sister in Christ

"I have known Cathy for over 40 yrs. As new believers, she and I lived together along with other women in a large dorm room in the parsonage of our church where she and I became close friends. Over the years since then, I have had many opportunities to watch her Christian life metamorphose into the beautiful grace-filled and faith-filled walk with Jesus that she and her husband now so passionately and freely share with all who will hear.

However, it took me a long time to grasp the joy and freedom they found through the gospel of grace given in God's New Covenant because I was still saturated with a mixture of law and grace. That mixture left me constantly looking inward and asking for God's forgiveness and acceptance.

Thankfully, God opened my eyes and heart as they patiently continued to pray and to teach this truly good news, and it has changed my life also. Reading Cathy's book helps me to remember how and why I can walk as an overcomer by His grace through this often overwhelming world. Thank you, Cathy, for laying down your life for all of us who have been blessed to know you personally and for all who will hear the message of God's amazing grace about which you have so lovingly written."

Janet Martin
Massage Therapist
Wife, Mother, and Grandma
Dear Life-long Friend

"I am thankful to Cathy for writing and teaching foundational truths that will enable us to BELIEVE God and love others as we are instructed to do under the NEW and BETTER Covenant which Jesus brought in through His death and resurrection. What is taught in this book has given me permission to believe that God is as good as He says He is, in spite of what genetics or our circumstances want to lead us to believe. This is a GOOD NEWS book about the unending love and presence of Jesus. Because of that, it will continue to be a resource to which I will refer back because when we BELIEVE Him, we are given supernatural strength (according to Ephesians 1:18-19). I haven't met a lot of people who couldn't use help BELIEVING GOD to overcome the overwhelming."

Mary Saip
Independent Consultant & Director for the Pampered Chef ®
Wife and Mother
Dear Friend

Acknowledgements

When your friend tells you that she's writing a book, of course, you will be excited for her. When you hear that she's almost finished, you might even offer words of encouragement. However, when you get an email requesting you to be one of the pre-readers for her book of nearly 400 pages, you might reasonably acquiesce. So, I cannot express how thankful I am to my dear friends who took the time to read this manuscript. Your input and encouragement are more valuable to me than I can ever express. I also wish to express appreciation to Mark Cermak and Job Vega Vargas for helping me with this revised edition.

I wish I could communicate to you what a beautiful influence my mother had on me. She showed me her love and God's grace each day of my life which would not be as blessed as it is today without the confidence she instilled in me.

I am thankful for all the love that surrounds me, especially the love of our family. My children encourage me constantly, and my grandchildren bring me so much joy and love that I can scarcely contain it. It is primarily for our children, grandchildren, and future descendants that I write with the hope that long after we are gone, they will be able to benefit from the truths God has taught us that have set us free.

My husband, David, is my biggest supporter in so many ways. First of all, he encouraged me to retire early. This gave me time to study and teach and eventually write. He works full-time in secular employment so that we both may minister the gospel of the grace of God. When I become weary, he encourages me. When success comes my way, he is there to celebrate. For over 40 years we have been best friends and partners in pleasing God. How thankful I am to share my life with him.

From a very young age, Jesus has been there for me. He was there as I sang songs to Him as a very little girl. He was there when I was roaming around my neighborhood in Imperial Beach, California searching for trap door spiders and floating on frog-filled ponds caused by rain on rafts made by who-knows-who. I knew His love intensely through the love that the members of our church gave to me. He comforted me when my father divorced my mother and left us. He understood why I forsook the church as a teenager, and He was with me as I tried not to believe in Him in college. Patiently, He brought me back to full faith in Him. As I became miserable trying to live by law, He guided me back to full faith in Him—again. When I faced many overwhelming losses, pain, and frustrations in life, He taught me how to have faith in Him—again and again. Jesus is everything to me. Through it all, this truth has remained: Jesus never fails.

Prologue

When I was young, my belief was that all human beings are basically the same with similar needs and desires. Now that I'm older and wiser, I know this not to be true. There are some people we simply don't understand. They go through life completely differently than we do. What vanity it would be on our parts to try and convert them to our ways of processing life, though many times when conflicts arise, we wish we could. When we discover that we are not all the same, we find freedom in knowing we don't have to understand someone to love them. That's what acceptance is. "I don't 'get' you, but I choose to love you 'as is'."

Being a relatively new author, I sometimes wonder, while in the process of trying to communicate, if people will be able to understand what I'm saying. My observation is that we all listen through a different filter consisting of everything we know, all we've experienced, and we are limited by what we don't know and haven't yet experienced. Keenly aware of this, I sometimes wonder if what I'm trying to express will ever be heard by anyone except by someone who processes life identically to myself.

Taking these things into consideration, it would be easy for me to conclude that I'm wasting my time. Thankfully, there is the Holy Spirit. I have complete confidence that He can take this 40-day feast that I am spreading before you, and distribute it to each reader as each one needs. This should also put you at ease. Even though you might not understand everything written, you can trust that God will speak words that will encourage your heart as you read.

For those who know me personally, please know that my thoughts here are not some silly attempt to secretly teach you something. Most of the examples given here are personal or very close to home or a response to incorrect teachings received in the past with which we do not any longer agree.

Let me also add that agreeing with everything shared is not required. Even though I believe God has called me to write this book and to inspire you to believe in Him completely, and even though, of course, I believe what I've written is true, I do not claim verbal plenary inspiration.[1]

Simply read this with the purpose of gleaning truths that will inspire you to believe in the character of God and the glorious grace He has provided and promised, and enjoy the journey toward rediscovering faith in God.

---

[1]   This is the belief that every single word of the Bible in the original Greek was inspired by God.

Introduction

*O*ver my nearly 62 years, I have faced many challenges in life as we all do, and most of them have been conquered by simply fulfilling what was needed for success. In my college years, I determined to manage my time well so that I could diligently study and complete the required coursework to gain the desired grade. As a young adult, staying out of debt by paying my bills on time and managing my money as frugally as possible kept me financially stable. When, as a married woman with children it became obvious that my house and life had become a disorganized mess, the remedy was simple: read books about organization and apply what I was learning so that my family could live in a clean and peaceful home. In many situations, reaching out to others for guidance about being a parent or improving my teaching skills has been of great benefit.

We could go on and on giving examples of how A + B = C, but most likely you understand what I mean. There are many situations we face in life which have logical solutions. Many of them are as simple as eliminating a destructive behavior or discovering a natural remedy. Given a challenge, we can accomplish much in this life simply by using the reasoning power God gives to all and doing what needs to be done to bring about change.

However—and this is a big "however", what do we do when our diligence isn't enough? What if all our hard work doesn't bring the desired results? Usually, we try encouraging ourselves by saying, "If at first you don't succeed, try, try again," or "Third time's a charm," or we "pull ourselves up by our bootstraps." We refuse to be conquered, so we dig in our heels until we finally reach our goals. This way of thinking can help us through many difficult situations in life, yet it also has the potential of starting us down a dead-end cycle of trying and failing leaving us in a hopeless state of defeat and pessimism.

Some of us evolve out of the trap of "trying harder" to Plan B. Sometimes Plan B is just what we need. Finding Plan B might involve some research and a new lifestyle, but we won't be daunted. So we follow Plan B and finally experience the success we always knew we could. If Plan B doesn't work, we try Plan C—and Plan D, E, F, and G until finally, we find something that works, but what if when we come to Z, we discover that nothing we've done has helped us? What are we to conclude if all our hard work gives us the opposite results? Yes, we can go back and try some of the other Plans again, as many of us do, but after years of trying what seems like "everything", with very little to no success, what are we to do? At what moment does beating one's head against the wall yet again become not only a waste of our time and energy but a destructive exercise in futility?

To top it off, in many situations, our problems are known to others—maybe to those who have supposedly faced what we are facing and have succeeded. Either our problems are visibly obvious, or we have dared to share our frustrations with others in hope of finally finding an answer. Many looking in on our struggles might "logically" conclude that either we aren't trying hard enough or that we secretly aren't trying at all. They think that if Plan X worked for them then surely it would work for us if we'd only work diligently toward our goal. We want to tell them that we've tried everything. In fact, more than once we've spoken up in our defense. However now, we hesitate to open our hearts at all because what's the point if they are to glare back in disbelief, offer yet another plan we know won't work, or watch over us like a hawk waiting to spot any mistakes we might be making so they can point them out?

What can happen to those who find themselves in such a lonely intolerable state is an acceptance of failure which, of course, requires living with a situation which is totally undesirable and completely unbearable.

Is anything coming to mind? I'm guessing that if you are reading this book, it is because you know exactly what I mean. You find yourself in just this place—overwhelmed. It seems insane to read yet another book about conquering your situation, but what else can you do? If this is the case, it might be that reading this book is accompanied by a reasonable amount of skepticism—even cynicism. In fact, you may have picked this book up and thought, "I don't know why I'm bothering to read this."

I don't blame you. Not at all. My heart aches for you as I remember my own crushing struggles and imagine yours. My objective in writing this is to set you on a path better than that of endlessly trying—one that can help you to overcome the overwhelming simply by believing in Him. My promise is to speak the truth in love without adding insult to injury. That is to say, this book is written to build up, not to burden you with yet another "spiritual discipline" or formula for success. I pray that while you read, the Holy Spirit will speak clearly to your aching heart and bring a lasting victory that you cannot at this moment imagine could ever be yours.

I speak as someone who has overcome what she never thought she would and as one who continues to face obstacles that need to be conquered. Feel free to disagree as you read, but my hope is that for the most part, you will find these words from my heart to yours a lasting comfort and a means of success.

You've blamed yourself. You've maybe even blamed others, and now, perhaps, you are considering blaming God. May the Lord help us to forsake the accusations and instead learn how to overcome the overwhelming by grace through faith.

For whatever is born of God
overcomes the world.
And this is the victory that has overcome the world—
our faith.
Who is he who overcomes the world,
but he who believes that
Jesus is the Son of God.

1 John 5:4-5

PART 1

By Grace through Faith
NOT Law

Day 1

FROM FRUSTRATION TO FAITH

Let me say this before we begin. If you have a life-threatening condition, please seek medical attention. If you need a lawyer, get one. If your life is in danger, seek out help. While I believe completely in miracles, we need to use God's wisdom as well. Don't add your name to the list of those, who in the name of "faith" or out of stubbornness or even religious zeal delayed or refused aid that could have easily helped them. Even though doctors, lawyers, and justice are not perfect, God can use these public servants as part of His answers to our prayers.

*M*ost of us have heard the pop culture definition of insanity as that of doing the same thing over and over expecting different results. You've been there and done that and are too tired (and sane, I might add) to do "that" again. You are ready to admit that what you've been doing is not working! You instinctively believe there must be an answer, but are completely baffled at this point as to what that could be. However exasperating this may be, you are actually perfectly poised to receive the relief you need.

I've been "there" too—more than once. I've prayed, studied, researched, tried my best, and then given up only to try again. There have been small successes, but not enough to completely vanquish my foe. Forlorn and confused, crying about situations which were completely over my head and seemingly out of my control, I've been tempted to throw in the towel and admit defeat—ready to give up all efforts, weary of the fight.

The frustration of wanting to explain my situation to someone—deeply desiring to be understood, but learning to hold back nearly paralyzed me. I learned the wisdom of not pouring out my heart, not wanting to expose myself once again to that incredulous expression staring back at me when I insisted, "I've tried that. It doesn't work for me." I longed for anyone to please believe me when I said, "It's not my fault that I have this problem." Yet, I knew that any logical human being would conclude that the blame was mine alone. Knowing this, I concluded that it just was not worth the risk of exposing the most painful area of my life to anyone if it meant once again being misunderstood.

Unsolicited advice—why do people feel they must toss it our way like a bone with no meat when it is clearly not requested? Yes, most of them mean well—they want to help, but when advice is given to someone who has tried it all, it can communicate painful unintended messages to the one who is struggling.

First, it can say that this person isn't aware that he has a problem that needs to be solved—that he is oblivious to his most painful "fault". "Informing" someone with an obvious problem that they have a problem is ridiculous and offensive.

Two, it implies that the individual hasn't researched the situation well enough—which translates to an exhausted heart that one is *willfully* ignorant. People who feel trapped financially, for example, have likely read multiple books and articles on how to manage money and have made themselves near-experts on the topic. When they are "encouraged" to be more frugal or offered the newest formula for success, it implies that they are merely meandering through life with no direction whatsoever—that they are so clueless that it hasn't even dawned on them to educate themselves.

Three, this unsought guidance implies someone hasn't tried *hard enough*—that he lacks self-control or is simply lazy. Consider someone who is troubled by a relationship. How he desires for that relationship to work! He's likely not only read books on fixing what is broken but has attended seminars and conferences to help improve himself. He's reached out in love to help mend the relationship, but his offerings of love have often been met with disdain. He lives daily with the reality that the relationship he believes could be wonderful, simply is not. He's repeatedly attempted to be a better friend, spouse, or family member, but nothing he's done has worked. He has tried but has experienced very few results. So, when someone offers up their words of wisdom, he listens, but often feels lectured instead of helped.

Four, and this can be the most painful—unsolicited advice can be perceived as a type of disapproval of someone personally. Oh, the individual might be sharing with all the love in his heart, but what is said goes through many layers of pain and frustration and comes to the other person through the other side, as a lack of love and acceptance of who he is right now. He might interpret advice as a message that he is not good enough to be loved unconditionally—he must be *fixed* first. He longs for someone to accept him without wishing he would change.

Writing and reading the above can be a little frustrating and even depressing, especially if you are experiencing it, so I'd like to encourage you. The name of this book is *Overcoming* the Overwhelming. That is to say, God has an *answer*. Although I have many times felt inundated by long-term struggles, amazing victories are now mine where I'd only known despair. Overcoming the overwhelming has brought great joy to me, and I now daily walk in peace, even when storm clouds linger and thunder rolls.

Even though many victories are now mine, not too long ago, I found myself in tears praying, "Lord, You have helped me overcome so many difficult situations in my life, even some that I never thought I'd conquer, and I thank You so much; but why, Lord, can't I overcome *this* one—the one that hurts me so deeply? You are the only One who knows my journey intimately. You're the only One who believes me when I say, "I can't." Lord, I believe You are the only One who can help me. It just seems that Your grace should be enough to conquer this. Please give me wisdom."

There have been many times I have asked God for wisdom that He gave it to me right on the spot which amazes me every time. This time was no exception. Suddenly, I saw it as plain as day. The wisdom had come right out of my mouth while I was praying.

**The answer was not to be found in a new formula
or renewed doses of diligence,
but in His grace—His grace *would* be enough.**

I became convinced of this truth but, at first, I was not sure how it would apply to "this mountain"—this unmovable obstacle I faced. Still, the good news that the answer was in His grace had come to me, and faith was rising in my heart! There was an answer to be found, and I would find it in His grace.

Day 2

OVERCOMING OVERWHELMING SIN

---

*T*his book is not about overcoming sin. It is about conquering certain areas in our lives that don't necessarily even involve sin. However, there are many Christians today who find themselves involved in an ungodly lifestyle that they either don't want to forsake because of the pleasure it brings them or that they cannot escape because the behavior has become addictive.

I could ignore or dismiss the topic of sin since it's not my focus, but I can't help but think that someone sought out this book for the express purpose of wanting to overcome overwhelming sin. If you aren't this person—if you are presently living in victory over sin (which is entirely possible) feel free to move on to Day 3.

We need to start at the beginning when discussing sin having control over you, and ask a very important question—are you really a Christian? I ask this question because Jesus came to save us from our sins. Christians are "free from sin", "dead to sin", and free from its dominion (Rom. 6). In fact, if a believer is walking in the grace of God, sin is not a daily struggle—even the thought of sinning is unwanted. While there are true Christians who are not currently living in this freedom, it is also true that there are some "Christians" who aren't experiencing freedom from sin because they aren't actually Christians at all.

If you are not sure if you truly are a Christian, it's important that you consider this: Many so-called "Christians" today, are not Christians. They might live in a "Christian" nation, so they assume they are Christian by virtue of where they were born. Or they've been brought up in a "Christian" church and have gone through the ceremonies that supposedly "make" them Christian, but they are not really Christians. Some attend churches with "Jesus" or "Christ" in the title, but the beliefs of their church couldn't be farther away from true Christianity. Others believe they are Christians because they keep the Ten Commandments or closely study and adhere to the teachings of Jesus—as if doing good and not doing bad is the way of salvation. Let me state this clearly—none of these have anything to do with what it means to be a true Christian. So, before discussing how to overcome overwhelming sin, allow me to explain clearly how it is that someone becomes a Christian.

John had much to write about the topic. One thing he clarified was that we can't make ourselves a Christian, nor can anyone else. We are *given* the right to become God's children by the will of God when we believe in the name of Jesus.

> ### John 1:12-13
> *But as many as **received** Him, to them He **gave** the right to become children of God, to those who **believe** in His name: ¹³who were born, **not** of blood, **nor** of the will of the flesh, **nor** of the will of man, **but of God**.*

Jesus declared that we must be born again. We are born physically, in the flesh, and have physical life. If we want to have spiritual life, we must be born again spiritually.

> ### John 3:3-6
> *Jesus answered and said to him, "Most assuredly, I say to you, **unless one is born again, he cannot see the kingdom of God**."*

> *⁴Nicodemus said to Him, "How can a man be born when he is old? Can he enter a second time into his mother's womb and be born?" ⁵Jesus answered, "Most assuredly, I say to you, unless one is born of water and the Spirit, he cannot enter the kingdom of God. ⁶That which is born of the flesh is flesh, and that which is born of the Spirit is spirit. ⁷Do not marvel that I said to you, 'You must be born again.'"*

If someone wants to see the kingdom of God, he must be born again. To be a Christian, that is to say, a child of God who is eternally saved from his sins and from the wrath that is to come, one *must* be born again. What does that mean, and how does one go about receiving this new birth? The only way to be born of God—to be saved, is by **believing that Jesus is the Lord**—that is to say, by believing that He is God. All the ceremonies and sacraments on earth cannot save one soul because salvation is by God's gift and our belief in the Gift He gave.

Allow me to demonstrate this by giving concrete examples and additional Bible verses that back this truth. The first example is found in Acts 16:16-34. Paul cast out a spirit of divination from a woman, and those who stood to profit from her skills were furious and wanted Paul jailed for what he'd done. He and Silas were beaten with rods and thrown into prison and secured with stocks.

At midnight, Paul and Silas were heard by the prisoners "praying and singing hymns to God." Suddenly there was an earthquake, and Paul and Silas were released from their chains and the prison doors were open. The jailor, being awakened from his sleep, was about to kill himself as he considered the dire consequences of prisoners escaping on his watch. Then Paul and Silas assured him that they were all there. Here is the account of the jailer's salvation—the moment he and his family were born again. Paul tells him exactly how to be saved.

Acts 16:29-34
Then he (the jailor) called for a light, ran in, and fell down trembling before Paul and Silas. ³⁰And he brought them out and said, **"Sirs, what must I do to be saved?"** *³¹So they said,* **"Believe on the Lord Jesus Christ, and you will be saved, you and your household."** *³²Then they spoke the word of the Lord to him and to all who were in his house. ³³And he took them the same hour of the night and washed their stripes. And immediately he and all his family were baptized. ³⁴Now when he had brought them into his house, he set food before them; and he rejoiced, having believed in God with all his household.*

The jailer wanted to be saved, so he asked Paul and Silas how to go about it. Their answer was simple, "**Believe** on the Lord Jesus Christ, and you will be saved." Paul and Silas "spoke the word of the Lord" to them. This means they told them of the good news that Jesus died to save them from their sins and rose from the dead to give them eternal life. Notice, they didn't ask the jailor to admit he was a sinner or to confess his sins or to ask for forgiveness. They didn't tell him "to make Jesus the Lord" of his life. He didn't have to take a class first, explaining the responsibilities of discipleship. He didn't have to go through any religious ceremonies. They didn't have to wait for Paul to declare that this man and his family were now officially born of God. He didn't have to be baptized to be saved because he and his family were not baptized until after they were saved. They instructed him only to **believe** on the Lord Jesus Christ.

Here is another touching story, surrounded by miracles, that demonstrates the same truth—that salvation is by faith (belief).

Acts 8:26-39

Now an angel of the Lord spoke to Philip, saying, "Arise and go toward the south along the road which goes down from Jerusalem to Gaza." This is desert. ²⁷So he arose and went. And behold, a man of Ethiopia, a eunuch of great authority under Candace the queen of the Ethiopians, who had charge of all her treasury, and had come to Jerusalem to worship, ²⁸was returning. And sitting in his chariot, he was reading Isaiah the prophet. ²⁹Then the Spirit said to Philip, "Go near and overtake this chariot."

³⁰So Philip ran to him, and heard him reading the prophet Isaiah, and said, "Do you understand what you are reading?"

*³¹And he said, **"How can I, unless someone guides me?"** And he asked Philip to come up and sit with him. ³²The place in the Scripture which he read was this:*

"He was led as a sheep to the slaughter; And as a lamb before its shearer is silent, So He opened not His mouth. ³³In His humiliation His justice was taken away, And who will declare His generation? For His life is taken from the earth."

*³⁴So the eunuch answered Philip and said, "I ask you, of whom does the prophet say this, of himself or of some other man?" ³⁵**Then Philip opened his mouth, and beginning at this Scripture, preached Jesus to him.** ³⁶Now as they went down the road, they came to some water. And the eunuch said, "See, here is water. What hinders me from being baptized?"*

*³⁷Then Philip said, **"If you believe with all your heart, you may."***

*And he answered and said, **"I believe that Jesus Christ is the Son of God."*** *[38]So he commanded the chariot to stand still. And both Philip and the eunuch went down into the water, and he baptized him. [39]Now when they came up out of the water, the Spirit of the Lord caught Philip away, so that the eunuch saw him no more; and he went on his way rejoicing.*

Notice that Phillip preached Jesus to the man. No requirement beyond faith in Jesus Christ as the risen Lord was demanded. Here is another verse that makes this perfectly clear.

Romans 10:9-10
*If you **confess with your mouth the Lord Jesus** and **believe in your heart that God has raised Him from the dead**, you **will be saved**. [10]For with the heart one **believes** unto righteousness, and with the mouth **confession** is made unto **salvation**.*

When we believe with all of our hearts that Jesus rose bodily from the dead and that He is the Lord God, and we confess this, we will be saved—born again. Once we are born again, our craving to sin diminishes as our desire to do what is right grows. To reinforce this truth, allow me to quote one of the most famous verses in the world followed by two lesser known verses that follow. Notice also that this is part of the same conversation with Nicodemus whom Jesus had just told he needed to be born again.

John 3:16-18
*"For God so loved the world, that He gave His only begotten Son, that whoever **believes** in Him will **not perish** but have **everlasting life**.*

*¹⁷For God **did not send His Son into the world to condemn the world**, but that the world through Him might be **saved**.
¹⁸"He who **believes** in Him is not condemned; but he who does not believe is condemned already, because he has not believed in the name of the only begotten Son of God."*

God loves you. He gave His Son to show just how much He loves you. He has made salvation as easy as it could ever be when it comes to what is required, and that is to believe on His Son, Jesus Christ. If you believe in Him with all of your heart and confess that He is the Lord God, you will be saved (born again), all of your sins will be forgiven, and you will be a new creation. All of this will happen because God's grace is extended to you in the form of His Son, and because you receive Him by faith (by believing in Him).

I Knew I Couldn't Resist Him[2]

*I knew I couldn't resist Him
When He looked at me.
He looked right past my sin and shame
Into the heart of me.
With arms wide open He beckoned,
"Come unto Me."
I yielded to His perfect will,
Now He belongs to me.*

Ephesians 2:8-9
*For by **grace** you have been saved through **faith**, and that not of yourselves; it is the **gift** of God, ⁹not of works, lest anyone should boast.*

---

[2]   A song by my mother, Enid Bennett Whitt (1922-1984)

However, what about those who can honestly say without any doubt that they have been born again and yet are still struggling with an overwhelming sin? They do love Jesus. They do want to please Him, but they keep falling again and again. They might be so overcome with sinning that they don't have any idea of how to stop. It isn't that they haven't tried, but that they keep giving in, or maybe they have stopped trying to resist, accepting sin as part of their life. They find themselves in the trap Paul described in Romans 7—doing the things they don't want to do and not doing the things they do want to do. Perhaps they've been told that this is the "normal" Christian life—an endless struggle with sin. There is good news for any Christian who is buffeted by sin. **Wrestling with sin is NOT the normal Christian life.**

There are three main reasons that a real Christian falls into overwhelming sin. While it might be that only one or two of these are in play, my observation is that usually, all three are at work, but I separate them here for the purpose of identifying them.

The first one is the most obvious. At some point in time, someone was tempted, and instead of resisting temptation he gave into a sin that now provides some form of pleasure or comfort that's become part of his life, and he does not want to forsake it. He is still a child of God but has become more like a prodigal son. Some common examples are getting drunk every night after work, turning to drugs or food to dull the pain and struggles in life, fits of rage sometimes leading to verbal or physical abuse of others, an obsessive grab for power, success, and riches, or sexual immorality. These things can become mentally and physically addictive because they offer a type of satisfaction and relief, even if it is only temporary, and even if it is damaging our lives and relationships.

The way to freedom for a Christian involved in sin for the reason above is not as complicated as one might think. Simply ask God to take the desire to commit sin away, and He will do it. One might, at first, find himself resistant to asking God to take away the desire to do something that he enjoys, but if someone wants to be free, this is a necessary first step. As we cooperate with the Holy Spirit, He will show us how to escape. When we allow Him to lead us gently away from these destructive behaviors, we begin to experience the joys of being free from them.

> **Philippians 2:12-13**
> *Therefore, my beloved, as you have always obeyed, not as in my presence only, but now much more in my absence, work out your own salvation with fear and trembling;* [13] ***for it is God who works in you both to will and to do for His good pleasure.***

Besides temptation which leads to addiction, most Christians bound by a sin do not know that living under religious laws plays a role in strengthening sin in their lives. They began their Christian walk with the joy of knowing they were forgiven and experienced increasing freedom from sin, but gradually, the joy of knowing they were forgiven and their freedom from sin got buried under laws and religious expectations. If what I just wrote made no sense or if it sounds vaguely familiar, I highly recommend reading my first book, Are We Preaching "Another" Gospel? In Day 9, I explain why teaching religious laws actually encourages sin. Here is an excerpt from that chapter which demonstrates my point.

> *We think that by preaching "hard" against sin, revival will break out, but actually, according to Scripture, the opposite is true. Shouting moral law at Christians does not set them free; it strengthens sin in their lives. Consider Prohibition which sought to stop the drinking of alcohol in the United States of America. Did it? No. In fact, by making drinking alcohol illegal, it was made more desirable. We think*

*we are doing the right thing shouting, "Thou shalt not," and, "Thou shalt," but in actuality, we are robbing from God's people what Jesus Christ **died** to give them: the assurance of eternal salvation, His very righteousness, and freedom from sin. This is because law strengthens sin. Paul makes this clear in **1 Corinthians 15:56**:*

> *The sting of death is sin, and **the strength (dunamis) of sin is the law**.*

*Perhaps some among us might be so bold as to declare this continual forgiveness, but would we be so bold as to tell people that the reason they are free from sin is because they are **free from law**?*

"Not so fast!" we would warn, fearing the path of lawlessness. For if proclaiming we are completely and continually forgiven doesn't cause believers to go on a sinning rampage; we think that certainly, teaching that we are not under law will! Yet, that we are free from the law is so obvious, my husband, David, and I still wonder how we missed seeing it for so many years.

Romans 6:14
*For sin shall **not** have dominion over you, for you are **not under law** but under **grace**.*

*How amazing is His grace? **It** is the precise reason sin does not have dominion over us.*

Jesus didn't die so that we would be *able* to keep the law. He died so that we could

be *free* from it so that we could live under grace which frees us from sin's dominion.

Romans 7:4-6
*Therefore, **my brethren**, you also have become dead to the law through the body of Christ, **that you may be married to another—to Him who was raised from the dead, that we should bear fruit to God.** ⁵ **For when we were in the flesh, the** sinful passions which were aroused by the law **were at work in our members to bear fruit to death.** ⁶ **But now** we have been delivered from the law, **having died to what we were held by, so that we should serve in the newness of the Spirit and not in the oldness of the letter.***

This could not be stated more clearly. We are dead to the law through the body of Christ. Prior to that, our sinful passions were aroused by the law. **Just to repeat that, law arouses sinful passions.** *It doesn't diminish them. Now, however, we are delivered from the law. This death allows us to experience the joy of being freed from sin as described in Romans 6 and being alive to God as proclaimed in Romans 8.*

If we don't teach this; if we insist that believers are still under law and that our right-standing with God is maintained or improved by keeping laws (the "dooties" and "don'ties" of "Christianity"), then we are preaching "another" gospel and making His sacrifice worthless or at best, provisional. As I quoted before, "If

*righteousness comes through law, then Christ
died in vain," (Gal. 2:21).-AWPAG*

The Christian life is a life lived by grace through faith—not by following religious laws. Too many churches today focus on sin. They not only reinforce weekly the things we are not to do, but also make not doing good things just as sinful (such as praying, fasting, giving, attending church, good works, and being involved in the ministry). I will repeat it. The strength of sin **is the law**. So, it may be that one reason a person is right now struggling with sin is that he has been fed law instead of grace. The process of freeing oneself from religious law is just that—a process. If you are permeated with religious laws and need some time to be freed from them, I again recommend the book mentioned above. I pray God will guide you into the freedom that is yours.

The third reason that many believers today live far below the freedom from sin than they could be experiencing is that they do not know who they are in Christ. This topic of our identity in Him is vast, so I will focus only our identity as it pertains to sin.

Most of us have heard the expression, "I'm just a sinner saved by grace," but this is not true at all. You were a sinner, but you have been saved by grace. Now, you are a saint. When Paul wrote to the churches, he addressed them as "the saints". "Saints" means "holy ones".

> **1 Corinthians 1:1-3 NASB**
> *Paul, called as an apostle of Jesus Christ by the will of God, and Sosthenes our brother,*
> *[2]To the church of God which is at Corinth, to those who have been sanctified in Christ Jesus, **saints by calling**, with all who in every place call on the name of our Lord Jesus Christ, their Lord and ours:*

³Grace to you and peace from God our Father and the Lord Jesus Christ.

I chose to quote 1 Corinthians because it is in this letter that Paul so strongly corrects their ungodly behavior. This is to point out that our standing as saints is not conditioned upon our perfect behavior, but on the fact that by God's grace, we have been called as saints. For a Christian to excuse his poor behavior by saying, "Well, I'm no saint," is to imply that we are saints based on how godly we live. Christians are saints *by calling.*

"Saints" means "holy ones". Yes, if you are a Christian, you are right now holy.

Colossians 1:21-22
*And you, who once were alienated and ene-mies in your mind by wicked works, yet now He has reconciled ²²in the body of His flesh through death, to present you **holy**, and **blameless**, and **above reproach** in His sight—*

"I'm only human," we say as if this is also an excuse to sin. No, we aren't "only" human.

1 Corinthians 3:1-3
*And I, brethren, could not speak to you as to spiritual men, but as to men of flesh, as to infants in Christ. ²I gave you milk to drink, not solid food; for you were not yet able to receive it. Indeed, even now you are not yet able, ³for you are still fleshly. For since there is jealousy and strife among you, are you not fleshly, **and are you not walking like mere men?***

Paul is reasoning with these Corinthians, whom he just called saints. Their behavior did not reflect that they had been changed into *spiritual* men. They were acting like "mere" men, even though they were not. Think about it. We have been changed. We aren't like the average person who walks around on this planet. We aren't *merely* human. It's time we begin to see ourselves and each other as we truly are.

> **2 Corinthians 5:16-17**
> *Therefore, from now on, we regard no one according to the flesh. Even though we have known Christ according to the flesh, yet now we know Him thus no longer.* ¹⁷**Therefore, if anyone is in Christ, he is a new creation; old things have passed away; behold, all things have become new.**

The word "sinner" is expressed in Scripture as the opposite of being righteous. We are right now righteous (justified). Righteous means that we have been made innocent or right before God. Many Christians today work hard at being righteous, but the truth is that under the New Covenant, righteousness is a gift given to us because of our faith in Jesus. Being a child of Adam made us sinners. Being a child of God makes us righteous. Notice how in these passages, "sinner" and "righteous" are opposites.

> **Romans 5:12-19**
> *Therefore, just as through one man sin entered the world, and death through sin, and thus death spread to all men, because all sinned—* ¹³*(For until the law sin was in the world, but sin is not imputed when there is no law.* ¹⁴*Nevertheless death reigned from Adam to Moses, even over those who had not sinned according to the likeness of the transgression of Adam, who is a type of Him who was to come.* ¹⁵*But the free gift is not like the offense. For if by the one man's offense many died, much more the grace of God and*

the gift by the grace of the one Man, Jesus Christ, abounded to many. *¹⁶And the gift is not like that which came through the one who sinned. For the judgment which came from one offense resulted in* **condemnation**, *but the* **free gift** *which came from many offenses resulted in* **justification**. *¹⁷For if by the one man's offense death reigned through the one, much more those who receive abundance of grace and of the* **gift of righteousness** *will reign in life through the One, Jesus Christ.)* *¹⁸Therefore, as through one man's offense judgment came to all men, resulting in condemnation, even so through one Man's righteous act the free gift came to all men, resulting in justification of life. ¹⁹For as by one man's disobedience many were made* **sinners**, *so also by one Man's obedience many will be made* **righteous**.

Righteousness is a gift by the abundance of God's grace to those who believe in Jesus. No amount of following the law or doing a long list of "spiritual disciplines" can make us more righteous than we have already been made by the gift of God. Again, we were sinners. Now, however, we are righteous.

1 Timothy 1:8-11
But we know that the law is good if one uses it lawfully, ⁹knowing this: that the law is not made for **a righteous person**, *but for the lawless and insubordinate, for the ungodly and for* **sinners**, *for the* **unholy** *and profane, for murderers of fathers and murderers of mothers, for manslayers, ¹⁰for fornicators, for sodomites, for kidnappers, for liars, for perjurers, and if there is any other thing that is contrary to sound doctrine, ¹¹according to the*

glorious gospel of the blessed God which was committed to my trust.

My friend, you are not only righteous before God; you are *His* very righteousness.

2 Corinthians 5:21 MOUNCE
*For He made Him who knew no sin to be a sin-offering for us, that in Him we might become **the righteousness of God** in Him.*

When we fully realize who we are in Jesus, that we are not a sinner, but a holy righteous saint indeed, sinning makes no sense at all. Sin no longer has dominion over us. We have dominion over sin. Don't allow yourself to be bullied by it. Stand up to it in Jesus' name and live in the victory that He won for you. Say it aloud. "I am not a sinner. I am holy and righteous. Sin does not have dominion over me because I'm under His grace and not under law. I am dead to sin and alive unto God. I am free from sin." Know who you are and then be who He has made you.

Romans 6:11-14
*Likewise you also, reckon (conclude) yourselves to be dead indeed to sin, but alive to God in Christ Jesus our Lord. [12]Therefore **do not let sin reign** in your mortal body, that you should obey it in its lusts. [13]And **do not present** your members as instruments of unrighteousness to sin, but present yourselves to God as being alive from the dead, and your members as instruments of righteousness to God. [14]**For sin shall not have dominion over you, for you are not under law but under grace.***

Day 3

NOT BY LAW

---

*G*race, not law, is the way of the Christian's life. We were saved by grace through faith, not by keeping the law, and we live by grace through faith, not by keeping laws. We also overcome overwhelming situations by grace through faith, not law.

We usually think of laws as a list of do's and don'ts, and yes, those are laws, but law takes on many other deceptive forms that I'd like to point out in this chapter. It is important to identify these things because as I showed in the last chapter, Paul wrote, "The strength (dunamis) of sin is the law." Even though it is likely that an overwhelming situation doesn't involve sin per se, if law is employed as the method of solving your problem, it will only make matters worse. We were born again into the kingdom of God's grace through faith in Jesus, and that is how we are created to function— not through applying law.

Blame and Shame

Law can take on a variety of forms. Here are a few that you have likely experienced. First of all, there are blame and shame. "It's all your fault," or "You should be ashamed of yourself for letting this situation get so out of hand." We can say this to ourselves or we might hear it from others. Accusations and condemnation are not helpful. In fact, they are contrary to the life God has for us. Think about it. Who is the "accuser of the brethren", and who "accuses the saints night and day before God" (Rev. 12:10)? Accusations are NOT from God. They are not meant to help but to defeat.

Shame is not from your Father either. In fact, even if your situation is your fault, your sins are forgiven, and He remembers them no more (Heb. 8:12). If He remembers them no more, do you really think he'll be endlessly reminding you or punishing you for them? He most certainly will not!

Sometimes our overwhelming situations involve someone else. Might we be allowing blame and shame to come from our corner to the person who is offending us? Think about it. God has extended His grace, mercy, and kindness to us. Shouldn't we do the same for our offenders?[3] Blame and shame are 100% counter-productive when it comes to resolving any situation. God might indeed correct our thinking and behavior as we go through the process of overcoming the overwhelming, but He will not shame us.

Here is something that helps distinguish between condemnation and correction. Condemnation is a dead-end street. It is like a final sentence of judgment. There is nothing you can do to fix the situation when you are condemned. Correction from God, however, while sometimes painful (no one likes to be told that what he thinks or does is wrong) offers hope and peace—and a solution.

Formula Living

Probably the most common form of law is the one I previously mentioned—formula living (also known as Plans A-Z). "Do this and your problem will be solved." "This" can be one thing or an ever-increasing list of things. The list usually consists of both practical and "spiritual" solutions. The clear implication is that if we do this list, things will go well with

---

[3] If you are in a physically or sexually abusive situation; that is to say, if a crime is being committed against you, God does not expect you to submit to this situation. Remove yourself from harm's way as soon as is safely possible.

us, but if we don't do the list, our lives will fall apart, and of course, this is our fault. So when our lives are falling apart, we are obviously not doing the list, and if we would just do the list, things would get better. This type of law can become a dizzying endless circle of despair.

Formula living is a reflection of the blessings and curses of the law—obey the law completely and these blessings will come upon you and overtake you; disobey the law and these curses will come your way (Deut. 28). Many Christians today live as if they are under the law of Moses instead of grace and faith. Or they try combining both the Old and New Covenants. However, the Law of Moses is the Old Covenant (Deut. 4:13), and the Old Covenant is obsolete (Heb. 8:13). Christians are under *only* **one** covenant, and that is the New Covenant. Even so, the Christian world today, not only obligates Christians to be guided by the moral law of the Old Covenant but adds new laws which they call "disciplines".

The clear but mistaken communication is that these practices are required for successful Christian living, and not keeping them will result in living below what God has for us. Often when someone goes in for counseling, they will be asked, "Have you been praying and reading your Bible?" This question trivializes the person's situation and sidelines his distress because the assumption is if someone isn't reading his Bible and praying, then this is the root cause of one's troubles—counseling session over, just go home, pray, and read your Bible, and everything with work out just fine. Excuse me for using caps and boldface in the same sentence, but

WE LIVE BY GRACE THROUGH FAITH; NOT BY PRAYER AND BIBLE READING.

Behavior Modification

Another evidence of law is that of behavior modification. Let me say that behavior modification can bring results, but doesn't always involve a change of heart, just of behavior. So, one might reach his goal of eliminating a certain behavior in his life, but deep inside he is still longing to do it. The law can motivate us to change our actions by the fear of punishment or the promise of reward, but only grace can change our hearts and thus our desires. The alcoholic redeemed or not redeemed can stop drinking using a variety of techniques, but only God's grace can make an alcoholic into someone who is *no longer an alcoholic at all*.

Some don't even believe it is possible for an alcoholic to be completely free—to rid himself of saying, "I am an alcoholic," for the—rest—of—his—life but we personally know those who are living in this freedom who were previously convinced that they would "always be an alcoholic".[4] Likewise, a person can put himself on a strict low-calorie diet, and he will lose weight, but until the person is healed of whatever it is that is causing him to be overweight (whether physical or emotional), the likely next step will be that the dieter will gain it all back. This is true of children as well. We can modify their behavior by using reward and punishment, but any parent knows the difference between a child whose

---

[4] Freedom from being an alcoholic (or any other sin) is not freedom to abuse alcohol, but complete freedom to abstain from it. An individual who is no longer an alcoholic is not free from the *temptation* to abuse it, for all face temptation, rather, he is free from the *desire* to abuse alcohol. You can't do this with will power. It is a miracle from God. When we receive Jesus, we are changed from sinner to saint. Who we *were*, we no longer are. Sin no longer has dominion over us (Rom. 6:14). *1 Corinthians 6:9-11*
Do you not know that the unrighteous will not inherit the kingdom of God? Do not be deceived. Neither fornicators, nor idolaters, nor adulterers, nor homosexuals, nor sodomites, [10] nor thieves, nor covetous, nor drunkards, nor revilers, nor extortioners will inherit the kingdom of God. [11] And such were some of you. But you were washed, but you were sanctified, but you were justified in the name of the Lord Jesus and by the Spirit of our God.

heart *wants* to please and the heart of a child who is forced to obey.

New Year's Resolutions

Each year, millions of people participate in what can be a futile exercise called New Year's Resolutions. I used to love that time right before the New Year because it was almost like a cleansing from all the ways I'd fallen short in the past year. I'd get out my new journal and write down each goal. I'd put them in categories such as Spiritual, Personal, Family, and Ministry. Each category would contain my deepest desire and how I'd go about it, yet little progress was ever made. Usually, I just felt guilty that I'd accomplished so little, but as the next year would draw near, I'd be right back at making my new list (which usually looked very similar to the previous list). "This year," I'd tell myself, "I am going to make some changes," but then "life" would happen and the list would fade away.

Self-Improvement

Some of the efforts we make include reading books and attending conferences. I don't put all books and conferences in the same box, but many of them amount mostly to new lists of laws on how to improve ourselves. If someone has been around the Christian community for very long, he has seen these philosophies come and go in waves.

Go to any Christian bookstore, and you will find so many self-help books that you have to wonder if Christians need to be told how to do nearly everything. When I considered writing Christian books, I asked myself, "Do I want to contribute to this madness?" There are Christian books that can help us, but when we are reading them, we need to "prove all things and hold fast to that which is good". Is the book pointing to Jesus as the solution or is it pointing to what we do as the answer and simply giving a new set of laws to employ?

Remember the strength of sin is the law. If we make law the basis of change, we are setting ourselves up for failure. We've been recreated to live by grace through faith, not by law.

Advice

Another thing that can be helpful or harmful, depending if it is grace or law, is advice. "There is victory in an abundance of counselors" (Prov. 24:6 NASB), but if our teachers are feeding us with the law instead of the good news; or even worse, combining the two, we won't be permanently helped. It is good to seek out counsel, but let us carefully consider the source and content.

Another aspect of advice, which was already discussed is that of unsolicited advice. You have likely struggled for years trying to overcome this battle. You've done much research. You've tried "everything". You have *lived* this. In fact, you've nearly made yourself an expert on the information available. Then someone, without knowing you or your circumstances at all, comes along with advice. This advice is usually premised on the belief that you are the cause of your situation; so, of course, you are the answer. It can be so wearying to hear unwanted advice from someone who has no idea of what we've been through.

One way to minimize being given unsolicited counsel is not to open the door to it in conversation. If your marriage is difficult, don't mention it to someone who will feel the need to "fix it". Don't talk about your financial woes if you aren't open to hearing about the latest and greatest seminar for success. Don't make reference to negative aspects about your physical frame unless you are ready to be told how to lose or gain weight or add muscle mass. Believe me, there will be those who offer advice, even if you don't open the door, but you can greatly lower your chances of this uncomfortable situation by not bringing it up.

Keeping our personal struggles private is not being unauthentic. Our personal problems are no one's business but ours and God's. If we choose to share them with someone, that is perfectly acceptable, but doing so is not proof that we are sincere. It can actually be the wise thing to keep private matters private.

Try Harder, Do More

After we have tried every method of improving ourselves or our situations, we will have to reckon with two more categories of law—trying harder and doing more. Yes, these are the answers to all problems we face, so we are told. Do it again! Do it better this time! Deep sigh!

Help Me Obey

The ultimate trap, after we've done more and tried harder is to ask God to help us follow a formula or keep a law. Maybe we've all prayed this, "God, help me to do this!" I have some news for you—God is not going to help us live by laws. He sent His precious Son to set us free from law. He is not going to use law to perfect us.

> **Galatians 2:21 YLT**
> *I do not make void the grace of God, for if righteousness [be] through law—then Christ died in vain.*
> **Galatians 3:1-3**
> *O foolish Galatians! Who has bewitched you that you should not obey the truth, before whose eyes Jesus Christ was clearly portrayed among you as crucified? ²This only I want to learn from you: Did you receive the Spirit by the works of the **law**, or by the hearing of **faith**? ³Are you so foolish? Having begun in the Spirit, are you now being made perfect by the flesh?*

I encourage you to ask the Lord to show you where law might be in operation in any overwhelming area of your life. Is there a list in the back of your mind that you got at church, from a book, at a seminar, one that you yourself constructed over time, or that is simply floating around in our popular culture so full of societal obligations? Ask Him to help you identify these laws.

God sent Jesus to set us free indeed from religious law. In Romans 7 we read that we have "died to the law" so that we could be joined to Christ. Shall we then return to our former spouse, the law, after we have died to him? Of course not. My experience has been that there are many layers of law lurking about us. It might take some time for us to see them all. As we identify them and declare ourselves to be free from them, we will experience a new sense of freedom where we previously only felt locked up. Enjoy this process of liberation!

Day 4

SIN CONSCIOUSNESS

---

*N*ot too long ago, I reached an impasse in an area of life with which I've struggled for what seems like forever. It is so "close to home" that I don't talk about it openly even with those I trust because, in the past, it opened the door for endless advice which I am no longer willing to hear.[5] If you've been the victim of well-meaning unsolicited advice, you will understand why I have chosen to circumvent my specific situation while discussing what God taught me, trusting that God can make the connections for you in your own private circumstances.

After realizing that the answer to my situation would be found in His grace, it seemed that God quite regularly was either making a change in my heart or revealing something to me I'd never seen before. One morning while groggily pulling myself out of sleep, two things were on my mind. One was the title of this chapter, and one was the image of something I owned.

Who wakes up thinking about "sin consciousness"? Since my husband and I teach about this from time to time, God knew He could get my attention with it. He might show you something completely different. It might be interesting to know that this was the morning I realized I would be writing this book.

---

[5] This difficulty does not involve sin or a lack of self-control.

"Sin consciousness"—at first, I had no idea why the words and this picture were in my mind or that God was about to show me something. It took a few minutes, but suddenly there was an awareness that God was actually trying to get through to me and that He was telling me that this item had become sin consciousness in my life. By it, my entire rightness was calculated—before self, before others, and before God. I had never seen it that way before, but I had to admit it was true. It seemed to me right then and there that God wanted me to eliminate this item from my daily life.

At first, the thought of letting go horrified me! Then every excuse that entered my mind just reinforced to me that it had to go. I thought, "If I get rid of that, how will I know how I'm doing? Don't I need it so that this problem doesn't get completely out of control? How will I know if I'm making progress?" The more excuses made, the more I had to recognize that this item was actually working against what God wanted to do in my heart. It was producing sin consciousness in my life!

When God speaks to us like that, it can be a bit painful. It was like asking a toddler to give up her security blanket. Can you picture a grown woman grasping for her blankie and putting her thumb in her mouth? That's kind of what I felt at first. At the same time, I sensed an excitement about the freedom God wanted to give me. Before I tell how it all worked out, let's discuss the meaning of sin consciousness.

This teaching should be taught as one of the foundations of Christianity, but I don't remember ever being instructed in this area; on the contrary, we were taught exactly the opposite (that we should constantly be aware of our sins), and as we've taught on the subject, we've observed that most Christians don't know much about it.

Do you know that Jesus wants us to be free from the consciousness of sin? **I am not saying He wants us to be free from having a conscience or that it's acceptable at any time to sin.** No, of course not! Nevertheless, Jesus became our sacrifice for sin so that we would be free from sin consciousness. If what I just wrote is something you have never heard, read this passage carefully.

> **Hebrews 10:1-13**
> *For the law, having a shadow of the good things to come, and not the very image of the things, can never with these same sacrifices, which they offer continually year by year, make those who approach perfect. ²For then would they not have ceased to be offered?* **For the worshipers, once purified, would have had no more consciousness of sins.** *³But in those sacrifices there is a* **reminder of sins** *every year. ⁴For it is not possible that the blood of bulls and goats could* **take away sins.** *⁵Therefore, when He came into the world, He said:*
> *"Sacrifice and offering You did not desire, But a body You have prepared for Me. ⁶In burnt offerings and sacrifices for sin You had no pleasure. ⁷Then I said, 'Behold, I have come— In the volume of the book it is written of Me— To do Your will, O God.'"*
> *⁸Previously saying, "Sacrifice and offering, burnt offerings, and offerings for sin You did not desire, nor had pleasure in them" (which are offered according to the law), ⁹then He said, "Behold, I have come to do Your will, O God." He takes away the first that He may establish the second.* **¹⁰By that will we have been sanctified through the offering of the body of Jesus Christ once for all.**
> *¹¹And every priest stands ministering daily and offering repeatedly the same sacrifices, which can never* **take away sins.** *¹²But this Man, after He had offered* **one sacrifice for sins forever,** *sat down at the right hand of*

> God, *¹³from that time waiting till His enemies are made His footstool. ¹⁴**For by one offering He has perfected forever those who are being sanctified.***

Jesus took away our sins and made us holy once for all time through the offering of His own body. The Old Covenant sacrifices could not "take away" sins, but Jesus offered **one sacrifice for sins forever**. By that one offering, He perfected us forever in regards to sin. He is the Lamb of God who took away our sins (Jn. 1:29).

However, we, the church, add on other requirements for forgiveness to this glorious revelation and in doing so nearly negate it entirely. We say, "Well, He forgave our sins *initially* when we got saved, but after we are forgiven for our past sins, we need to *maintain* our forgiveness through repentance and confession." If this is true, wouldn't that mean that we can only be free from sin consciousness the day we are saved or immediately after confessing our sins? **We would need to be aware of our sins *constantly* so that we'd remember to confess them**. It would also mean that we don't really have a one-time forgiveness for all sin, but that we still need to follow the pattern of the Old Covenant and "get" our sins forgiven, or as some have erroneously taught, "put our sins under the blood".

Good news! Our sins, all of them, are already forgiven by the one-time offering of the body of Jesus Christ, and to top that off, "our sins and lawless deeds, He remembers no more," (Heb. 8:12). Why won't we allow ourselves to accept this glorious truth? Are we afraid that if we really understood it, we would begin to sin more horrifically than we did before our salvation? **What part of "no more" don't we understand?**

Bible translators chose "no more" for **oume eti** in the Greek, but does "no more" impress our English-speaking brains the way that it should? I don't think so. **Eti** means "any longer". If only the word **eti** was present in this sentence, we'd have, "Our sins and lawless deeds he remembers no longer," which sounds the same as "no more" to English readers. Interestingly enough, the Greek text doesn't just say **eti**. It reads **oume eti**. **Oume** is defined by Strongs as "a double negative strengthening the denial[6]; not at all, any more, at all, by no means, neither, never, in no case, not at all". In other words, we have the denial, **eti**, and then a double negative strengthening the denial, **oume**. How could we translate this emphasis into English? Perhaps we can draw from the Amplified Version's translation of Hebrews 13:5 where oume is used to say that He will never leave us or forsake us. The Amplified reads, "[I will] not, [I will] not, [I will] not in any degree leave you helpless nor forsake nor let [you] down (relax My hold on you)! [Assuredly not!]" Using this translation, Hebrews 8:12 would read, "Their sins and lawless deeds I will not, I will not, I will not any longer remember; assuredly not!"

Does this make someone want to run out and begin sinning wildly? Of course not. It makes our hearts want to dance for joy! It causes us to love Him more than ever. God is NOT AT ALL by any means EVER holding our sins against us. Why not? It is because His Son *took away* our sins *forever*.

After we rediscovered the gospel of the grace of God, this truth of sin consciousness was already evident in most areas of our lives. We were experiencing this freedom long before we started pointing it out in our teachings. Yet, without knowing it, this object that God pointed out to me that winter morning was a constant reminder of my shortcomings and provoking sin consciousness in my heart—preventing me from being truly free.[7]

When I saw what He was revealing, I let go of it, but not without quite a bit of trepidation. (Picture, here again, a little girl handing her treasured security blanket to her Daddy.) It

---

6 Underlining, boldface, and italics in definitions are that of the author.

7 By the way, sometimes there is a person in our lives who takes it upon himself to point out our faults. This is more difficult to correct especially if it is a family member. However, you can draw boundaries with such a person making it perfectly clear that it is not acceptable for him to serve in this role.

had been my helper and guide for most of my life, and now it was gone.

What happened next was shocking to me. In only a couple days, a new freedom began to grow in my heart. I felt God's grace and mercy extended to me where I had previously felt daily guilt and shame. In fact, new faith began to grow in my heart. If God could show me this one little thing that I never knew was hurting and binding me and set me free from it, what else would He do to help me to overcome this overwhelming area of my life? My heart began to joyfully anticipate what He would do next.

This is not to say that God will wake each of you one morning and reveal to you exactly what He revealed to me, but I'm pretty sure that for those who are facing a hopeless situation, sin consciousness is at play somewhere. Are you or is someone or something reminding you of what a "failure" you are? Those thoughts are not from God. By faith, may you begin to hear the heart of God saying to you, "My dearly loved child, I will not, I will not, I will not ever again at all remember your sins. Assuredly not!"

Day 5

LIVING BY GRACE THROUGH FAITH

*M*any Christians have lived most of their Christian lives by law, so much so, that they haven't a clue as to how it is we live now if not by law. There is beautiful, good news for us in this area. We have been created in Christ to live in Him in the exact same way that we were saved—by grace (God's undeserved favor) through faith (by believing in Jesus).

Here is a verse most believers know.

> **Ephesians 2:8-9**
> For by grace you have been saved through faith, and that not of yourselves; it is the gift of God, ⁹not of works, lest anyone should boast.

It was not of yourself—it was God's gift. "Gift" in the Greek is **doron** which means "a present; specifically, a sacrifice: - gift, offering." It was by His sacrifice and our faith in Jesus that we were saved. I hope that most true Christians understand this at least—that their initial salvation was not because of anything they did, except to believe in what He already accomplished.

Assuming that you do understand that your salvation was by grace through faith, I need to ask you this, what about afterward? Isn't this the message that is commonly taught?

Efarceus 2:8-9
For by law you continue to be saved through obedience, it is by your diligent discipline and sacrifice; the requirement of God, ⁹by your works, so that you may humbly boast.

How is it that we live after we've been born again? Some of you understand the gospel of God's grace (Acts 20:24), and you know where I'm heading, but others perhaps have been burdened down with so many Christian expectations that they aren't even sure where to start responding. Some answers might include, "God gave His best. Now I'll give my best," or "God did everything I need, so now it's up to me," or "The important thing now is to obey God and please Him," or "It's important for me to pray, read the Bible, and go to church," or "I'm just gonna hold on until He returns."

Notice how in all of these sayings, the focus has shifted off of what God does and onto what we do. Thankfully, that is not how we live. Simply stated, we now live in the same way we were saved—by grace through faith.

Colossians 2:6-10
As you therefore have received Christ Jesus the Lord, <u>so</u> walk in Him, *⁷rooted and built up in Him and established in the faith, as you have been taught, abounding in it with thanksgiving. ⁸Beware lest anyone cheat you through philosophy and empty deceit, according to the tradition of men, according to the basic principles of the world, and not according to Christ. ⁹For **in Him** dwells all the fullness of the Godhead bodily; ¹⁰and **you are complete in Him**, who is the head of all principality and power.*

We walk in Him the same way we received Him. We are born again by faith in Him, and now are built up and established by grace through faith in Him.

Hebrews 13:9

Do not be carried about with various and strange doctrines. For it is good that the heart be **established by grace**, *not with foods which have not profited those who have been occupied with them.*

Instead of thinking we need to do something more, we are to thank God that *He* has done it *all*. Immediately after telling them how to walk, Paul warned them that there would be those who try to cheat them of this glorious rest. The Amplified gives us a clearer picture of what he meant.

Colossians 2:8 AMP

See to it that no one carries you off as spoil or makes you yourselves captive by his so-called philosophy and intellectualism and vain deceit (idle fancies and plain nonsense), following human tradition (men's ideas of the material rather than the spiritual world), just crude notions following the rudimentary and elemental teachings of the universe and disregarding [the teachings of] Christ (the Messiah).

It is hard for us to imagine that there are individuals who want to carry us "off as spoil", but there are. They want to make us their disciples for less than noble reasons. Paul warned the Ephesians about these deceivers as he was saying his farewell.

Acts 20:29-30
For I know this, that after my departure savage wolves will come in among you, not sparing the flock. ³⁰Also from among yourselves men will rise up, speaking perverse things, to draw away the disciples after themselves.

Sadly, there are wolves among us. They take people captive by "speaking" (teaching) perverse things. Then Paul made an incredible declaration: "You are complete in Him." We have everything we need right now to live our entire lives in Him. Yes, we will grow and mature. God's grace will teach us how to live godly. We will be transformed by the renewing of our minds as we learn many wonderful things about God's nature, what He has done for us, and who we are in Him, but we are already right now complete in Him.

We live, truly and abundantly live, by **fai**th in God's super-abounding **grac**e toward us. How thankful we will daily be when we understand this simple truth about the Christian life. What rest we know when we are free from the yoke man has made, and wear His alone—for it is easy, as He said, and we will find rest for our souls as He promised. In any situation we face, His grace has us covered already. We don't need to add what amounts to law to improve on what God the Father accomplished through Christ by His grace.

Day 6

ALLOWING GRACE
TO PERMEATE YOUR LIFE

*I*t is one thing to know that we walk by grace through faith and not by law and another to actually live it. We began this journey to understanding these truths in 1987 when God miraculously showed me that prayer was not a requirement for Christian living but rather a beautiful privilege and joy. For many years, God gradually set my husband and me free from an abundance of "Christian" rules and regulations which we had no idea were oppressing us. Each time it was as if a knot deep inside was being untied, and when that happened, it was almost as if our whole beings sighed with relief, "Ahhh! Thank-You, Jesus!" This process took years.

Perhaps there are reasons that this all took so long. One, we were very busy living life. We were happy for what God was showing us but didn't really have time to study it closely with both of us working full-time and raising three children. Another factor was that there were very few resources available on the topic in the late 1980's and 1990's. Finally, try as we did, we could not find a fellowship that was teaching these truths.

The only source we knew at that time that spoke of this life of grace through faith was Bob George's radio show "People to People", and his then recently published book <u>Classic Christianity</u> (1989). Even so, our eyes remained blind to many of the glorious truths he shared, and more importantly just how this amazing grace would affect our lives and relationships. When I read his book now, I nod in total agreement. I get it now. It's not about me. It's about Jesus. When I read it then, it was through the dim eyes just coming to light after fifteen years of living under a mixture of law and grace.

My point is that even though most of us receive the glorious truth of God's grace with a great sense of relief, it usually takes some time for grace to permeate the different areas of our lives and root out the devastating destructions of law—especially the areas that overwhelm us. For many of us, we begin to realize, much to our sorrow, that living under a mixture of grace and law had damaging effects on our closest relationships.

Parents may realize that they raised their children mostly under law (the way the church told them they should), thinking all the while they were doing what was right, but which they now see caused their children to harden their hearts toward them, and even concerning the things of God.

Marriages which may have begun with all the love in the world were slowly eroded with the constant bombardment of marital formulas gained from endless books and teachings based on what amounted to law. Marriage—which was supposed to be a glowing example of Christ and the church—was turned into something far from it. Many of these marriages fell apart perhaps without the participants even understanding that religious law had undermined them. Others, who stuck it out, even though perhaps just as miserable as those who gave up, ended settling for something exceedingly less than the beautiful picture Paul paints of marriage in Ephesians 5.

I'd like to share with you how grace completely overhauled our marriage—which was for us for many years completely overwhelming. When we first met, we liked each other right away, but it would be almost two years before we got married. We first became close friends and then realized this friendship had blossomed into love. We were both so blessed to have found each other.

At first, there was the normal tension of learning to get along, then somehow, law crept into our relationship in the form of religious expectations. It was so subtle that we didn't notice it was taking place. Gradually, a true friendship of two equal partners in life and ministry became lopsided as a result of accumulating false perspectives on submission. No wonder we struggled. This distorted view of marriage surrounded us!

On top of that, anything we might have done to enjoy each other's company involved breaking the religious laws that were "understood" among those who attended our church. We couldn't go out dancing together. We couldn't attend a concert. We couldn't go to the movies and share a bag of popcorn. We didn't even have a television. It seemed no matter which way we turned, all we could do together involved the church.

The two of us were longing for grace but often ended giving each other quite the opposite. In between fantastic days of love and friendship, we would engage in intense arguments that devastated us both for days. It was very confusing because David and I sincerely and deeply loved each other. We were best friends. We lived together and were learning to enjoy life together. We worked on our house and yard together. We were committed to each other and to staying married. We were dedicated to our children. When we weren't arguing, we enjoyed our life together.

Eventually, the frequent arguments became overwhelming for me. I felt like a complete failure and couldn't comprehend how we could endure another blowout.

"Lord," I whimpered, "I'm not willing to live like this any longer. I love David. I want to live a long life with him, but not like this. Help me, Jesus. Give me wisdom."

Without having the understanding of how to overcome the overwhelming like I do now, I unwittingly took the first step toward victory. I gave up trying and asked God for wisdom. There was something inside of me that just gave up. Nothing we'd done to fix our relationship worked, and I was convinced nothing new would either.

God gives wisdom when we ask Him for it in faith, and He did not let me down in my moment of mourning. As clearly as ever, I heard the Holy Spirit speak to my heart, "Cathy, the only behavior you can change is your own." Looking in, one might think that God was being harsh with me considering how much pain I was experiencing, but that is not how my broken heart received it. Though He was clearly correcting me, at the same instant, He set me free. Suddenly, I had faith that I could let go of trying to coerce change out of David and let God do His work in me.

After a few years, our argument cycles mostly ceased. Both of us began to experience a new enjoyment in marriage, and not only did I change, but so did he—all without my meddling. Imagine that! Did he become the perfect spouse? Did I? No and no. However, grace began to operate in beautiful ways. No, he wasn't perfect, but neither was I. Joy came when we learned to accept each other—flaws and all. Believe me, only the grace of God could work this in our hearts. We stopped trying to fix each other. What a relief!

You see, even though we thoroughly understand that God loves us unconditionally and that our sins and lawless deeds He remembers no more, it really is another thing entirely to love others unconditionally and to remember their sins no more. We fall into this way of thinking: **"Grace for me but no grace for you!"** Not until we learn to extend to others the grace that God is extending to us can we really deeply know what grace means—for those who are closest and dearest to our hearts and even for the nameless crazy drivers who cut us off on the freeway.

"Love one another as I have loved you." Jesus did not mean to feel love for each other. He meant to *demonstrate* love for each other. If there is a relationship in your life that might right now be devastating you, the answer is to be found in accepting His grace toward you and allowing that same grace to flow through you. "Grace for me and grace for you."

Ephesians 4:29-32

*Let no corrupt word proceed out of your mouth, but what is good for necessary edification, **that it may impart grace to the hearers**. [30]And do not grieve the Holy Spirit of God, by whom you were sealed for the day of redemption. [31]Let all bitterness, wrath, anger, clamor, and evil speaking be put away from you, with all malice. [32] **And be kind to one another, tenderhearted, forgiving one another, even as God in Christ forgave you.***

Day 7

NEEDING NEW FAITH

I find it curious in my personal life that I will have faith for one miracle and then struggle to have faith to receive another. One good example is my health. We have experienced many physical healings in our family, some of which I will share in this book. Suffice it to say for now that in our home we sincerely believe that Jesus is our Healer.

Even though divine healing was commonplace in our family, four years ago my health became an overwhelming situation for me. I did believe. I really did, but for some reason, I was not seeing results as I had in the past. Why wasn't what I'd believed before "working" now?

God hadn't changed. His provisions and promises hadn't changed. I rightfully concluded that my health problems were not His fault or doing. I'd long forsaken the heresy that God sends sickness to "teach me something". I knew that it was by His grace and His Spirit that He instructed me; He didn't need to use evil to bring about good. I completely believed that He wanted me healthy. So, what was going on? Since God wasn't to blame in any way, who was? I thought I had a thorough understanding of the topic of healing but had to admit that for reasons I didn't yet understand, there was something going on in me that needed to be mended or strengthened or to grow.

What I'm about to say is a very touchy subject for many Christians, especially those who were wounded by the movements that put a heavy emphasis on faith. When someone even slightly suggests that the solution to their struggles is the need for more faith, they buckle and tighten up inside—and with good reason. In their minds, they've already attempted to have more faith, and it didn't work for them. There is another group of people who squirm when the topic of faith comes up—those who have always thought such teachings border on heresy.

I don't want to lose either group here, but I do want to discuss faith from a grace perspective. I know a first reaction might reasonably be, "Well, I don't want to hear it!" I get that. I really do. May I ask you to please listen without plugging your ears for a bit—without assuming that what I'm going to say will be the same thing you've heard before?

Although it made me a little uncomfortable, I had to admit, that for some reason, my faith was not rising to the occasion during my health crisis. I found myself praying "Lord, increase my faith. Show me what I'm missing here." I didn't do this with an ounce of guilt or shame, only with the acute awareness that I needed His help.

Notice Jesus' response when His disciples made the same request.

> **Luke 17:5-6**
> *And the apostles said to the Lord, **"Increase our faith."***
> *⁶So the Lord said, "If you have faith as a mustard seed, you can say to this mulberry tree, 'Be pulled up by the roots and be planted in the sea,' and it would obey you."*

We learn from this that it doesn't take a superabundance of faith to see great miracles happen. Imagine how amazing it would be to see a tree pull itself up by the roots and go plant its roots in the sea! All we need is a very small amount of faith to see immense problems solved. This should bring a certain amount of peace when it comes to believing.

So, from here some conclude that we don't need to ask for more faith at all. Yet, there is evidence which indicates that our faith can grow, not just grow a little bit, but exceedingly.

> **2 Thessalonians 1:3-4**
> *We are bound to thank God always for you, brethren, as it is fitting, because **your faith grows exceedingly**, and the love of every one of you all abounds toward each other, ⁴so that we ourselves boast of you among the churches of God for your patience and faith in all your persecutions and tribulations that you endure.*

One might say, well, he was referring to persecutions, and I agree; if I began to be threatened and persecuted for my faith, my faith would need to grow exceedingly because right now, I live in a country where persecuting someone for their faith could get one arrested. I've never known the fear of possibly being killed for my faith. If my country ever turned a blind eye to this, though, my faith would need to grow in that area.

I do not think it is a leap in logic at all to conclude that if faith can grow exceedingly to endure increased persecutions and tribulations, it can also grow exceedingly to help us to overcome the overwhelming in our lives. Indeed, our faith can grow to reach any need that we have, and when faced with a mountain of health problems as I was, my faith needed to grow, and it needed to grow exceedingly.

Where people go astray at this point of realizing that their faith needs to grow, is taking it upon themselves to make it happen. (Let the grunting and groaning begin.) No matter what faith-growing formula I might have employed in the past, it all came down to me doing something to bring about more faith—about me somehow convincing myself to believe. Yet, as I prayed one late night, experiencing pain and surrounded by fears, wondering if I should once again head for the emergency room, I knew the answer to my need was not to be found in me at all.

Through my tears, I began to confess in the form of praise what I already sincerely and honestly believed. "God, I trust You completely. You have never failed me, and You never will. I would rather go to my grave trusting You than ever even to hint that these troubles are from You or that You are withholding Your gift of healing from me. You know this, Lord. I trust You completely. I don't understand this, but I do know You, and You are faithful. You are my Healer. You keep Your promises. Help me believe in You."

I'd heard the teaching again and again that faith comes by hearing and hearing by the word of God. Perhaps I didn't understand the teachings very well, but what my mind always heard was that if I would immerse myself in the Bible, I'd have more faith. The fact was, though, that I had immersed myself in the Bible. I was studying it constantly. We were *teaching* from the Bible. I was so full of Scripture that it was overflowing from me as I wrote my first book. Previously, I would have been discouraged and maybe even dared to ask, "God, what more do You want from me?" but I knew better. I experienced an increase in my faith before; not only for our family's health but for our difficult marriage. Now, I needed new faith to face this mountain. I didn't know the answer, but I knew where I would find it.

It would be almost two years before my health crisis ended, and I'm happy to say that the many physical challenges I faced during that time have all been resolved, some by practical solutions and others by healing. How I thank God for His faithfulness and for helping my faith in Him to grow.

Day 8

FINDING FAITH

---

*T*here is good news about how our faith can grow to over-come the overwhelming areas of our lives. The answer is as sweet and simple as it can be. God wants to give us something that will cause our faith to grow. I'll give you a hint—it is found in His grace! Yes, His amazing grace!

So, let's discuss a commonly misunderstood verse. Context, of course, will shed the light we need to understand it more accurately.

> **Romans 10:13-17**
> *For "whoever calls on the name of the Lord shall be **saved**."*
> *¹⁴How then shall they call on Him in whom they have not **believed**? And how shall they believe in Him of whom they have not heard? And how shall they hear without a preacher? ¹⁵And how shall they preach unless they are sent? As it is written:*
> *"How beautiful are the feet of those who preach the **gospel** of peace, Who bring **glad tidings of good things!**"*
> *¹⁶But they have not all obeyed the gospel. For Isaiah says, "Lord, who has believed our report?" ¹⁷**So then faith comes by hearing, and hearing by the word of God.***

Just what does "word of God" mean here? As I said, when I used to read "word of God", I thought of Scripture and specifically of my NKJV Bible. Yet, predominantly in the New Testament, the term "word of God" refers to the gospel—the good news of God's grace and love demonstrated in the giving of His Son and His subsequent resurrection. After only a few minutes of searching this phrase in the book of Acts, this becomes obvious. The proof in this portion of Scripture is found in the preceding verses. The word of God is the gospel of peace.[8] It is the glad tidings of good things. **Faith for salvation comes by *(originates from)* hearing the glad tidings of good things preached.**

We can see this principle at work in the natural realm quite easily. Someone might tell us the good news that there is a sale at our favorite store. We believe what we hear and head off to buy something fully convinced and confident that we are going to get a great deal. Or, maybe we like someone, but aren't sure he likes us, but then a friend tells us that he does. Faith rises, and we might even find the courage to give him a call. Perhaps we hear that they are hiring at a place we'd like to work. So, we get dressed and go! You can see then, even with everyday things, that good news brings faith to our hearts, and faith results in taking action.

Many of us heard the good news that Jesus rose from the dead and that whoever believes in Him will not perish but have everlasting life. After hearing these glad tidings, faith came to us. When faith arrived, we took action, and confessed Jesus as the Lord, and were saved. The Biblical pattern of saving faith looks like this.

---

[8]   There is only one gospel and it is referred to in many ways. It is called the gospel of the kingdom, gospel of Jesus Christ, gospel of the Son of God, gospel of the kingdom of God, gospel of the grace of God, gospel of God, gospel of His Son, gospel of Christ, gospel of peace, gospel of the glory of Christ, gospel of your salvation, and the gospel of the blessed God. Paul called the gospel "my" gospel not only because he taught it, but because he received it by revelation from Jesus Christ.

- The GOOD NEWS of His grace exists.
- The good news is PREACHED.
- We HEAR the good news.
- FAITH COMES-WE BELIEVE the good news.
- We CONFESS-SPEAK what we believe about His grace.
- SALVATION COMES.

We don't need to work up faith at all. Faith finds its origins in hearing good news. This is simply how it works. If we find that our faith is not quite rising to the occasion in our overwhelming situations, this is the miraculous pattern of finding the new faith we need.

Faith isn't something we work up or earn or force ourselves to have.
Faith comes to us when we hear of His grace toward us.

My favorite example of this is the night my husband was born again. He had just transferred to a new university, and as the downtown was alive with other college students, he was walking around hoping to hear of a party. He wasn't looking for God that night. He wanted to have some fun. Unknown to him, there was a group of Christians also walking the streets and inviting anyone who might be interested, to come to a concert at a Christian coffee house. It so touches my heart to see God's perspective of this scenario. David was looking for a party. The Christians were looking for someone who would hear. Then it happened. One of the Christians greeted David. David was impressed that this fellow had hair down to his waist—a signal to David that this guy was "cool" and might know where a party would be. So, he willingly went with him to the concert.

The coffee house was alive with college students. The concert began and was followed by a message, both of them presenting the good news of God's love for him. David heard the message and saving faith came to him right then and there. When the invitation came, David went forward and prayed a prayer he can't even remember now, but one in which he surely declared his belief in the Lord Jesus Christ. For the first time in His life, he "saw" Jesus and fell instantly in love with Him. The message was preached. David heard the good news. Faith came. He confessed. He was saved. Glory to God!

Just as faith comes to us for salvation by hearing about God's offer of salvation, so faith comes to us to receive other things from God. Let us first look at one example of how faith to be healed came to someone who heard the good news that Jesus would heal her.

Mark 5:25
Now a certain woman had a flow of blood for twelve years,

Consider this Jewish woman's social condition. First of all, she was considered unclean according to the law (Lev. 15:25, 20:18). Anyone who touched her or anyone whom she touched would also be unclean. Friends and family had to steer clear of her. Not even her husband could be with her without being unclean, and would have to go through ceremonial cleansing if he even touched her—that is, if she was even married. Who would want to marry or stay married to a woman with such an intimate problem? She was likely lonely and undesirable.

Since this problem had gone on for twelve years, it is probable that everyone in the community knew about her health. Privacy was limited; embarrassment was abundant. Imagine the amount of unsolicited health advice and home remedies this engendered.

Then of course, as "good" friends sometimes do, she was surely encouraged to repent of whatever sin she'd committed that had brought on this curse so that she could be healed. She likely searched her heart repeatedly to see if she could pinpoint what was causing this. Long-term overwhelming situations have a way of bringing about unwanted advice and accusations.

Mark 5:26
And had suffered many things from many physicians. She had spent all she had and was no better, but rather grew worse.

The fact that she had "suffered *many* things from many physicians" is a testimony to the fact that she wanted to be healed and was doing everything she could to get well. (Notice also that "she" spent all she had—another possible indicator that she was not married.) I don't even want to imagine what these treatments might have been, and whatever they were, it was costing her "all she had" and to no avail.

Can you relate to this? My experience is that doctors can be of great help to us—until they just aren't. Have you ever stopped getting care because you just couldn't afford it or because you got weary of test after test with no diagnosis, or a diagnosis with no helpful treatment? Did you ever have to face the fact that instead of getting better after all of your efforts, time, and money, you were actually getting worse? This woman was overwhelmed by her health. Surely such a condition resulted in serious weakness. She doubtless had little time for anything else. Her senses reminded her continuously that she was not well.

Mark 5:27
When she heard about Jesus, she came behind Him in the crowd and touched His garment.

She heard about Jesus, and what she heard was good news. Jesus was healing all who came to Him—completely and instantly healing them. The blind were seeing. The lame were walking. The deaf were hearing. Leprosy, another disease resulting in one being unclean, was removed. Surely He would heal her condition. Faith came to her by hearing of His grace, and that faith propelled her to reach out to Jesus. She, even in her current frailty, pressed through the crowd casting aside her shame until she touched the hem of His garment.

> **Mark 5:28-29**
> For she said, "If only I may touch His clothes, I shall be made well."
> 29Immediately the fountain of her blood was dried up, and she felt in her body that she was healed of the affliction.

She heard good news, and faith came to her which lead her to confess what she believed, even though it was only to herself (Mt. 9:21). She didn't just believe Jesus could heal her but that He would. Her healing was so thorough that she could tell immediately that she was whole. How different her story would have been if she hadn't heard that Jesus was healing, if faith hadn't come, if she hadn't confessed what she believed, and if she hadn't determined to reach out to touch His garment.

Perhaps you are thinking, "I'm happy for her and for everyone else who has been healed, but I've tried all those healing teachings, and they didn't work for me." May I ask you, with all due compassion, how you would respond to someone who said, "I tried to get saved, but it didn't work for me"? Surely you would know that the person was missing something. Maybe he never heard the true gospel. Maybe he thought salvation comes to those who go to church each week, or who attend classes, or who are deemed saved by someone else, or those who are baptized, or those who confess they are a sinner and ask for forgiveness, or to the ones who live a holy life. One way or another, you would seek to help the person see that the promise of salvation is for all who believe that God raised Jesus from the dead and who confess that He is the Lord. I hope you would never say, "Yeah, maybe God doesn't want to save you personally. Maybe He didn't die for you."

Perhaps you have many conflicting thoughts on this topic, but at least be open to what we can see in this woman's story. She heard about His willingness to heal, faith came to her, and she let nothing get in her way of receiving the miracle she needed.

> **Mark 5:33-34**
> *But the woman, fearing and trembling, knowing what had happened to her, came and fell down before Him and told Him the whole truth. ³⁴ And He said to her, "Daughter, **your faith has made you well**. Go in peace, and be healed of your affliction."*

Jesus tells us exactly how this woman was healed when He said, "Your faith has made you well." Faith in what? In Him—in the good news she'd heard about Him—faith which motivated her to confess what she believed and then to take action based on her belief in His grace. So, at the risk of being too repetitive, let me present again the Biblical principle of grace and faith this time as demonstrated in her story.

- God's healing grace existed.
- Someone told her about His healing grace.
- She heard it.
- Faith/belief for her healing came to her.
- She confessed that she would be healed.
- She took action.
- She was healed.

What I am hoping to communicate is that when we hear the good news of God's grace, faith comes to us. We don't have to work it up, pretend we have it, or take some risky action to prove we have faith in an attempt to force God's hand. It isn't about us. It is about what God has done through His Son.

I hope you are beginning to hear the good news that I am preaching right now. It is this: Just as faith to be saved came to my husband by hearing the good news of Jesus' offer of salvation preached to him; and just as faith to be healed came to the woman with the flow of blood when she heard that Jesus offered healing to the masses, **faith will also come to us for our specific overwhelming situations when we hear the good news pertaining to our own particular problems.**

Faith is not an area of our lives in which we strive. It is meant as a place of rest for us. Think about it. Read through the gospels and the book of Acts. You will see this principle in action again and again. Faith comes by hearing, and hearing by the preaching of glad tidings of good things.

Day 9

GOOD NEWS

---

*N*ow for some good news that will be very helpful and comforting as you face tough times. These are truths you can preach to yourself when you are feeling discouraged, or it seems you can't go on. Since faith comes by hearing good news, we miraculously find that as we speak these truths to ourselves, we discover the grace and faith we need to endure and overcome. All of these are woven together by God's love for us. (You might want to bookmark this chapter to read again the next time you feel the walls crashing in.)

God Sees and Hears You

Sometimes it feels like we are almost completely alone in the struggles we face. It seems that even those who are closest to us can't reach the lonely place where we are. We can rest assured that even when others cannot see or understand what it is we are experiencing, God sees us and our pain, and He has deep compassion for us.

In fact, one of His names is El Roi, the God who Sees. We learn of this name as we read of Hagar in the desert alone and pregnant. Even though it was Sarah's idea that Hagar go into Abraham for the express purpose of conceiving a son, it was unacceptable that she despised Sarah when the union was fruitful. Sarah complained to Abraham about her, and he gave her permission to deal with her as she pleased. When Sarah treated Hagar harshly, probably after being fed up with her attitude, Hagar fled.

So, there she sat at a spring of water in the wilderness. It wasn't her fault that Sarah gave her to Abraham so that he could have a son, but it was her arrogance that created the rift between Sarah and herself. It was also her fault that instead of changing her attitude toward Sarah, she ran away.

What was God's response? Did he leave her alone in the wilderness to suffer so she could see the error of her ways? No, He gently corrected her. He sent an angel to help her see where to go from there. The angel instructed her to go back and submit herself to Sarah. He even told her to name her son Ishmael, which means "God will hear". So blessed by this heavenly visitation was she, that we read, "Then she called the name of the Lord who spoke to her, You-Are-the-God-Who-Sees (El Roi); for she said, 'Have I also here seen Him who sees me?'" (Gen. 16:13) Think of this, in just one story of one woman's *mistake*, we have revealed to us two very important characteristics of God. He sees you, and He hears you. You are not alone—not ever.

So many times when we face hard times, the blame game begins. How did we get ourselves into this? "If I'd only—. I wish I hadn't. I shouldn't have. It's all my fault. I deserve this." Here is the good news. Even if our problems are our own doing or partially so, God still sees and hears us. He will help us. Consider, too, the superior relationship we have with God—that we are called his sons and daughters. Would you leave your own child in the wilderness *to die* to "teach him a lesson"? He will take care of us when we call on Him—even if the mess we are in was caused by us, even if we were acting irresponsibly. He will cause all things; yes, even our wrong decisions, to work together for our good.

"Father, I thank You that You see me right now—that I am not alone. You see me, and You hear me. You will bring me from this place of weakness into a position of strength."

Psalm 40:1-3
I waited patiently for the Lord;
And He inclined to me,
And heard my cry.
²He also brought me up out of a horrible pit,
Out of the miry clay,
And set my feet upon a rock,
And established my steps.
³He has put a new song in my mouth—
Praise to our God;
Many will see it and fear,
And will trust in the Lord.

God Knows the Truth

Sometimes we want help, but when we try to explain it to certain people, their only response is to try and fix us. The thinking is that all of the problems we face are somehow our own fault. Now, it may be that we had some part to play in getting where we are today, but what good does it do to keep proving it's our fault—as if repeatedly admitting we were at least partially to blame solves the problem? Whatever the situation, whether we are to blame or not, we can't redo yesterday.

God is not holding our sins against us. We are forgiven. While "sin" has natural consequences that might be affecting us and we may need to make it right with those we have offended, God is not punishing us for our sins. He already punished Jesus.

People looking in may visibly see our struggles and be making all sorts of conclusions and passing judgments, but we can rest assured that God knows the truth. He knows if we are still believing or doing certain things to contribute to it all and whether we are not. We don't need to prove ourselves to Him or to anyone. It's such a joy just to sit down with Him and know He knows. We can be completely open before Him because we don't need to hide or pretend.

"Jesus, You are the only One who knows the whole truth about this problem in my life. I know that to everyone else looking in, this is all my fault, but God, You know the truth. You know how I got into this mess, and You are the only One who can get me out."

> **Romans 8:26-27**
> *Likewise the Spirit also helps in our weak-nesses. For we do not know what we should pray for as we ought, but the Spirit Himself makes intercession for us with groanings which cannot be uttered. ²⁷Now He who searches the hearts knows what the mind of the Spirit is, because He makes intercession for the saints according to the will of God.*

God Cares for You

Especially when it comes to difficult relationships, it is easy to start to feel that no one is concerned at all about what we are going through. Financial struggles, too, can bring about these thoughts of no one caring. Please be encouraged to know that God does care. We are instructed to weep with those who weep, and we know that when Jesus saw the pain of Mary and Martha, he wept. **God will not be less than He asks us to be.** He is compassionate. We are told to cast all of our cares on Him because He cares for us. God isn't in heaven apathetically looking down on our demise. Still, it's easy to think He's on His throne with His arms folded waiting for us to fix things. We cry out for help and picture Him too busy even to listen, or we imagine Him turning away in disgust. These thoughts couldn't be further from the truth. He sees you. He hears you. He cares about you. When you feel that you can't go on, take a minute to remind yourself that *God cares for you personally.*

My mom told me about something she did when she was worried about my brother and me which is an illustration of casting your cares upon the Lord. She said that, in her mind, she took a napkin in her hands and put my brother and me inside. Then she folded it up and handed us to Jesus. She said that once in a while, she'd check inside the napkin, but then she'd give us right back. So many times in life this has helped me—just to take whomever or whatever it is that's over my head, place it in a napkin, and hand it to Jesus.

"Lord, I can't bear this situation. It's just too much for me. So, I place this in Your hands because I believe that You care for me."

> **1 Peter 5:6-7**
> *Therefore humble yourselves under the mighty hand of God, that He may exalt you in due time, [7]casting all your care upon Him, for He cares for you.*

God is for You Not Against You

Many Christians have been exposed to teachings that paint God as someone who is constantly working against us. When something goes wrong we see God more as our antagonist than the helper He claims to be.

Not too long ago while sitting in a church we'd attended over two years, the pastor said, "I really believe God sends evil to bring about good in our lives." This shocking statement left me stunned, but surely in the two and a half years we'd attended there, he had said something similar. Maybe in the past, we overlooked such statements thinking he didn't really mean it the way we heard it. On that Sunday, though, the horror of what he just said was staring me in the face, and I said to myself, "I really don't believe that."

Knowing David also heard it the way I just did, I whispered in his ear, "I am leaving. If you want to stay, that's fine. I'll be in the car." I remember sitting in the car still baffled but now in tears asking God, "Do we need to write down what we believe and nail it to the church doors?"

Hear this! God is not against you. He is for you. He is not sending evil to teach you. Yes, He really is on your side. He wants you to be successful. He wants your relationships to be enjoyable. He is right this very minute working all things together for your good, not for your downfall—no matter how you feel, no matter what it looks like, God is for you.

God is not "putting us in a pressure cooker so that our flesh will fall off and rise to the top." He doesn't need to do this because life is difficult enough to provide us with multiple opportunities to mature. No, instead, He is there with us when these hard times come, working to build us up! He is not trying to crucify us, and we certainly don't need to crucify ourselves. We were already crucified with Christ and now live risen with Him.

"Father, You are for me not against me. You gave Your Son for me in death even while I was your enemy. How much more will you provide for me now?"

> **Romans 8:31-32**
> *What then shall we say to these things? If* ***God is for us***, *who can be against us? [32]He who did not spare His own Son, but delivered Him up for us all, how shall He not with Him also **freely give** us all things?*

Nothing is Impossible for God or for You

Christians are convinced that God is all-powerful, but when the threat of death or disaster seems to be looming over us, it is easy to forget that **nothing is impossible for God**. Before you let fear take you over, stop and remind yourself of this: nothing is impossible for God who is living inside of you.

What is also equally amazing is that Scripture teaches us that **nothing is impossible to him who believes**. Nothing. No matter what, we can trust Him. Even if we die tomorrow, we win. We will be with Him. If we live, that will give us the opportunity to serve Him even longer.

"Jesus, I look to You right now. This situation looks impossible, but it isn't, because nothing is impossible for You. **I believe in You, and therefore, nothing is impossible for me.** I trust You even though this looks really bad. You are my Deliverer. You are my Savior. You are my Healer. You are my Provider. I ask You to do the impossible in me and through me."

> **Luke 1:37**
> *"For with God nothing will be impossible."*
> **Matthew 17:20**
> *"Assuredly, I say to you, if you have faith as a mustard seed, you will say to this mountain, 'Move from here to there,' and it will move; and* **nothing will be impossible for you.**"

God is Willing

I am assuming that you already believe that God is able to do the impossible, but sometimes we wonder if He is willing to do a miracle for us individually. Consider this, Jesus Christ is the visible image of the invisible God. When we look at His life on earth, we begin to see what His will is. God the Son we see in Scripture is the exact representation of God the Father in heaven (Col. 1:15).

Since He is able, and He is willing, then He will help us if we believe. "Jesus, I believe that You are not only able to help me and that You want to help me, but also that You will help me."

> **Matthew 8:1-3**
> *When He had come down from the mountain, great multitudes followed Him. ²And behold, a leper came and worshiped Him, saying, "Lord,* **if You are willing**, *You can make me clean."*

*³Then Jesus put out His hand and touched him, saying, **"I am willing;** be cleansed."*
Immediately his leprosy was cleansed.
2 Corinthians 1:20
*For all the promises of God in Him are **Yes**, and in Him **Amen**, to the glory of God through us.*

Following is a wonderfully amazing illustration of this concept. It is written by my cousin, Nancy Morin, who is also one of the editors of this book.

> *Just three months after celebrating his second birthday, our precious and only son suffered his first seizure. Stunned and even angry, I sought God for the "why?" answer. I prayed that God would heal my baby, Joseph, and my husband and I thought God had healed him, until months later, he suffered repeated seizures. At our doctor's strong and frightening urging, we finally succumbed to medication.*
>
> *I cried out to God asking Him if it was sin in my life. I continued to pray for healing, but really, I just slowly accepted it, assuaging myself that this was God's will and that God would bring good from this heartbreak. Oh, I believed my Almighty God could heal Joseph. Yes, indeed; I believed my Savior, who died on the cross, by whose stripes we are healed, could heal him. I just didn't believe he **would** or **had already** healed him.*
>
> *My lack of faith seized both Joseph and me for seven years until the Holy Spirit exhorted me, "Enough!" I dropped to my knees and prayed, "Father God, in the name of Jesus Christ, heal my son!" From that moment, I knew he was healed—knew it! "But, Father God, how can I now convince Joseph's doctor*

to take him off the powerful medication that has kept him seizure-free for seven years?"

Amazingly, two weeks later, the doctor called me. Based on blood tests, he wanted to withdraw slowly Joseph's medication. Stunned! But now with incredible joy! I laid prostrate on my bedroom floor rejoicing in tears, overwhelmed that Jesus had overcome for me, for Joseph. My five-year-old daughter, Ciara, walked in, saw me, and immediately dropped to the floor with me and began praising God. Then we all danced, rejoicing like never before.

Today Joseph lives in faith with the powerful, triumphal knowledge that he was made whole because I exercised whole faith in our Healer and our Victor, Jesus Christ.

God Wants Us to Ask

There have been different teachings over the years that tend to disparage the concept of asking from God for personal needs. As a child in the 1960's, we were taught to pray for five things using our fingers on one hand. I don't remember exactly how the formula went now, but I've never forgotten that the last prayer was the pinky finger (the smallest one), and those were the prayers for ourselves. At such a young age, the idea of praying for my own needs was presented as less significant, perhaps even selfish. As an adult, we learned of other prayer formulas with similar overtones. Some claimed that after worshipping and praying for others' priorities first, we wouldn't even want to pray for our own needs. Again, the idea is that to pray for one's own needs borders on being self-centered.

Nothing could be further from the truth, and God does not want us to feel ashamed about praying to Him for our needs. God not only *wants* us to ask but also delights in seeing the joy we experience when He answers our prayers. It's like a parent who savors the moment when he sees the happiness of his child receiving a much longed-for gift. Any sacrifice that went into that gift is forgotten as our children's eyes widen, and they shout for joy with the realization that what they hold in their hands is the very thing they requested. They feel loved. They feel joy. They express gratitude.

We all want to please God, but seldom give thought to the truth that God wants to please us. He *wants* to answer our prayers.

"Father, I thank You that I am Your child. You tell me to ask. You want to bring joy to my heart by answering my prayers. So, I confidently ask You to meet this need in my life."

Matthew 7:7-8
"Ask, and it will be given to you; seek, and you will find; knock, and it will be opened to you. ⁸For everyone who asks receives, and he who seeks finds, and to him who knocks it will be opened."
John 16:23-24
"And in that day you will ask Me nothing. Most assuredly, I say to you, whatever you ask the Father in My name He will give you. ²⁴Until now you have asked nothing in My name. Ask, and you will receive, that your joy may be full."
Luke 12:32
"Do not fear, little flock, for it is your Father's good pleasure to give you the kingdom."

God is Right Here Right Now

When you pray, where do you see God in relationship to you? Is He in heaven and are you on earth? Do you visualize a certain distance between the two of you? Do you calculate your nearness to God by how consistent you've been in prayer?

Let's think about this together. Yes, God is in heaven, and yes, we are on earth, but we are also in heaven seated with Him, and He is also on earth living inside of us. In fact, God is so close to us at all times that Paul wrote that we are "one spirit" with Him. We cannot be closer to God than we are right now.

I'm going to say something that might sound a bit shocking—something that might make you buckle inside, but hear me, prayer does not bring us closer to God. It is the blood of Jesus that brought us close to God. Nothing we do can improve on the blood He shed that brings us into the holiest place. We don't pray so that we can be closer to God. We pray because we are close to God.

**We don't need to enter His presence
because His presence has once and for all time
entered us, and we have once and for all time
entered His presence.**

This makes a profound impact when we pray. When you pray, be conscious of the fact that God is present with you and in you and that you are present with Him seated with Jesus in the heavenly places—and that even more amazingly, consider this truth—you are one spirit together with Him. All of these things are true simultaneously.

> ***Hebrews 10:19-23*[9]**
> *Therefore, brethren, having boldness to enter the Holiest **by the blood of Jesus**, [20]by a new and living way which He*

---

[9] *This entering into the Holy of Holies which the Messiah inaugurated for sinners was by way of a freshly-slain and living road, and this road went "through the veil, that is to say, His flesh." The inner veil of the tabernacle separated the Holy Place from the Holy of Holies. It barred man's access to God... When the Messiah died on the Cross, the veil of the temple was rent by the unseen hand of God, showing Israel two things, that the Messiah had now provided the actual entrance for the sinner into the presence of God, and that the symbolic sacrifices were to be discontinued, for the Reality to whom they pointed had come (9:7-10).*
- Wuest's Word Studies from the Greek New Testament – Vol. 2

consecrated for us, through the veil, **that is, His flesh,** [21]and having a High Priest over the house of God, [22]let us draw near with a true heart in full assurance of faith, having our hearts sprinkled from an evil conscience and our bodies washed with pure water. [23]Let us hold fast the confession of our hope without wavering, for He who promised is faithful.

Colossians 1:27
To them God willed to make known what are the riches of the glory of this mystery among the Gentiles: which is **Christ in you,** the hope of glory.

Ephesians 2:4-7
But God, who is rich in mercy, because of His great love with which He loved us, [5]even when we were dead in trespasses, made us alive together with Christ (by grace you have been saved), [6]and **raised us up together, and made us sit together in the heavenly places in Christ Jesus,** [7]that in the ages to come He might show the exceeding riches of His grace in His kindness toward us in Christ Jesus.

1 Corinthians 6:17
But he who is joined to the Lord is **one spirit with Him**.

He Will Never Leave You or Forsake You

When we face hard times, we need to know that everything between God and us is right, but sometimes our overwhelming circumstances are so intense that we might feel as if we are forsaken by God. This is especially true if someone has been taught the error that hard times are God's way of disciplining us or that we have become separated from His presence because we've fallen short in some area.

However, He has promised never to leave us. The Amplified translation demonstrates to us just how sure this promise is.

> **Hebrews 13:5b AMP**
> *For He [God] Himself has said, I will not in any way fail you nor give you up nor leave you without support. [I will] not, [I will] not, [I will] not in any degree leave you helpless nor forsake nor let [you] down (relax My hold on you)! [Assuredly not!]*

In fact, it is precisely when we have weaknesses that we can come boldly and confidently before Him. He understands everything about us.

> **Hebrews 4:15-16**
> *For we do not have a High Priest who cannot **sympathize with our weaknesses,** but was in all points tempted as we are, yet without sin. [16]Let us **therefore** come boldly to the throne of grace, that we may **obtain mercy and find grace to help in time of need**.*

When we "come before Him", we don't need to see ourselves approaching Him as if He is in heaven and we are on earth. He is inside of us. We are in the holy place with Him at all times. There is no separation. We don't need to "enter" His presence. We are one spirit with Him. When we come before His throne of grace, we are already in the throne room! Glory to God. We simply speak to Him. No formulas are necessary.

In those moments when you are tempted to despair (give up hope), remind yourself of this gift of knowing you are right now with Him and that He will never forsake you, especially in your times of need.

"God, I thank You for promising never ever to leave me or let go of me—not ever. You are here with me right now in my time of need even though I am not 'perfect'. You are my friend, my brother, my Father, and my God."

Nothing Can Separate You from His Love

We might think it goes without saying, but God loves us. He does. Let us not diminish this fact by putting emphasis primarily on our love for God. My husband and I were caught up in this frame of mind for many years. The twisted thought is that if we focus on God's love for us we can become self-centered instead of God-centered. It makes me dizzy thinking about it now, but previously, that idea made perfect sense to us.

Actually, the complete opposite is true. Putting our emphasis on our love for God is what makes us self-focused. It becomes all about us and what we do for Him instead of on what He did and does for us. Let us settle the argument here and now.

> ***1 John 4:9-10***
> *In this the love of God was manifested toward us, that God has sent His only begotten Son into the world, that we might live through Him.* ¹⁰*In **this** is love, **not** **that we loved God, but that He loved us** and sent His Son to be the propitiation for our sins.*

"Loving God" was so ingrained in me, that even after 26 years of learning about the gospel of His grace, I still have to force myself to focus on His love for me. On top of the poor teaching received in this area, my personality is very task-oriented. It is the easiest thing ever for me to get consumed with any ministry I am doing for God. I purposely have to take time during the day to remember how much He loves me.

This is one reason I now enjoy taking communion. Jesus said to "do this in remembrance of Me". For so many years, though, I took communion in remembrance of myself. Did I love God enough? Had I sinned? Was I living a holy life?

Had I offended anyone? With so much self-reflection, I don't know how I ever concluded I was worthy to take communion at all. However, now when I take communion, the focus is on Him—on what He did for me because He loves me.

> **Romans 5:8**
> *But God demonstrates His own love toward us, in that while we were still sinners, Christ died for us.*

If He loved us enough to die for us when we were His enemies, shall He not now love us all the more now that we are His children? Shall God only have compassion on the lost, but then turn His back on us? This is completely illogical.

There are Christians today who travel the world to "experience God's love" for them by attending churches or ministries that supposedly have a "great presence of God", but notice in the verse above that God demonstrates, present tense, His love for us in that He sent His Son to die for us even when we were still sinners.[10]

So many times when I have been at the end of my strength in certain situations, the only way to survive was to camp out in His love for me. "God, I believe that You love me and that nothing, not even this situation can separate me from Your love for me. I thank You for this love. I trust in Your love. I need Your love. I receive Your love right now for this situation." When our worlds are upside down, when it seems like all is lost, nothing can separate us from God's love for us.

God loves you.
That is something you cannot change.
He loves you
As you are
Where you are
No matter what you are doing.

---

[10] Notice also, that we WERE sinners.

He loves you
Even if you don't love Him
Even if you don't believe in Him
Even if you hate Him.

His love for you is E N O R M O U S.
His love for you is not based on how successful you are.
His love is not withheld from you if you are a failure.
He loves you, even if no one else on earth loves you.

He loves you because He created you.
He loves you because He is love.
Loving is who He is and what He does.
He simply and completely loves you.

God has some things to say to you.
"You are not alone.
I see you.
I know you.
I love you.
I am not mad at you.
I am not holding your faults against you."

Can you hear Him speaking to you?
He is saying, "Come to Me and I will give you rest."

You might ask, "How?"

God says, "Believe in my Son, Jesus."
He came to earth, gave His life for you, rose from the dead, and lives forevermore.`

Do you believe this?
If you do, there is one more thing for you to do.
Believe in Him as the Lord.

You might say, "Well, I don't believe this."
God already knows this, and yet
He still loves you.

Why don't you ask Him to help you believe?
He will. Why would He do that?
Because He loves you even if you don't believe in Him,
Even if you don't love Him back.

No matter who or what may have hurt you
No matter whom you may have hurt
He cares and wants to help you.
He wants to heal your pain and use you to help others.

Sound impossible? Nothing is impossible for Him.

If you don't believe in Him
He already knows.
If you ask Him
He will open your eyes to see.

If you believe in Him
And you've been taught
That His love for you is conditional
He wants to show you
That this isn't true.
If you ask Him
He will open your eyes to see.

No matter how you feel right now
God loves you.
He wants to give you His life.
Reach out to Him because He's reaching out to you.[11]

---

[11] C. D. Hildebrand

Day 10

DISCOVERING SPECIFIC GOOD NEWS

*T*hankfully, God provides many different means to give us the good news that we need to help us overcome our overwhelming circumstances. It doesn't matter what the situation is, He is able to help each one of us personally and specifically, and He knows just how best to reach our hearts. If you are looking for a cookie-cutter formula for success, this might not be the best chapter for you, but if you are ready to tap into the supernatural source needed finally to obtain the victory you so desire, read on.

Before we begin examining the many ways God speaks to His children, let us first differentiate between how God spoke to His people before the resurrection and how He speaks to us now. The writer of Hebrews sums it up best.

> **Hebrews 1:1-4**
> *God, who at various times and in various ways spoke **in time past to the fathers by the prophets**, ²**has in these last days spoken to us by His Son**, whom He has appointed heir of all things, through whom also He made the worlds; ³who being the brightness of His glory and the express image of His person, and upholding all things by the word of His power, when He had by Himself purged our sins, sat down at the right hand of the*

*Majesty on high, ⁴having become so **much
better than the angels**, as He by inheritance
obtained a more excellent name than they.*

What a glorious privilege is ours! Previously, God spoke
to mankind through prophets and angels, but we have the
honor of being spoken to directly by the Son Himself. We,
believers, have only one Mediator between God and us, and
He is Jesus Christ.

1 Timothy 2:5-6
*For there is one God and one Mediator
between God and men, the Man Christ
Jesus, ⁶who gave Himself a ransom for all, to
be testified in due time,*

Jesus, who became a man, is far superior to angels or
prophets because He is, in fact, God.

Hebrews 1:5-10
For to which of the angels did He ever say:
"You are My Son,
*Today I have begotten You"?
And again:
"I will be to Him a Father,
And He shall be to Me a Son"?
⁶But when He again brings the firstborn into
the world, He says:*
"Let all the angels of God worship Him."
*⁷And of the angels He says:
"Who makes His angels spirits
And His ministers a flame of fire."*
⁸But to the Son He says:
"Your throne, O God, is forever and ever;
*A scepter of righteousness is the
scepter of Your kingdom.*

> *⁹You have loved righteousness and hated
> lawlessness;
> Therefore God, Your God, has anointed You
> With the oil of gladness more than Your
> companions."*
> **¹⁰And: "You, Lord, in the beginning laid the
> foundation of the earth,
> And the heavens are the work of
> Your hands."**

How are Christians to regard prophets?¹² Let us first look
at the role of prophets before Jesus came to earth. They
were seen as God's voice to the people. Their writings were
considered Scripture.

> **Matthew 11:11**
> *"Assuredly, I say to you, among those born of
> women there has not risen one greater than
> John the Baptist;* **but he who is least in the
> kingdom of heaven is greater than he."**

We might consider ourselves "least" in the kingdom of
God, but observe the status we've been given in Christ—
that of being "greater" than John the Baptist whom Jesus
declared to be greater than all who came before him. We
may feel like a worthless speck of dust on the earth, but we
are more and have much more than John the Baptist or any
prophet before him.

Today God speaks to believers through His Son directly.
We don't need a prophet or an angel to bring a message to
us from God. Each of us has individual communication with
the very God who created the universe.

It's important to keep the above in our minds, because
when we face stressful situations in life that seem out of our

---

¹² My doctrinal perspective, based on the book of Acts, is that there are prophets
in the body of Christ today, but it is clear from the examples given that their role
and authority is not the same as it was prior to the coming of Christ.

control, we can easily be seduced into seeking angelic visitations or prophetic words instead of going to Jesus.

I don't negate that there are prophets in the body of Christ and that angels minister to us as we see in the book of Acts, *but they are not our mediators.* We have only one Mediator. His name is Jesus. He will speak to us directly. There is no record in the book of Acts of Christians seeking "a word" from the Lord via a prophet. There simply isn't. Yes, prophets did speak and foretell, edify, exhort, and comfort as the Spirit gave them faith, but nowhere do we see people standing in lines to hear from God via a human medium. We don't need a seer to hear from God. How offensive it must be to God who sent His only Son so that we could indeed know Him personally and speak directly to Him, for us to seek out so-called "words" through human beings—for us to seek out other mediators. Is this not akin to idolatry? Why should we seek prophetic or angelic advice when we have Jesus? In these last days, God speaks *to us through His Son.* Let the one who listens hear.

When we need to hear from God specific good news that will bring us the faith we need to see lasting change, it is important to draw our understanding of just how it is God speaks to us today through Scripture. This will prevent us from falling prey to yet another formula for success which is usually based on conforming to religious laws.

By His Spirit NOT by Law

> **Romans 8:14-15**
> *For as many as are led by the Spirit of God, these are sons of God. [15]For you did not receive the spirit of bondage again to fear, but you received the Spirit of adoption by whom we cry out, "Abba, Father."*

The law promised blessings for obedience and curses for disobedience. Since the people were still dead in their sins, they needed an outward motivation to obey. Falling short of having a heart that was redeemed, the blessings were so wonderful and the curses so extreme, that many worked diligently to follow it. Thankfully, Christians are led by His Spirit, not by law.

It is different for us. We received, not the spirit of bondage leading to fear, but rather the Spirit of adoption that causes us to cry out to God as our Father. We are not His slaves. We have been made His children with hearts that long to please Him.

He leads us by His Spirit. This isn't a commandment. It is a statement of fact. He leads us by His Spirit. This does not require something from us. It is a gift. I say this because many believers are "trying" to be led by the Spirit as if the burden is on them to make something happen. They've been taught to believe that if they will just pray enough, study enough, give enough, sacrifice enough, and worship enough, they will mystically be led by God. No, this verse says that the sons of God **are** being led by the Spirit. This gift might be buried under years of putting the focus on ourselves to "be more spiritual", but it is liberating to realize that we need only respond. He is already speaking to us and leading us.

We don't need "signs" from God, nor should we allow our circumstances to dictate His guidance. God's ability to communicate to us is far higher than that. He speaks to us directly, and we hear His voice.

John 10:27
*"My sheep hear My voice, and I know them,
and they follow Me."*

When I began to be set free by this truth, an enjoyable journey began. I admitted to God that I was quite clueless about how being led by the Spirit worked, especially if it didn't involve me working something up.

I started by paying attention to thoughts that would run through my mind instead of always assuming they were just my thoughts. If a certain person kept coming into my mind, instead of ignoring those thoughts, I'd give her a call. Most of the time, the person would reveal that she needed the phone call or that she'd been thinking of me also. If I was heading one direction and suddenly had a desire to go somewhere else, it was often confirmed that God was guiding me. This might be something as mundane as finding what I was looking for at the best price or running into someone we hadn't seen in years to whom we could minister in some way. While teaching, a thought would come into my mind that I hadn't planned to say. So, I would just say it, and sometimes I could perceive by looking on faces that God had led me to say it. What a delight to let go of trying to be led and simply be led. Eventually, things seemed to click in this area. It is amazing and miraculous every time.

We don't need to get ridiculous about this, my friends. We don't need to be guided about whether or not to eat scrambled eggs or an omelet for breakfast, but if we have a strong sense that we should or shouldn't do something, we should consider taking that seriously.

Being led by the Spirit won't cause fear. It will cause us to cry out, "Abba Father!" We can rest assured that God isn't going to speak anything to us that we can't clearly perceive as Him speaking. If He is speaking to us, there will be a sense of clarity and peace in our hearts about it.

James 3:17
But the wisdom that is from above is first pure, then peaceable, gentle, willing to yield, full of mercy and good fruits, without partiality and without hypocrisy.

God is an expert at speaking to us, and when we ask for Him to give us wisdom, He will see to it that we get the information we need. Consider this too: God knows just how long it will take for you to hear Him, and He is more than willing to work on your heart and mind in advance so that you can make the right decision in time. He delights in leading us. Here is one example of how God led me to be healed from a very scary situation. For months, I'd been concerned that my memory was becoming very unreliable. I'd always been forgetful now and then, but I was beginning to forget the sentence I just uttered or couldn't remember if I'd completed a task one minute prior. At my age, this can be disconcerting. Of course, I'd prayed about it and was speaking to my brain to function and rejecting the thought that I was losing my memory completely, but the problem persisted.

One day I "randomly" ran across an article about a study that had been done using a derivative of chocolate.[13] Brain scans were taken before and after the experiment, and they revealed a significant change in memory function in the group of those who had used this chocolate formula. The end of the article was disappointing, though. This derivative of chocolate was not yet available, but I did learn through reading this that the researchers believed it was the flavonoids in chocolate which made the difference. I then searched "foods high in flavonoids", and the number one food high in flavonoids was green tea. I thought, "I could drink green tea once a day," and promptly ordered some. After about a month my memory was as sharp as ever. One might say, "Well, anyone could have figured that out," and I agree, but I know in my heart that this was an answer to my prayer for wisdom. God led me. I followed. Now, I have my brain back. Praise His name!

Shepherd or Sheepdog

Psalm 23 is one of the most beloved passages of Scripture. We see the Lord as a loving and gentle Shepherd caring for His sheep—meeting all of their needs. Although the Amplified Version of this passage isn't as poetic as my favored NKJV, it brings out the meaning in a beautiful way.

---

[13] I apologize that I was unable to relocate this article.

The Lord is my Shepherd [to feed, guide, and shield me], I shall not lack.
²He makes me lie down in [fresh, tender] green pastures; He leads me beside the still and restful waters.
³He refreshes and restores my life (my self); He leads me in the paths of righteousness [uprightness and right standing with Him—not for my earning it, but] for His name's sake.
⁴Yes, though I walk through the [deep, sunless] valley of the shadow of death, I will fear or dread no evil, for You are with me; Your rod [to protect] and Your staff [to guide], they comfort me.
⁵You prepare a table before me in the presence of my enemies. You anoint my head with oil; my [brimming] cup runs over.
⁶Surely or only goodness, mercy, and unfailing love shall follow me all the days of my life, and through the length of my days the house of the Lord [and His presence] shall be my dwelling place.

Do we see God this way, as someone who is always ministering to us? Or might we sometimes (or even often) think of Him more like a sheepdog than a shepherd, distressing us by always nipping at our heels to keep us on the right path, barking out our shortcomings day and night so we'll repent and improve? Do you catch yourself feeling a sort of hopelessness because you don't measure up to some standard that someone else set? Do your thoughts sometimes sound more like this?

The Lord is my Sheepdog; He doesn't care that I lack. He just cares that I obey Him and produce more sheep.

> *²He leads me into uncomfortable situations. He wants to keep me hungry, thirsty, and broken.*
> *³ He wants me to be desperate, so He allows me to suffer. He lets me know that I am still unrighteous, but leaves making myself righteous up to me.*
> *⁴ When I go through dark times, He lets me sink or swim. With His rod, He beats me. He grabs me by the neck with His staff to keep me in line.*
> *⁵ He allows my enemies to devastate me and watches me suffer instead of helping me. He leaves me for dead, and He makes sure that my cup is never quite full so I will keep seeking after Him.*
> *⁶ All the days of my life, I will seek after His goodness, mercy, and unfailing love, but without completely finding them. I will seek to be close to Him and to enter His presence all the days of my life, but I'll never know the joy of actually being as close as I can be.*

Or perhaps, like many Christians today, do we live with mixed messages—good Shepherd, mean Sheepdog? Do we believe on one hand that Jesus paid it all and yet feel we will never ever be good enough to "pay the debt of love we owe" even though we are doing everything that we think we should? Do we know theologically that God can be pleased, but have no idea *how?* Does it seem God is always demanding more from us—never satisfied with us at all ever?

These mixed messages, Beloved, are not from God. He is our gentle, loving Shepherd. Don't allow these lying thoughts to infiltrate your heart. Reject them! May the Lord set us free to see Him as He truly is, our loving Shepherd who loves us and is gently leading us by His love.

I love the gospel of Mark. It seems that he noticed details that some of the other gospel writers didn't record. See in this account its similarities with Psalm 23 and witness the acts of a loving Shepherd for His sheep who were in need.

> **Mark 6:34, 39-42**
> *Jesus, when He came out, saw a great multitude and was **moved with compassion** for them, because they were like **sheep not having a shepherd**. So He began **to teach them** many things.*
> *[39] Then He commanded them to make them all sit down in groups on the **green grass**. [40] So they sat down in ranks, in hundreds and in fifties. [41] And when He had taken the five loaves and the two fish, He looked up to heaven, blessed and broke the loaves, and gave them to His disciples to set before them; and the two fish He divided among them all. [42] **So they all ate and were filled**.*

By His Grace that Teaches

Under the Old Covenant, the law instructed the people concerning what was right and what was wrong. Under the New Covenant, His grace, not law, teaches us.

> **Titus 2:11-14**
> *For **the grace of God** that brings salvation has appeared to all men, [12]**teaching us** that, denying ungodliness and worldly lusts, we should live soberly, righteously, and godly in the present age, [13]looking for the blessed hope and glorious appearing of our great God and Savior Jesus Christ, [14]who gave Himself for us, that He might redeem us from every*

lawless deed and purify for Himself His own special people, zealous for good works.

Formerly, the people were guided like small school children by the law. It is the complete opposite for us. We don't need to be guided from without because we are taught by His grace from within.

> **Galatians 3:23-26**
> **Before faith came**, *we were kept under guard by the law, kept for the faith which would afterward be revealed.* 24*Therefore the law was our tutor to bring us to Christ, that we might be justified by faith.* 25**But after faith has come, we are no longer under a tutor.** 26*For you are all sons of God through* **faith** *in Christ Jesus.*

One evening as we shared verse 25 with a friend, he said in amazement, "That's not in the Bible, is it?" Yes, indeed it is. Faith has come, and we no longer need the law to teach us from without. Grace teaches us from within.

His Grace is Sufficient

We hear of Paul's thorn in the flesh when we read of the extreme persecutions Paul faced during His ministry. He asked the Lord that these would be removed from Him, just as Jesus asked that "this" cup (the sufferings and death He was about to endure) be removed from Him. God's answer to Paul was, "My grace is sufficient for you for my strength is made perfect in weakness." Let me add here that Paul wasn't asking God to remove sickness from him or some annoying person in his life. In context, it is perfectly clear that he was referring to the attacks against him motivated by Satan and perpetuated by those who opposed him because of his faith.

Many of us know the pain of having a friend or family member patronize us or treat us with disdain because of our faith. After confessing their faith in Christ, many suffer the loss of friendships, even employment. Others have been threatened and even killed for their faith.

We expect that the world will hate us, but there is another type of persecution, one most painful—that of being persecuted by one's own Christian brothers. Those perpetuating this intimidation scoff, seeing themselves as religious enforcers and proceed headlong into destroying the lives and reputations of their own brothers and sisters in order to discredit their teachings (and exalt themselves). There are plentiful examples of this in the book of Acts, and most of them involved the law coming against those who taught grace in Christ. As it was then, so it is now. The meanest people within the church that we've ever met are also the most legalistic.

I wish I could open my heart here and share with you some of the details of an experience within the church that broke our hearts, but there is no way to do so without potentially defaming those who mistreated us, and we have no desire to do that. If you've been "wounded in the house of your friends", you probably have your own story to tell. If so, insert that experience here. It is extremely painful to be falsely accused by people we love.

When we went through this overwhelming time, part of us wanted to come to our own defense, but we sensed that doing so would cause damage within the fellowship, so we chose to walk away knowing that neither we nor the message of God's grace that we taught were any longer welcome. My husband calls it "receiving the left foot of fellowship".

We were *d e v a s t a t e d*. We felt used and spit out. Day by day, we would surrender the pain of what we were experiencing, but in the evening, we would feel the pain again. One night, as I sat weeping and anxious because the pain I was experiencing was so intense, I cried out to God for grace, "Father, I believe that Your grace is sufficient for me at this

time, but I have no idea how to access it. I just don't know how I can go on one more minute. Please help me, Lord."
    Picture me in the depths of anguish ready to pass out due to the intensity of my emotional state and the sorrow and loss of friendships. I wasn't expecting an immediate response, but suddenly, I saw in my mind a cartoon figure. It was my husband. He was on a surfboard navigating his way on a big wave. (David doesn't and has never surfed.) His long blonde hair was being tossed by the wind and waves. (He had been growing his hair for several months in silent protest of what was happening to us.) His arms were extended to give him balance, and he was obviously enjoying the ride.
    Immediately, I laughed at the sight of this scene and was jolted out of my pain by the beautiful way God's grace was ministering to me. I was profoundly touched by this. It was unexpected. It was tailor made just for me. It was exactly what I needed. His grace reached through the agony that I didn't know how to handle and touched me in a way no one on earth could. Later I understood that when the waves of persecution come, we can ride above them full of joy instead of getting sucked into and plummeted by them.
    This is the story of a dear friend of mine who went through a similar trial in which God's grace reached down and calmed her stormy seas. In the midst of her anguish, when the pain of false accusations and the threat of impending injustice caused her mind to whirl beyond what she thought she could endure, the following took place.

> *As I lay in the darkness of my room reeling with tormenting thoughts of rejection and accusations, I was overwhelmed by grief and could find no peace or rest. Looking up into the blackness I cried, "God You are good, and I love You!"*
> *Suddenly, the words, "You are counted worthy to suffer for my name's sake," appeared above me. Then the word "worthy" floated*

toward me growing larger as it approached and enveloped me like a blanket, wrapping me in an incredible peace which remained for a long time into the night.

In that place of comfort, the idea that He saw me as "worthy" filled my heart with His love and I sensed that I was treasured and valued by Him. The total chaos and anxiety I'd experienced were completely dispelled, and I was able to fall asleep.

When God touches us in precious ways like this in our deepest moments of need, we take that comfort with us on our journey. As the days went by, it mattered less and less to her the opinions of others. It only mattered what God saw in her. The emphasis was taken off of the suffering she was experiencing and was placed on the fact that God had considered her worthy to suffer for His name. There would be much more pain to endure, but she was able to go back to that moment of grace and be blessed.

His grace is enough. We may feel that there is no way out of the pain thrust upon us at times. You might be in the midst of a similar situation being tossed by the wind and waves of persecution. I don't know what God will do for you, but I can promise you that His grace is sufficient, and He will help you.

In the meantime, do as Paul and Silas did when falsely accused and imprisoned unjustly in Philippi. Praise Him. His grace will reach you right where you are and work this horrible experience for your good. Paul and Silas saw an entire household come to the Lord after what they went through. After our horrid experience, the Lord opened a door of new ministry for us—the very one we are in now. If man unjustly slams the door in your face, God will open another. Our callings are not limited by time or location.

2 Corinthians 12:9

And He said to me, "My grace is sufficient for you, for My strength is made perfect in weakness." Therefore most gladly I will rather boast in my infirmities, that the power of Christ may rest upon me.

His Anointing Abides in You

Hopefully, you are beginning to see that God is not limited in His ways to speak to us personally. He has also put many persons in the body of Christ who are called to teach us and build us up (Eph. 4:11-16). As long as they are teaching the pure message of the gospel of grace and peace, there are many things they can share with us that will help us to navigate the trying times in life. As an author who is teaching my readers, I take this responsibility very seriously (James. 3:1). I want to represent the word of God accurately and share the truths that can set free—to comfort others with the comfort with which God has comforted me.

2 Corinthians 1:3-4

Blessed be the God and Father of our Lord Jesus Christ, the Father of mercies and God of all comfort, ⁴who comforts us in all our trib-ulation, that we may be able to comfort those who are in any trouble, with the comfort with which we ourselves are comforted by God.

Yet I want to encourage you in this also. Even if there were no teachers in the body of Christ, God is still teaching you by the anointing that is within you.

1 John 2:27

But the anointing which you have received from Him abides in you, and you do not need that anyone teach you; but as the same anointing teaches you concerning all things, and is true, and is not a lie, and just as it has taught you, you will abide in Him.

This is important for us to know because sometimes teachers fail us. They are either somehow too involved in the situation, are too busy, don't have the information we need, or they are teaching a mixture of grace and law—mixing in the Old Covenant principles with the New. Other times, our problems are so intensely personal that we don't want to share them with anyone else. We don't have to be overly concerned when these situations arise. We need not fear that because our troubles are too intimate that we will be led astray because we aren't discussing them with others. No, we have an anointing abiding within us that is teaching us concerning all things.

Again, I say this not to diminish the legitimate ministry gifts that God has set in the body of Christ. They obviously have their important place, but in these last days, God has spoken to each of us directly through His Son. Too often we elevate these people to a king-like status, placing them several levels above us in their ability to hear from God. This is simply not correct. You can hear from God as well as the minister whom you admire most. Each of us knows Him, and each of us can hear from Him equally.

Jeremiah 31:34
"No more shall every man teach his neighbor, and every man his brother, saying, 'Know the Lord,' for they all shall know Me, from the least of them to the greatest of them, says the Lord. For I will forgive their iniquity, and their sin I will remember no more."

His Written Word

It is imperative that everything we believe God is saying to us regarding our situations agrees completely with the written Scriptures of the New Covenant. If you have not yet read the New Testament, today would be the best day to start. Knowing the written word of God, will not only prevent us from being deceived but give us a treasure trove of information that can change the course of our lives.

Let me give an example of how this works in the natural. When we need to take on a project but lack information, what do we normally do? We get the information we need. We might take a class, buy a book, research online, watch an instructional video, ask for help from experts and friends who seem to be in the know—in short we begin to gather information. If we lack skill, we might take an hands-on training course.

Everything I know about gardening and landscaping I learned from books that my mother gave me and the information she shared with me personally. If I want to improve my organizing skills, I research. If I want to decorate a room but lack ideas, watching several DIY shows on the TV will give me the needed input. Eventually, as information is gathered, a picture begins to formulate in my mind, and at some point, the confidence I need arises to give it a try.

The Bible is overflowing with so much good news, that unless someone is reading with his eyes closed and his fingers in his ears, or he is blinded by mixture[14], he can't help but see faith grow in his heart. **Remember faith comes from** *hearing the good news* **in the Bible, not by the discipline of** *reading* **the Bible.**

For me, it is like going on an exciting treasure hunt. When we wanted to understand better, topics like the gospel of grace, divine healing, money matters, and just about any topic we have ever taught or that I write about, the Bible was

---

[14] "Mixture" refers to teachings that negate or try to "balance" the good news of God's grace.

our source[15]. When you want to know for yourself what the Bible teaches on a certain subject and formulate your own conclusions based on that study, take the time to study the Scriptures.

Don't deny yourself this amazing journey of finding out for yourself what God's good news is to you for your individual overwhelming situation. Open the Book. Ask God to open your eyes. Start reading. You will be blessed before five minutes are over. He is speaking to us through the written word.

Gleaning from the Examples of Mature Believers

It's normal to feel all alone in our struggles, but the truth is, the problems we face in life are really more common than we know. There are other human beings who have walked in shoes similar to ours who might be able to help us if we are willing to open up to them. Choose carefully, though.

If you don't know of anyone, you might be able to get helpful hints from a variety of sources that are less personal and yet which originate from other human beings who've walked similar paths.

Counselors should be people who are very knowledgeable in the word of God, who teach the gospel of grace accurately, whose lives are respected, and in whom one can deeply trust.

Some of the truths others share with us might have multiple applications as we walk through life, like the one my mother gave me saying, "People will fail you, Cathy, so keep your eyes on Jesus. He will never fail you." So many times

---

[15] There are many great Bibles available, but I advise you to seek out an excellent translation, not a paraphrase. I use the NKJV Nelson Study Bible because I've found it to be quite forthcoming and the notes provided below the text, the charts, the maps, and word studies are very helpful. Keep in mind, though, that a commentary is not Scripture. It can give you much historical and cultural and interpretive information, but even the most careful commentator sometimes reflects individual doctrinal bias. My husband uses the NASB which is also an excellent translation. The Amplified Bible is also very helpful because it uses Greek definitions of keywords to expand on the meaning. Wuest Expanded Translation is also based on the original Greek.

this has proven to be true in my life and helped me navigate through disappointing situations.

Specific Wisdom

> ### James 1:2-8
> *My brethren, count it all joy when you fall into various trials, ³knowing that the testing of your faith produces patience. ⁴But let patience have its perfect work, that you may be perfect and complete, lacking nothing.* **⁵If any of you lacks wisdom, let him ask of God, who gives to all liberally and without reproach, and it will be given to him.** *⁶But let him ask in faith, with no doubting, for he who doubts is like a wave of the sea driven and tossed by the wind. ⁷For let not that man suppose that he will receive anything from the Lord; ⁸he is a double-minded man, unstable in all his ways.*

It is appropriate that this verse about asking God for wisdom is put in the context of "various trials" for it is when we are in the midst of them that we need wisdom most. Knowing that God will speak specific wisdom to our hearts is one of the most comforting blessings we can know and experience. I've already shared how specific insight from God began my path in regaining a beautiful marriage when it looked like I would never be completely at peace, but believe me, there have been hundreds of times when I've found myself in a difficult situation, or I'm feeling down, or can't figure out why there seems to be no victory over something, that I will just remember this verse and ask Him to give me wisdom. He has never let me down. There is no limit on this truth. If you need wisdom from God, even if you need it *right now*, even if you think you don't deserve His wisdom, He will give it to you if you ask in faith.

Let me share one health-related matter in which God gave me wisdom. A few years ago, I woke up in the middle of the night because my heart was racing and my blood pressure was out of the roof. I called the advice nurse thinking she'd have me come into the ER. Instead, she talked with me for a while as these symptoms subsided and said it sounded like I had sleep apnea. What? How could someone who didn't even snore have sleep apnea? I dreamed like a maniac (or, at least, I used to). How could I have it? Sure enough, the sleep test came back positive. I was going to have to sleep with a CPAP machine the rest of my life.

This was all so unacceptable to me. It would NOT be possible for me to sleep with one of those contraptions on my face as I don't go to sleep easily when all conditions are perfect, but my health care provider said they didn't offer any other device. So, I sought a second opinion in hopes of being prescribed a smaller device which fits in one's nostrils, which the second doctor was happy to do. I asked that doctor how I would know if the device was working. She said, "You will start dreaming again."

It was a huge disappointment that those little vents prescribed for my nose made falling asleep impossible. What would be the next step—the CPAP machine? After doing all there was to do with no results, I just asked God to show me what was going on. I'd always been an avid dreamer and had never snored or woken like that before so I asked the Lord for wisdom about this because I was so baffled as to why all of this happened so suddenly.

Over the next few days, God brought some thoughts to my mind. I remembered the purchase of two new pillows because my neck, which I'd injured in an accident several years prior, would tighten up on me when I slept. The curved neck pillow was used to support my neck, and another small pillow under my chin near my throat helped to support my neck so my head would stay in a painless position since I slept on my side. Suddenly, I just saw it. At night, I was relaxing into these pillows, and I was choking myself!

So, I adjusted my curved pillow so that it supported my head right at the base of my skull instead of supporting my neck, and used the other pillow to keep my head from going too far forward but on my forehead, not at my neck. This allowed me to breathe with ease. Just as the second doctor predicted, I started dreaming like crazy. No more sleep apnea.

Even though I was thrilled that this problem had a simple solution, it caused considerable anxiety in me for many months. Many times before I could fall asleep, I would remember Philippians 4:6-7 and make my request to God that I would breathe and sleep in peace. I'm so thankful for the wisdom God gives us when we ask.

Steps of Faith

When God gives us wisdom, sometimes it will require steps of faith. Don't be afraid to experiment a little here as long as you act prudently. If you think God is giving you wisdom about something, go ahead and test it out. If you didn't hear correctly, that's OK; ask again.

It is interesting to explore in this area and to experience the joy of receiving wisdom from God. Sometimes God's grace will come to us in grand ways such as what my friend and I experienced visually when our hearts were breaking about persecution. Other times, His grace just enters our lives in ways that might not even seem supernatural such as when I ran across the research on memory loss or when I realized I was choking myself with my new pillows.

Specific Good News

Remember, "Faith comes by hearing and hearing by the word of God,"—the glad tidings of good things. If you need to find new faith in order to face what is overwhelming you, then you need to discover good news that will help you specifically, and as I've demonstrated above, God is able and willing to give it to you, if you will only ask for it. He's done all the work already to make you capable of having this personal access to Himself, and He delights in answering you. If you need good news, go get it, my friend.

> ### Luke 11:9-10
> "So I say to you, **ask, and it will be given to you**; seek, and you will find; knock, and it will be opened to you. [10]**For everyone who asks receives**, and he who seeks finds, and to him who knocks it will be opened."

Day 11

"FAITH" PITFALLS

---

*O*ften in our pursuit to finding new faith, many become sidetracked by teachings that are so not true about faith that they aren't faith at all. Some of those who read this chapter will do so nodding their heads, perhaps even letting out a little chuckle because they've experienced the temptation to veer off the true road of faith or have even fallen into some of these traps.

Let me say this, God sees our hearts. He knows that we are learning, and He knows all about these pitfalls. Many of His children in their desire to please God have made some of these mistakes in thinking. Perhaps He even smiles at us trying so hard to believe in Him, like a Father might when His child is learning new skills. If we see we are heading down a wrong path, we can simply turn around and head back toward the true faith that *originates from* hearing the glad tidings of good news.

FAITH PITFALL #1: Presuming Deity

We are NOT God nor shall we ever be. There is only one God. He alone created the heavens and the earth. He spoke, and there was light. He made the sun, moon, and stars and everything in the universe into infinity. He spoke, and the water of the earth was separated into sky and seas. By His power, He created all living plant life and animals. From the dust of the earth, He formed man and breathed life into him. From the side of man, God formed a woman. When He was done, He rested having given to Adam and Eve everything they needed.

We have not been given such power. Yet, sometimes, people can get a little arrogant when they begin to learn that their words do have power—some even bordering on delusions of deity. They start proclaiming things that aren't theirs to declare.

While we were studying about the power of our words one day, my husband pointed out this distinction, and it makes such perfect sense. When God speaks, those things which do not exist come into being. He hasn't given us that authority. **What we speak is that which God has already made true by what *He* has spoken.** In this way, we *participate* in *His* divine nature, but we still are not God (2 Pet. 1:3-5).

He has provided the way of salvation, for example. He did this through the death and resurrection of His Son. We didn't resurrect Jesus, but we can confess our faith in Him and be saved. Our words speak His promises and provisions. They already exist. We believe and confess these things. God did His part by speaking into being what did not exist before. We simply receive what He has already done by confessing our faith in Him.

You will find that this takes a lot of pressure off you. You aren't God, and you don't have to be God—not in your life and not in the life of others. We can rest in what He has done and in what He has promised to do.

FAITH PITFALL #2: My Way or No Way

Although God will meet us where we are and help us, bringing us to where we need to be when it comes to understanding true Biblical faith, let us not be sidetracked by thinking that we may dictate to God how He will meet our needs by bypassing what He has already set in motion. God is the King of His kingdom. He is the One who determines how things will operate. It is not our place to demand that God sidestep faith and submit to us on our own terms.

"If God wants to save me, He'll save me," isn't any more presumptuous than, "If God wants to heal me, He'll heal me," or "If God wants me to have the victory, He'll give it to me." The person who says these things is putting his faith in a principle that he has set forth and is not submitting to God's principles. He tells us to ask, for example. Shall we be so arrogant as to refuse to ask? Let's say there is a generous king in the land who has unlimited resources. If the king were to announce that he would give land to anyone who *asked,* would we really be so stubborn as to say, "No, if the king wants me to have that land, he'll give it to me without me asking"? Of course not!

Yet many people express this haughtiness when it comes to God's promises and provisions. He tells us to ask, to seek, and to knock believing He will give us what we need. He wants to answer our prayers, and He will, but we need to respond to His grace with faith.

FAITH PITFALL #3: Allowing Experience to Undermine Scripture

This is a very sensitive and highly emotional point, but it must be addressed so that we can correct our thinking. Please know that I write these things as one who has experienced them. Many of us have asked God for miracles and have not seen those miracles come to pass. Or, we know someone who didn't seem to receive from God when they asked, and so we don't ask thinking we will get the same result.

Instead of digging deeper into the written word of God to discover "what went wrong", we invent our own doctrines and begin to base our faith on our own experiences or that of others.

While it is perfectly acceptable to rethink our beliefs, it is not proper to conclude that God sometimes doesn't do what He has promised to do which is the same thing as calling Him a liar. Experience is highly personal. We don't know what is in the hearts of others. We don't know what they are believing. Shouldn't we instead form our theology on the written word of God which speaks of His provisions and promises? Let us search the Scriptures more earnestly and fortify our faith by learning of His grace instead of letting it be undermined by experience. Let us not retreat from believing that what God promises, He will indeed do.

> **Hebrews 10:23**
> *Let us hold fast the confession of our hope without wavering, for He who promised is faithful.*

PITFALL #4: Going at Things Backward

God has given us clear evidence of how faith comes to us. First of all, His grace exists. We hear of this good news from a preacher, which these days could be a face to face person or through a book or recorded teaching, and of course, we can preach to ourselves. When we hear of His love and grace toward us, faith comes, which, in turn, causes us to respond to God, and miracles such as salvation, healing, and victory happen.

However, we can't go at this backward. We can't start at the end and work our ways back to try and get faith. We can't "confess and possess" *in order* to produce faith in our hearts. We need first to hear good news, then wait until faith grows in our hearts, *then* speak what we believe. Speaking it doesn't make it true. **It *is* true, we believe it, and *therefore*, we speak.** Taking "steps of faith" when we don't really have faith doesn't produce faith.

2 Corinthians 4:13
And since we have the same spirit of faith,
<u>*according to what is written,*</u> *"I believed and*
therefore I spoke," **we also believe and**
therefore speak.

Believing comes first, and it is why we speak.

FAITH PITFALL #5: Trusting in Your Works

We were clearly taught and also taught others that if we wanted to see "revival" and "miracles" in and through our lives, it was dependent on us. If we would pray for an hour a day, read ten chapters a day in the Bible, go to church when the church doors were opened, give ten percent and more, get heavily involved in ministry, become increasingly holy, live righteously, and on and on, then and only then God would be able to use us.

We did the list. It didn't happen. "Revival" didn't come. What were we to conclude? For us it meant that since doing the first list didn't bring results, we then needed to all of those things more and more diligently. So, we did that, and guess what? Nothing. It never dawned on us that the whole premise was faulty.

God doesn't do miracles based on our adherence to any law. Being perfect and living flawlessly is not required to receive a miracle from God. It's by hearing good news and responding in faith.

Galatians 3:5
Therefore He who supplies the Spirit
to you and works miracles among you, does
*He do it by the works of the **law**, or by the*
*hearing of **faith**?*

We need to stop basing our confidence before God on our ability or lack thereof to follow laws. The life we live is by grace through faith, NOT law! How I rejoice that this is the case because, in myself, that is to say in my own humanity, there dwells nothing worthy of a miracle.

FAITH PITFALL #6: Faith without Works

If you have been trying to communicate the message of grace to friends and family, you have likely heard a quotation from James about how "faith without works is dead". The idea is to prove that works are required for right-standing with God, but this is not true.

What James is really saying in his letter is that living faith causes us to take action. We say we believe in God. So what? Satan and the demons believe in God, too. (I'm loosely quoting from James here.) If we have true faith, our actions will demonstrate it. If our actions don't, then we have a dead faith—no faith at all.

True faith causes us to speak what we believe. It causes us to take steps of faith. If we refuse to speak our "faith" and refuse to do what He shows us to do, then we don't really have faith at all. Authentic faith gives us the motivation and confidence to take action.

I'm not saying simply to take action. That would be akin to Pitfall #4. What I am saying is that if you do have faith, speak it. Move forward. Do what God is telling you to do.

FAITH PITFALL #7: Foolishness

I don't mean to insult anyone by saying this, but allow me to err on the safe side by expressing this point. God is NOT going to ask us to do something that will endanger us or someone else, and we won't force God to do something by taking a daring supposed "step of faith".

He won't ask us to drive without our glasses if we need them to see. He won't tell us to stop taking medicine that we need to live. He won't ask us to walk across a lake or to tell Mount Shasta to be removed and cast into the sea. If someone jumps out of a skyscraper to prove that God will save him, that person will die. Anything God tells us to do will be wrapped in wisdom and peace. He won't ask us to risk anyone's life to prove we have faith.

FAITH PITFALL #8: Giving Up

This last pitfall is one most tragic. Sometimes after years of "believing God" for a certain miracle, some will simply stop believing and eventually forsake Jesus altogether. While we certainly have compassion on those who are suffering to this extent, crossing the line from discouragement into apostasy is serious business.

Instead of putting Him on trial for not doing what we thought He should do, let us reexamine our own beliefs and actions in light of the written word of God. Let us seek His wisdom in our situations with the understanding that Jesus is our wisdom. Let us continue to put our faith in Him—no matter how difficult the journey may be, He is still our Savior and is worthy of our praise.

Day 12

GOOD GIRL, BAD GIRL

When we began this journey of learning to live by grace through faith and not by law, it was like entering a new and living road—one which Jesus already prepared for us. How beautiful it was to behold! It seemed that daily our eyes were opening to Scriptures we'd read so many times before without knowing what they meant. The truths were in our hands all those years, but we were blinded by our bent perspectives of what it meant to please Him.

Diligently seeking to be close to Him and seeking to love Him with all of my heart, my soul, and my strength, yet not being totally convinced of how deeply He loved me brought emptiness and misery.

As I was heading down a prescribed road to righteousness, I was convinced I was correct in my pursuits. "I" would please God. "I" would live a holy life. "I" would practice my spiritual disciplines. "I" would love God with all of my being. "I" would be a good wife and mother. "I" would make sure that every thought and word and deed of mine was honest and pure. "I" would give. "I" would love others as Christ loved me. "I" would overcome the overwhelming areas of my life. Please understand this, I didn't see this as self-righteousness, but as my desire to please God and be holy—to be diligent and faithful.

In my zealous pursuit of holiness, I lost sight of the fact that by "His" blood, once and for all, "He" made me holy. "He" brought me close. "He" forgave all of my sins. By "His" grace through faith, "He" made me "His" righteousness. By "His" wounds I was healed. "He" was my wisdom. By "His" doing I was in Christ. "He" gave me an anointing. "He" brought about revival. "He" loved me, yes, me personally, and "He" loved me without condition. All these things that "He" did, I was trying to better.

No wonder God seemed far away! Of course my perception of His love for me, the love I knew the first day I believed in Him, was diminished. Religious laws and goals mixed in with societal expectations had snuffed out nearly every trace of the life that was in me. Seeking my own righteousness through my own efforts, caused me to be "estranged from Christ" even though I was not involved in sin and desired so greatly to please Him and glorify His name.

Anyone who seeks to be justified by law
will fall from His grace.
It is automatic.
God loves us too much to allow us
to feel comfortable continuing down
the dead road of self-effort.

How wonderful it was to see Jesus once again. How marvelous it felt to have Him peel the burden of law off of our backs and replace the loss with His grace. Even so, the law is very pushy. We may think we have banished it completely from our lives, but then discover it is still lurking somewhere we didn't detect.

This became apparent to me again recently when the evening was winding down, and I was getting things ready for the next day. A thought was running around in my mind without me really "hearing" it. Not unlike me, I began to speak my thoughts aloud. "Today," I began, "I was a good girl because I took my vitamins, had my fiber three times a day, and didn't snack." I was nearly patting myself on the back for these great accomplishments. Then I said, "But I was a bad girl because I didn't stretch like I planned, and had a dessert."

When I heard myself, it hit me—this Good Girl, Bad Girl routine was not only an integral part of my existence, but it was LAW in operation. I sat motionless, stunned yet delighted by this revelation from God. I wasn't just feeling justified or guilty before God based on what I did or didn't do—something I'd observed and eliminated many years before, but I was evaluating my *goodness* and *worth* as a person on how well I met the goals I'd set. Instantly, I rejoiced that God was going to set me free from *this* operation of law, too.

I share this so that you will not be alarmed or discouraged to discover that some aspects of law are still in operation in your life. **This is because we can be walking by grace through faith in many areas, but when it comes to overcoming the overwhelming situation that we currently face, we might still be layered in law and self-effort which is restricting us in ways we have not yet identified.** Even after many years of recovery from "living" by law, you will likely realize as you walk down this new life of grace through faith that there is yet another layer of it at work in your heart attempting to rob you of the liberty that is yours in Christ.

Since that night, when it became apparent that I was evaluating myself as either good or bad based on keeping a list of self-imposed rules, God has helped me stop this bad habit dead in its tracks. Increasingly I'm learning that my goodness is based on the truth that He made me good, and even if I don't do everything perfectly, I'm still good because who I am now is based on *His* work, not mine.

God delights in setting us free, truly free. When we see the lies that are holding us back and come to know the truth, we will be free indeed. As we begin to apply these truths to the different areas of our lives, we begin to see the victory in life that He has provided for us.

132

PART 2

Walking by Faith
Not by Sight

Day 13

SUPERNATURAL SOLUTION

When we face situations that seem impossible and we are not sure where to go from "here", we begin to realize that overcoming the overwhelming will require a supernatural solution. When the faith we've experienced in other areas of our lives doesn't seem to reach our current circumstances, I believe this is when we need to find new faith. This new faith comes from hearing good news, and this includes applying the good news we already know to the new situation. We listen again to who He is. We remember all of His beautiful qualities and power. We remind ourselves of who He has made us by the power of His death and resurrection. We focus on what He has already provided for us. We open our hearts to the veracity of His promises. We allow ourselves to believe again that He loves us—unconditionally, completely, and forever, and we do so in the context of our difficulties.

As we cast our cares upon Him and ask Him to give us wisdom while recognizing that He is our wisdom, He carries our pain by His grace and leads us by His Spirit. Little by little we begin to discover if we believe things that are not true. We find out if some law principles are in operation giving strength to continued defeat. Over time, we begin to experience progress here and success there, and eventually, we realize that what previously so crushed us is finally overcome.

There is usually a period of time before the full solution becomes reality. Especially if the situation involves another human being, we may experience small victories but need years to resolve the situation fully. In some instances, the other person might completely resist God's grace, and we will need to learn how to live victoriously without that person's cooperation. This section of my book is meant to help you walk through the storms that might still rage while you reach for the peace He desires to bring.

Sadly, many of us were exposed to teachings about faith which left us bewildered and disappointed. To put it simply, faith became a work, a bondage, a cruel taskmaster which put all the emphasis on "me" and sidelined Him. True faith will cause us to take action, but once again, we don't take action to find faith.

We can't deny, however, even though we may have been deeply damaged or repulsed by false teachings about faith, that **faith is crucial**. Yet, faith does not stand alone. I find it helpful, in light of my former confusion about faith, to finish the phrase. Not just "faith", but "faith in **Him**". By *God's* grace through faith in *Him*, I am saved. By **God's** grace (His loving character, His provisions, and His promises) by faith in **His Son**, I live. **We don't put our faith in our faith. We put our faith in Jesus.** Faith in Him is the way we overcome in this life.

> *1 John 5:4-5*
> *For whatever is born of God overcomes the world. And this is the victory that has overcome the world—our faith. [5] Who is he who overcomes the world, but he who believes that Jesus is the Son of God.*

Day 14

SUPERNATURAL FAITH

Hebrews 11:1
Now faith is the substance of things hoped for, the evidence of things not seen.

*R*emember, true Biblical faith originates in hearing the good news. Faith is an amazing miracle, and Chapter 11 of Hebrews repeats again and again how the miracle of faith caused ordinary people to do supernatural things. I could spend some time here taking apart the scripture above, but this is the best interpretation I've seen to date.

> *Vincent says...* **"Faith apprehends as a real fact what is not revealed to the senses. It rests on that fact, acts upon it, and is upheld by it in the face of all that seems to contradict it. Faith is real seeing."**[16]

The most obvious example is one's belief in Jesus. Most believers haven't seen Jesus, but they still believe in Him completely. Even though we can't touch Him, if we are a Christian, He is as real to us as the sun in the sky. No matter

---

[16] Wuest's Word Studies from the Greek New Testament – Volume 2.

what happens to us in this life, we can't deny Him because we know He is real.

> **John 20:29**
> *Jesus said to him, "Thomas, because you have seen Me, you have believed. Blessed are those who have not seen and yet have believed."*

In our quest to understand supernatural faith, let us first examine an example of natural faith in action.

If someone buys a new house and lives where the summer days can easily be in the 90's and 100's, he will likely make sure his house has air conditioning. He moves in, and turns it on! Ahhh, what a relief.

What would happen, though, if he did not know he had air conditioning? Wouldn't he still have air conditioning? Yes. Would he be benefitting from it? No. Why? It would be because he **didn't know** he had it.

Perhaps a friend visited and after seeing the thermostat, revealed to the new house owner that he did indeed have air conditioning. Wouldn't that be good news? Of course, but if the person did not believe his friend, his house would still be hot. Would he have air conditioning? Yes. Would he be benefitting from it? No. Why? It would be because he **didn't believe** the good news.

What if he heard the good news and believed it, but was afraid to turn on the AC because he feared it might not work? He wouldn't want to feel like a fool turning it on and he wouldn't want to be disappointed if it didn't happen. Would he have air conditioning? Yes, but he would not benefit from it because of **fear**.

Yes, of course, these examples are just plain strange, but play along here because many of us respond similarly to the good news of what God has given us.

What if this person felt that getting up to turn on the thermostat shouldn't be necessary—that if the electric company really wanted him to have air conditioning, they could simply arrange it so that it would turn on automatically. It still would be true that he had it, but if he **refused to take the required steps** to turn it on, he would be miserable all summer.

Perhaps the man has a friend who also bought a house, and was so excited that he had air conditioning, but when he went to flip the switch, nothing happened. Perhaps it would seem **unfair** for him to have AC if his friend didn't have it. So, instead of figuring out why his friend's AC isn't working, he might conclude that air conditioners **don't work at all; they are a cruel hoax**. Clearly, air conditioners work, but because he would be basing his faith on his friend's experience, he would still not enjoy the air conditioning that came with the house.

Natural faith is similar to supernatural faith. We hear the good news, for example, that our house has a cooler. We believe this good news. We act on that good news. We are blessed by that good news. Of course, all of these things are still tangible. We might not understand all there is to know about an air conditioner and just flip a switch with confidence, but there is an actual unit that can be installed and repaired. As long as our unit is functioning and we pay our electric bill, we are set.

When it comes to supernatural faith, we witness something much more magnificent, for instead of relying on physical facts, **we are putting our confidence in God whom we cannot see to do something for us that we cannot do for ourselves.** By faith in Jesus, I know that I have eternal life and that I will not perish. I don't have an individually signed document to this effect. I haven't gone to heaven to check out the premises there, but it is more real to me than anything here on earth that I can see.

Using Vincent's definition above, consider this perspective:

My faith is the proof that I have what I hope for, even though my senses and this world say that there is hope only in this life. I rest on this fact. I live according to this fact. I am upheld by this fact in the face of all that seems to contradict it. I "see" it, even though I cannot yet see it.

This amazing faith is a result of hearing about His amazing grace. If we lack faith, we know what to do! We fill our hearts with glad tidings of good things from our benevolent God! Faith will then supernaturally come to us as we hear of His great love for us.

Day 15

THE GIFT AND FRUIT OF FAITH

*H*ave you ever been listening to a sermon in which the preacher focuses in on one verse to substantiate his point, and by the time he is finished dissecting it 30 minutes later using the original Greek and various cross-references, he manipulates the verse into saying something it doesn't say at all? The uncanny thing I've often noticed is that the point he is trying to prove might be perfectly valid. There may be dozens of verses that would easily substantiate the truth he's trying to bring forth, but instead of using those references, he chooses one which has nothing to do in the slightest with what he's trying to say.

Sometimes when we're studying a passage, we'll notice that the translators chose a word which doesn't perfectly capture the meaning of the original word. Most of us are by no means experts in Greek, but even an amateur knows that A ≠ B. My hope is that these errors aren't intentional, but rather an attempt to clarify. Here is an example pertaining to "faith" that makes me wonder.

> **Galatians 5:22-23**
> *But the fruit of the Spirit is love, joy, peace, longsuffering, kindness, goodness, **faithfulness (pistis)**, 23gentleness, self-control. Against such there is no law.*

Pisits is the Greek word for "faith". I find it curious that the older versions of the Bible, including those in Spanish, translate the word **pistis** in the above verse as "faith", but the relatively newer versions of the Bible translate **pistis** as "faithfulness" in this one verse. Why is this? Might it be a reflection of the church's modern-day emphasis on obedient works instead of emphasizing the grace of faith? We have no way of knowing for sure, but it is important we understand what the original Greek says: **Faith is a fruit of the Spirit.**

Hearing this good news causes me to take a deep breath as if to inhale a lovely fragrance, and then to exhale as if renewed by its scent. We not only receive faith by hearing good news, but just by the fact that the Spirit of God dwells within us, the fruit of faith grows.

Perhaps this is why it seems that out of nowhere we sometimes have faith about a certain area of our lives seemingly without even focusing on hearing good news. Have you experienced this? You've had a bad attitude perhaps for days; you have avoided teachings that might have encouraged you to believe, and you might have even given God (and everyone else around you) the cold shoulder. You certainly have done nothing to nurture faith, and then suddenly, faith is simply there for you as if it sprouted while you slept. I love the way God seems to cover all the bases for us. **We never need to stress out about faith.** Since His Spirit permanently dwells within us, we can trust that faith will grow.

Another amazing verse is this one.

1 Corinthians 12:7-9, 11
But the manifestation of the Spirit is given to each one for the profit of all: [8]for to one is given the word of wisdom through the Spirit, to another the word of knowledge through the same Spirit, [9]to another faith by the same Spirit, to another gifts of healings by the same Spirit... [11]But one and the same Spirit

works all these things, distributing to each one individually as He wills.

The gifts listed above are given "for the profit of all"; in other words, these gifts are given to build up and encourage the body of Christ. Laying aside the debate about spiritual gifts, let us take a look at this amazing "gift" of faith. We can see in verse 11 that it is a working of the Holy Spirit given to individuals as He wills. Some might see this as a gift given to a particular person and that this gift will always be in operation in that person's life. I won't deny this possibility. However, it seems reasonable to also make way for the idea that the Holy Spirit gives this gift as needed to anyone He wills whenever He wills, perhaps for just that particular situation.

It is crucial to remember that no matter what we are facing in this life, someone else we know is also suffering. We are told to "desire" spiritual gifts (1 Cor. 14:1), so it is appropriate to desire this gift of faith. Do you know that even though we may be maxed out emotionally and physically, God can still drop this gift into our hearts to encourage someone else? This is a beautiful and amazing thing about faith. It isn't limited by our feelings or strength. It can walk right over waves and silence storms. God can use us whenever He wants to minister to others in the body of Christ. Don't discount ministering to others because you are presently overwhelmed personally, because His strength is made perfect in weakness.

The flip side of this is that God can give this gift of faith to others in the body to minister to us. I consider myself a woman of faith who believes God for miracles, but often for whatever reason, I just need someone else to pray for me. I don't necessarily need to share the details of my situation. I can just say, "I don't want to go into it, but will you please pray for me today?" If the person is willing, it seems God drops a gift of faith into that person, and to my amazement, I am not just comforted by someone caring to pray for me, but their faith ministers to me and brings results almost instantly.

Galatians 5:6

*For in Christ Jesus neither circumcision nor uncircumcision avails anything, but **faith working through love***.

Faith works through love, and we will never fathom the depths of God's love for us and the effects of faith working through love. Will we let ourselves be loved? Can we receive the faith of another to minister to us from God? We aren't alone in this life. We have each other. It might be that no one really knows our frustrations or they might think that we are handling them perfectly well. Perhaps we will need to reach out to someone to pray for us. Find someone who doesn't need to know the details, who will accept that you don't want advice, and ask them to lend their faith to your situation. It might be that God will give a gift of faith to someone else for you.

Paul, the apostle, probably the greatest of all, understood this principle. Although he had the faith to shake a venomous viper off his hand and not be in any way affected by it, and though amazing miracles were done through him in his ministry, he did not hesitate to ask for the prayers of others.

2 Thessalonians 3:1-2

*Finally, brethren, **pray for us**, that the word of the Lord may run swiftly and be glorified, just as it is with you, ²and that we may be delivered from unreasonable and wicked men; for not all have faith.*

Why would Paul ask for prayers? Certainly he had enough faith to ask God for the same thing and see results! Yet, here we see him humbly asking the Thessalonians to pray for him. He sincerely believed that their prayers would be effective, and they were.

We know that God gives to each one of us a measure of faith (Rom. 12:3), yet God surrounds us with many sources of faith to help us face the storms of life. Perhaps someone will share good news with us, and faith will come to our hearts through hearing good news, or faith will simply grow in our hearts since it is a fruit of the Spirit of God who lives within us, or God will give us or someone else a gift of faith to minister to our needs. No matter what be the source of faith, God's love for us and the love we have for each other are the channels through which faith works. Let us open our hearts to love and be loved so that faith may flow.

1 Corinthians 13:13

And now abide faith, hope, love, these three; but the greatest of these is love.

Day 16

JOYFUL ANTICIPATION

---

*I*ntricately woven together with love and faith is hope. Godly hope bears little to no resemblance to the hope of which we speak in our day to day conversations. Worldly hope is quite a bit more like doubtful wishing. When we say, "I hope so," we aren't necessarily saying that we believe that the good we desire will happen, just that it would be nice if it did, but we can't be sure that it will.

Godly hope is a joyful and confident expectation of good.[17] Unlike the doubtful "hope" we normally witness, **true hope includes no doubt at all**. When we hope for something in the spiritual realm, we do so joyfully because we are completely confident we will receive it. Hope sees as already possessing by faith what our senses cannot yet perceive.

> **Romans 8:24-25**
> *For we were saved in this hope, but hope that is seen is not hope; for why does one still hope for what he sees? [25]But if we hope for what we do not see, we **eagerly wait** for it with perseverance.*

For those of us who speak English, there is an obstacle to fully understanding the meaning of hope because in English,

---

[17] This definition is derived from Strong's and Thayer.

the word "hope" does not carry with it the idea of waiting. In many languages, though, the verb "to hope" also means "to wait". The words are interchangeable. Knowing this helps us better understand hope. If one is waiting for a train, the reasonable thought behind this is that the train will be there. Imagine saying in English, "I'm hoping for the train." Most English speakers would conclude that you were not sure it was coming rather than believing it would.

If you are waiting to receive a package you ordered, you expect (hope) that it will come. If it contains something you really want, you might even wait for it (hope for it) with joyful anticipation.

Waiting implies there might be some time before you actually see that for which you hope. That is where faith comes in. Faith is the proof that you have the thing for which you hope, and hope, just like faith, is wrapped up in God's love for us. **The more we know that we are loved by God, the more easily we will hope.**

Romans 5:5
*Now hope **does not disappoint**, because the **love of God** has been poured out in our hearts by the Holy Spirit who was given to us.*

Hope also does not stand alone. We have faith in God. We also hope in God. If He has provided or promised something for us, we can joyfully anticipate that we will see it one day.

The clearest example we have of hope and faith is Abraham. He was given a promise by God that he would be the father of many nations. Even though everything "proved" the contrary, Abraham believed God and was fully convinced that what God promised, He would do.

Romans 4:16-22 NASB
For this reason it is by faith, in order that it may be in accordance with grace, so that the

promise will be guaranteed to all the descen-
dants, not only to those who are of the Law, but
also to those who are of the faith of Abraham,
who is the father of us all, ¹⁷(as it is written,
"A father of many nations have I made you")
in the presence of Him whom he believed,
even God, who gives life to the dead and calls
into being that which does not exist. ¹⁸In hope
against hope he believed, *so that he might*
become a father of many nations according
to that which had been spoken, "So shall
your descendants be." ¹⁹Without becoming
weak in faith he contemplated his own body,
now as good as dead since he was about
a hundred years old, and the deadness of
*Sarah's womb; ²⁰**yet, with respect to the***
promise of God, he did not waver in unbe-
lief but grew strong in faith, giving glory
to God, ²¹and being fully assured that what
God had promised, He was able also to
perform. *²²Therefore it was also credited to*
him as righteousness.

Everything Abraham could see with His physical eyes
said the complete opposite of what God promised. He saw
his own body "as good as dead", and knew that long ago,
Sarah passed the age of being able to bear a child. How
much more impossible could his situation have been? Still,
God promised him a child. So, contrary to all he could see,
He believed (had faith) and joyfully anticipated (hoped) that
the good that God had promised him would come to pass.

What about you? Are you facing an impossible situation
that gives not one hint that things might ever improve? Are
your finances such a mess that there is no logical way out?
Are you struggling with a relationship that keeps going around
and around in destructive circles? Is your health a completely
tangled web of so many problems that no matter what you

do, you still don't feel well? Do you "live" with depression or are you one day on top of the world, and the next day in the pit of despair? Are you suffering the loss of a marriage or loved one? Do you feel you missed God's calling in your life somewhere along the way and that now God can't use you? Have you been damaged by the misdeeds of others? No matter what you are facing, God sees you. He knows you. He cares. He has the answer, and He will not withhold it from you. You can trust Him.

Allow your heart to once again believe that God loves you and that His intentions toward you are good. Allow yourself to hope in Him and His promises again—to joyfully anticipate and wait for His promises to be realized. I'm not suggesting you just jump out of your chair and shout yourself into believing. I'm not saying, "Get over it!" or "Chin up!" in the face of grief. On the contrary, simply open your heart to God who loves you, who only desires good for you, and who will do all that He has promised. Just allow your heart to hope in Him.

> ### 2 Corinthians 1:10 AMP
> *[For it is He] Who rescued and saved us from such a perilous death, and He will still rescue and save us; in and on Him we have set our hope (our joyful and confident expectation) that He will again deliver us [from danger and destruction and draw us to Himself].*
> ### Isaiah 40:29-31
> *He gives power to the weak,*
> *And to those who have no might He increases strength.*
> *30 Even the youths shall faint and be weary,*
> *And the young men shall utterly fall,*
> *31 But those who wait on (hope in) the Lord*
> *Shall renew their strength;*

They shall mount up with wings like eagles,
They shall run and not be weary,
They shall walk and not faint.
Psalm 43:5
Why are you cast down, O my soul?
And why are you disquieted within me?
Hope in God;
For I shall yet praise Him,
The help of my countenance and my God.

Day 17

PLEASING GOD

When I first believed in Jesus, there was nothing I wanted more in life than to please God. How glorious it was to appreciate daily that God was my Father and that His love for me was immense. I was so full of joy and peace and love for God that reading the Bible was a glorious treasure. What a joy to finally understand it. Prayer was like breathing. It was non-stop. Almost immediately, I longed to be in the presence of other believers who knew God as I did. So, I sought out fellowship. Oh, how we worshiped God together in those days. Our songs would rise effortlessly as we praised Him for all He had done.

Generosity simply happened. We were happy to help anyone we could and putting something in the offering was a joy. As time went by and opportunities of ministry came up, we were honored to be asked and happy to serve God in any way we could. We were thankful to be able to pray, to read and understand the Scriptures, to fellowship with others, to give, to share our joy with our friends, and to serve.

Everything we did was motivated by love for Jesus. We didn't have the sense that we had to do anything. We *wanted* to do what we were doing and what we were doing was motivated by our *faith* in Jesus.

Over time, however, we started to see these graces as *requirements*. What was overflowing from our hearts was converted into a systematic regimen which our leaders called "spiritual disciplines". Gradually, this working of law in our lives robbed us of the joy we'd known originally. Our initial love and willingness was viewed as our "honeymoon period" and was expected to end eventually as we "matured" in Christ. That enthusiasm motived by the Spirit that we would see in the faces of new believers was looked upon with fond memories but with the clear view that it wouldn't last forever, and indeed, it didn't.

Much to our disappointment, being a Christian became a matter of how we pleased God by doing a long list of things. Yes, Jesus saved us by grace through faith, but we were taught that we'd be judged by what we did with that salvation. Every good and every bad deed and thought was being judged by God. Our lives were constantly under God's not-so-glorious magnifying glass. Added to this grief was the growing sense that nothing we did would ever be enough anyway. If we prayed one hour, there was always someone else who prayed two. If we read ten chapters in the Bible, someone else would boast of reading fifty. Fast one day? Well, that's fine if it's the best you can do, but what about three days or ten or 40?

If you've read my first book, then you know that God set us free from this way of "living". I'm so thankful, too, because I'm not sure I could have "lived" one more day in that heap of misery.

All believers desire to please God. This is a glorious miracle, but this longing combined with wrong explanations about what it means to please God, can also cause us to stumble. When we are new believers, we instinctively know we have much to learn. We want to please God, so we look to our elders in Christ to teach us how. In many instances, however, the ones we are trusting to teach us about how to please God were themselves taught incorrectly. Believing that what they were taught was correct, they teach us the same false doctrine—to please God by doing good and not sinning. Someone needs to stop this not-so-merry-go-round of law and works so that we can truly discover what it means to live by grace and faith.

John 6:26-29
Jesus answered them and said, "Most assuredly, I say to you, you seek Me, not because you saw the signs, but because you ate of the loaves and were filled. ²⁷Do not labor for the food which perishes, but for the food which endures to everlasting life, which the Son of Man will give you, because God the Father has set His seal on Him."
²⁸Then they said to Him, "What shall we do, that we may work the works of God?"
*²⁹Jesus answered and said to them, **"This is the work of God, that you believe in Him whom He sent."***

We can see in their question that the Jews wanted to know what God wanted them to do in order to have "the food which endures to everlasting life". Perhaps they sensed that Jesus meant there was something "else" besides the law that God wanted them to do. Instead of giving them something to do, Jesus surprises them by saying that the work God wanted from them to do was to believe in the One whom God had sent.

I can picture everyone's brain going in a different direction after Jesus said that. I can almost see a cartoon, with one person's head spinning and looking dumbfounded. Another might have his hand on his beard pondering how to do believing. Surely others looked on scoffing at such a thought. Some, though, had to feel a sense of relief even though they didn't completely understand. I can see them smiling with their shoulders relaxed and pondering what this good news might mean. Even we, looking on at this scene find it impossible, even perhaps irresponsible to think that simply believing in Jesus is what God desires from us.

In the book of Hebrews chapter 11 we are given multiple examples of people who did mighty things for God. Notice, though, how each example begins. "By faith—". We tend to focus on the courageous deeds they did, but from God's perspective, it wasn't the doing that pleased Him. It was their *faith in Him* that brought about the doing that brought Him joy. If you have a few extra minutes, read Hebrews 11 again.

Hebrews 11:6
*But without **faith** it is impossible to please Him, for he who comes to God must **believe** that He is, and that He is a rewarder of those who diligently seek Him.*

Wuest wrote, "The idea is, 'Without faith it is impossible to please Him at all.'" No matter what we are doing as Christians, if it is not motivated by our faith, it doesn't please God—at all. Even Paul, in a different context, wrote, "Whatever is not from faith is sin."

If we examine each example of faith in Hebrews 11, we see the verse above on display. They believed that God existed, and they believed He would do what He said He would do—that He would reward them.

In the beginning of my walk with Jesus, all that I did was a result of my faith in Jesus. He was pleased with my faith. The good works flowed from my faith just as the mighty deeds described in Hebrews 11 originated in their faith. All of this was turned upside down when we began to believe that what we *did* pleased God. What we did no longer was a result of our faith; it became a requirement. If we did good deeds and didn't do wrong, then God would be pleased with us. It became an endless cycle of trying to do more and more to please God better and better. Sadly, the opposite was also in view: if we weren't doing, we didn't please Him. **We no longer lived by grace through faith. We were living by law through works.**

God was not alarmed that we got off track. Many throughout the church's history did the same. How difficult it must have been for those whose whole righteousness had been based on obeying the law, to embrace the concept of righteousness based on faith.

Philippians 3:4-9

*If anyone else thinks he may have confidence in the flesh, I more so: ⁵circumcised the eighth day, of the stock of Israel, of the tribe of Benjamin, a Hebrew of the Hebrews; concerning the **law**, a Pharisee; ⁶concerning **zeal**, persecuting the church; concerning the **righteousness** which is in the law, blameless. ⁷But what things were gain to me, these I have counted loss for Christ. ⁸Yet indeed I also count all things loss for the excellence of the knowledge of Christ Jesus my Lord, for whom I have suffered the loss of all things, and count them as rubbish, that I may gain Christ ⁹and be found in Him, **not having my own righteousness**, which is from the law, but that which is through faith in Christ, the **righteousness which is from God by faith**.*

If there was someone who had a right to boast about how righteously and zealously he lived under the law, it was Paul. Many have said, "Well, no one can follow the law perfectly," but Paul seems to be claiming here that he did.[18] When Paul wrote that He was willing to give up the things that were gain to him, did he mean what we commonly think today, that of giving up self, worldly riches, and sin?

No. He clearly declared in this passage that he was blameless according to the law. Although, from our perspective, we can see he was sinning because he persecuted the church, but from his perspective, before He knew Jesus, his zeal only amplified his righteousness which was based on keeping the law.

---

[18] Doubtless, there were others. Consider Luke 1:5-6, "There was in the days of Herod, the king of Judea, a certain priest named Zacharias, of the division of Abijah. His wife *was* of the daughters of Aaron, and her name *was* Elizabeth. ⁶**And they were both righteous before God, walking in all the commandments and ordinances of the Lord blameless.**"

Then what was it exactly that Paul gave up? What did he consider "rubbish" so that he might gain Christ and be found in Him? Looking a bit closer we can see that he gave up his own righteousness based on keeping the law and received the righteousness which is through faith in Jesus—a righteousness which "is from God by faith". This is how we are born again—by faith in Jesus.

"Without faith, it is impossible to please God." This is true, but this can also be said in this way:

Faith pleases God.

Yes, that's right. We can please God simply by believing in Him. When returning to this truth, my husband and I saw this as too good to be true. He prayed, "God, I wish you were really this good!" I personally thought at first that I was being led down a road of deception (and some of our friends thought we were off our rockers, too). Could it really be so wonderfully simple that what God really wanted from us wasn't performing the long list of "spiritual disciplines" we'd collected, but rather to just believe in Him?

Let's look at the verse again in order to extract more of its glorious goodness.

> **Hebrews 11:6**
> *But without faith it is impossible to please Him, for he who comes to God must believe that He is, **AND that He is a rewarder of those who diligently seek Him.***

Yes, there's more. We not only believe that He exists but also that He rewards those who seek Him. (We'll discuss the word "diligently" in the next chapter.) Let me restate the obvious:

**God wants us to believe
that He rewards those who seek Him.**

Many of us used to pray because we saw prayer as a requirement and a means of remaining close to God and even as a way to get closer to Him. Over time, we lost the idea that He would actually answer our prayers. As David and I began to break free from the false teachings that entombed us for so long, this simple truth stunned me. God *answers* prayers. Otherwise, why pray? Indeed! What did all the time I put into praying accomplish? From my warped perspective answered prayer wasn't the point. The act of praying had become the focus. As my eyes began to open once again, I returned to praying with the understanding that God would reward me—answer my prayers. So amazing was it to me, that I wrote this song to express my joy.

*I'd been frustrated and condemned for years
By the rules and laws of man
That taught the only way God will hear
Is on my knees and at six a.m.
I would try with all my might
To perform this awesome task
Trying to stay awake
Thinking this was doing as He asked.
When for weakness or by circumstance
I could not this law fulfill,
I would think that He was angry
And my life out of His will.*

*So I started to pray all day
Doing dishes or in my car
Trying to find my way
Back to the desire of His heart.
To my amazement, He met me there,
And my spirit He set free.
Now, I'm thanking you, my Father,*

For this precious liberty.

There are troubles we cannot share
With even the dearest friends.
There are burdens that we bear
That seem to never end.
When we come to God in prayer
For one minute or for an hour,
His Spirit meets us there
Giving wisdom and giving power.

It's so amazing what God will do
When we take the time to pray,
And just a little time with Jesus
Goes a long, long way.

God rewards those who seek Him, and it should be pointed out that a reward is a good thing. He wants us to believe this, and believing this pleases Him. He isn't concerned about how long our prayers are. He doesn't answer them based on how spiritually disciplined we've been lately as if we accumulate His grace by what we do. (Now, that is a twisted thought!) He doesn't refuse to answer them because we've had a bad attitude lately or aren't living up to some expectation we or someone else has placed on us. As Vincent puts it, "He who approaches God has, through faith, the assurance that his seeking God will result in good to Himself." We pray because He answers.

When we face impossible situations, how much more we need to believe that He exists and that He rewards those who seek Him with good. No, we don't deserve it. That's the point. It is our faith God sees. It is our faith in Him and our trust in His goodness toward us that pleases Him.

Romans 4:1-5
What then shall we say that Abraham our father has found according to the flesh? ²For

*if Abraham was justified by works, he has something to boast about, but not before God. ³For what does the Scripture say? "Abraham **believed** God, and it was accounted to him for righteousness." ⁴Now to him who works, the wages are not counted as grace but as debt. ⁵But to him who does not work but **believes on Him** who justifies the ungodly, his faith is accounted for righteousness.*

Day 18

"DILIGENTLY" SEEKING HIM

What does it mean to "diligently" seek God? Due to the teachings many of us once received, just the words "diligent" and "seek" can send chills of horror through our beings. If you have never "lived" under a mile-long list of spiritual disciplines which were perceived as diligence, you may think I am overly dramatic here. However, if you, perhaps even more than we, were driven by a never-ending list of religious expectations, it's likely your heart also sinks at the remembrance of teachings on "diligently" seeking God.

First of all, let's make clear one important matter. Christians do not need to seek God in the sense of finding Him, for He has already found us and brought us into His throne room. We are one spirit with Him. He's not "out there somewhere", He is ever-presently with us. We don't need to "chase after Him" or "be where He is". We already have all of Him, and He has all of us, and He's promised never to leave us not ever.

When I first worked on a lesson about diligently seeking God, it never dawned on me to challenge the word in the first place, but when we later did a study on Hebrews 11, my husband pointed out that the word "diligently" in verse six isn't present in the Greek text.

"Oh, there those grace preachers go again. They don't agree with something, so they just say that the word isn't there!" Let me assure you of this, as one who considers herself to be a preacher of the gospel of grace, there is no desire in me at all to water-down the meaning of this verse or any other passage of Scripture. On the contrary, I want to understand every verse and this one in particular to the fullest extent possible because there is nothing more important to me in this life than pleasing God. If my faith pleases God, then I want to understand what that means. If seeking Him is evidence or part of my faith, I want to go about it correctly and with a proper understanding.

First of all, "diligently seek" in the Greek is actually one word, **ekzeteo**, not two separate words as it is translated in some versions in English. This can be significant or not, for there are many compound words in the Greek which translate better into English with two words, and this is true of many languages. No big revelation there, but when we come upon a word in an English translation that isn't specifically there in the Greek, it's worth our time to check and see if the Greek word actually needs an extra word to translate it or not.

It is curious once again that many of the older translations and more literal translations of this verse simply translate **ekzeteo** as "seek" with no mention of the word "diligently". Here are a few examples.

> *New American Standard Bible: He is a rewarder of those who <u>seek</u> Him.*
> *Young's Literal: To those <u>seeking</u> Him He becometh a rewarder.*
> *Wycliff Bible: He is [a] rewarder of men that <u>seek</u> him.*
> *1599 Geneava Bible: He is a rewarder of them that <u>seek</u> him.*
> *Mounce Reverse-Interlinear New Testament: He rewards those who <u>seek</u> Him.*

So, setting aside the word "diligently" for one moment, let us simply examine the meaning of the one Greek word that is actually in the text. The word **ekzeteo** is a compound word, **ek-zeteo**, but one part doesn't mean "diligent" and the other part "seek". So, let's look a little closer.

When we take apart a Greek word, it can help if one of the parts has a really clear definition, but that still doesn't guarantee that we will then have the right meaning as the other part of the word can amplify the other word or even negate it. This is also true in most languages. A good example is the word "amoral". We all know what "moral" means, but "amoral" is nearly the opposite of "moral", meaning "without morals". We need to keep this in mind before we form conclusions about what a word means. In this instance, however, the definition of **zeteo** is very helpful in ascertaining the meaning of **ekzeteo**. Here is Thayer's definition. (I've underlined some things I find interesting.)

Thayer Definition:
1) to seek in order to find
1a) to seek a thing
1b) to seek [in order to find out] by thinking, meditating, reasoning, to enquire into
1c) to seek after, seek for, aim at, strive after
2) to seek, i.e. require, demand
2a) to crave, demand something from someone

So, we have then our first clue as to why some translators added "diligently". This word **zeteo** isn't a passive seeking. It implies seeking with the intention of finding. Perhaps they were trying to pull out the purposefulness of the seeking that is indicated by the definition.

The first part of the word, **ek**, is a preposition which has a two-layered meaning "out from and to".[19] Now, that would be hard to translate using one word, and certainly, "diligently" would not bring this meaning forth. Let me try explaining it in a sentence. Now, admittedly, this is my opinion, but I think it is safe to conclude that **ekzeteo** can be understood as a

---

[19] Helps Word Studies copyright © 1987, 2011 by Helps Ministries, Inc.

seeking out from me to God with the purpose of finding an answer from Him. More simply stated, when we seek something from God, we expect to find. Completely stated:

God is pleased by those who believe that He is a rewarder of those who seek Him out expecting to be rewarded.

Having a better understanding of what it means to seek, let us amplify our understanding by examining some examples in life and in Scripture.

Seeking God Means to Pray and Not Faint

If we put a dollar into a vending machine, we have the reasonable expectation (hope) that what we just purchased will come out. I use this example deliberately because so many times I've heard people say, "Well, God isn't a vending machine," and, of course, He isn't. Yet, He is a dependable God. He will do what he has promised, and we can joyfully anticipate that we will receive what He has promised to give us.

If we put a dollar in a machine and nothing comes out, it is highly unlikely that we are going to shrug our shoulders and walk away. No, we will likely shake the machine, maybe give it a kick or a punch; or as I have done on more than one occasion, even feed it another dollar hoping this time, it will give me what I purchased, and if that doesn't work, I will probably go find the manager responsible for the machine and demand my money back. We will likely not give up until we get justice. Am I saying we should get mad at God if He doesn't give us what we ask? Should we complain to His manager? Well, that's just silly because as we all agree, God is not a vending machine, and He doesn't have a manager. No. **God is far better than a vending machine and much more reliable.** The point I'm making is this: We expect something as basic as a machine to give us the promised product. How much more should we believe and joyfully anticipate that the living all-powerful and faithful God who just so happens to be our loving Father will keep His promises to us.

Following are several examples given in Scripture that help us have a fuller view of what it means to seek God. This first one has to do with asking Him for something and not losing heart while we wait for the answer.

> **Luke 18:1-8**
> Then He spoke a parable to them, that men always ought to pray and not lose heart, ²saying: "There was in a certain city a judge who did not fear God nor regard man. ³Now there was a widow in that city; and she came to him, saying, 'Get justice for me from my adversary.' ⁴And he would not for a while; but afterward he said within himself, 'Though I do not fear God nor regard man, ⁵yet because this widow troubles me I will avenge her, lest by her continual coming she weary me.'" ⁶Then the Lord said, "Hear what the unjust judge said. ⁷And shall God not avenge His own elect who cry out day and night to Him, though He bears long with them? ⁸I tell you that He will avenge them **speedily**. Nevertheless, when the Son of Man comes, will He really find faith on the earth?"

What does real faith look like? It looks like a woman seeking justice and not giving up asking until she gets it. Now, God is no more an unjust judge than He is a vending machine. **God is far better than an unjust judge and much more reliable.** He will not only answer our prayers, He will do so without resentment, and "speedily" if we will pray (seek/ ask) and not give up.

The widow knew her rights and insisted upon them. In like manner, we are to know what God has provided and promised and ask Him with confidence knowing we will receive. Jesus then asks the question, "When the Son of Man comes, will He really find faith on the earth?" Can you hear the heart of God in this question? What brings Him pleasure? What is He hoping to see on the earth? Our faith!

Seeking God Means to Keep Asking, Seeking, and Knocking

My husband and I don't like inconveniencing people—not our friends or our family. We do everything we can not to be a burden on anyone for anything. However, when anyone we know has a need we absolutely love being able to help them. If you've ever had a need, and you were in the painful position of needing to ask for help (as we have been from time to time), I'm sure you can imagine how horrifying it would be if a friend from whom you sought help seemed resistant to give it.

Luke 11:5-10

And He said to them, "Which of you shall have a friend, and go to him at midnight and say to him, 'Friend, lend me three loaves; ⁶for a friend of mine has come to me on his journey, and I have nothing to set before him'; ⁷and he will answer from within and say, 'Do not trouble me; the door is now shut, and my children are with me in bed; I cannot rise and give to you'? ⁸I say to you, though he will not rise and give to him because he is his friend, yet because of his persistence he will rise and give him as many as he needs.

⁹"So I say to you, ask, and it will be given to you; seek, and you will find; knock, and it will be opened to you. ¹⁰For everyone who asks

*receives, and he who seeks finds, and to him
who knocks it will be opened.*

Thankfully, a good friend would help us right away. There would be no hesitation or stress. In like manner, God doesn't give to us because if He doesn't, we will keep pestering Him. Of course not! **God is a far better friend than that and much more reliable.** In fact, Jesus encourages us to ask, seek, and knock. Not only that, He makes one of the most beautiful statements that our overwhelmed hearts could hear.

**"For EVERYONE who asks receives,
and he who seeks finds,
and to him who knocks it will be opened."**

This has everything to do with Hebrews 11:6. He wants us to believe that He rewards those who seek Him.

Was Jesus using hyperbole? Was He teasing us? Could it be so marvelous that if we ask, we will receive? Notice, it doesn't say here that God answers our requests with, "Yes," "No," "Maybe," or "Later". It says that if we ask, we will receive.

Seeking God Means to Believe and Not Doubt

Having gone through the process of needing to rediscover what Biblical faith truly is, I hope something I share will liberate you from seeing faith as a work and instead see it as it truly is—a response to His grace.

One thing that has helped me personally when I find myself going off course on the topic of faith, is to substitute the word "believe" for "having faith". In the Greek, the word for both of these is **pistis**.[20] To believe means to have faith. Faith/belief pleases God.

---

[20] Since there is no verb form of "faith" in English, for example, "faithing", we use believe. There is no difference in what they mean. Faith = belief, to have faith = to believe, having faith = believing.

Another characteristic of faith that brings us victory is that it does not doubt. Doubt comes not only to challenge God's promises but to cast aspersions on God Himself. When we believe God to be who He says He is and that He will do what He says He will do, we must choose to do so without doubting.

> **Mark 11:23**
> *For assuredly, I say to you, whoever says to this mountain, 'Be removed and be cast into the sea,' and **does not doubt in his heart**, but **believes** that those things he says will be done, he will have whatever he says.*
>
> **James 1:5-8**
> *If any of you lacks wisdom, let him ask of God, who gives to all liberally and without reproach, and it will be given to him. ⁶but let him ask in faith, **with no doubting**, for he who doubts is like a wave of the sea driven and tossed by the wind. ⁷For let not that man suppose that he will receive anything from the Lord; ⁸he is a double-minded man, unstable in all his ways.*

I'd like to add here that we would think a person to be insane who daily placed orders online and then never expected them to arrive. If we place an order, we expect it will arrive and on time, or else we are on the phone asking where our order is and demanding a refund if it doesn't make it to our doorstep. How doubly ridiculous would it be for us to pray and not expect God to "reward" us with an answer? Is our God an online catalog? Of course not! **He is far better than that and much more reliable.**

Seeking God Means Praying According to His Will

Critics of teachings about faith, and maybe even on the attempts I'm making to represent faith more accurately, worry that unstable souls will start "naming and claiming" and "blabbing and grabbing", and then be disappointed when nothing happens. They reason that it's better not to get one's hopes up so that we are not disappointed.

Of course, there will be people who misunderstand true Biblical faith and then try to make things happen just as there are those among us who misunderstand righteousness and are trying to make themselves righteous. Try not to be too critical of these confused souls. At least they are trying to please God with their faith. He's seen it all before and isn't shocked if someone gets a bit off kilter while trying to learn or relearn how to believe in Him.

The verse below takes care of most of our wild child behavior, in my opinion. When we pray, it is according to His will. If we don't know what His will is, we have Bibles to read. If we need to know if something is His will that isn't exactly written in the Bible, we can ask God for wisdom.

1 John 5:14-15

*Now this is the confidence that we have in Him, that **if we ask anything according to His will**, He hears us. [15]And if we know that He hears us, whatever we ask, we **know** that we have the petitions that we **have** asked of Him.*

We need to be reasonable. It isn't God's will for one man to ask God that another man die so that he can marry his widow. It obviously isn't God's will that everyone be the president of his country. We can't speak to the local mountain and command it to be removed and be cast into the sea because thousands of people would be killed in the process.

We will not have faith to believe God for anything if we do not first have faith that what we are praying is His will. It is important to take some time to discover what His will is, and then ask and receive with confidence.

Seeking God Means to Live in Thanksgiving after We Have Asked

Seeking God isn't only about asking. If you've asked God for something that you know is His will, He won't be bothered if you ask Him again, but maybe you could find a way to reflect the fact that you already asked Him. The best way to do this is to pray with thanksgiving. Instead of, "Father, I ask You again to help me find a good job," try, "Father, I thank You that you are helping me to find a job. I am looking forward to the job You are going to help me find. I'm so happy I don't have to worry about this." We can also use Scripture when we give thanks. "Father, I thank You that Your word says that I should provide for my own household. This means that You want me to make money so I can do that. I thank You that You want me to always have an abundance for every good work. This means I not only need money to take care of my family, but I need extra money so that I can give. So, I thank You for getting me a well-paying job so I have something to share with others." In doing this, we are giving thanks, but we are also reminding ourselves of what is written.

> ***Colossians 4:2***
> *Continue earnestly in prayer, being vigilant in*
> *it (watch over it) with thanksgiving.*

We needlessly let ourselves get anxious about so many things. Sometimes, we worry without being completely conscious of it. We seem to find ourselves suddenly all tied up in knots and frustrated, and we wonder how we got so bound.

Some say, "It's a sin to worry," but I don't think that is correct. Worry is natural for all human beings. In many families, worrying, though perhaps verbally criticized, is also viewed as a virtue. If I worry about you, that means I care for you; at least, that's how it is on my mom's side of the family. Everyone agreed that our grandmother was "such a worrier". We'd tell her not to worry. On the other hand, though, it was seen as a compliment. It meant she loved the people for whom she worried. The truth is, though, that her worrying never helped any of us (though certainly her prayers did). In fact, being anxious is completely counterproductive because it is very difficult to hear God speak to us when we are a jangled mess of emotions. That is why He blessed us with this instruction.

Philippians 4:6-7
*Do not be anxious about **anything**, but in **everything** by prayer and supplication with thanksgiving let your requests be made known to God. [7]And the peace of God, which surpasses all understanding, will guard your hearts and your minds in Christ Jesus.*

I am a mom to three and grandmother of ten and taught elementary school for about four years before moving on to teaching high school, and I can tell you that children often worry. They get so frustrated sometimes that they will just throw themselves on the floor and have a hissy fit. They can get so mad at a classmate or sibling that they will push them or insult them. Sometimes they will get so upset they'll say, "I hate you!" It's quite comical, actually, though certainly disruptive. Teachers and parents know that we have to teach children how to express their frustrations with *words*.

We adults can be just as immature as little kids sometimes. Things aren't going our way, so we begin to pout. Someone isn't cooperating with us, so we walk off. Someone says something on Facebook, and we unfriend or block them—even good friends and family members. We have needs we think other people should meet without even telling them what our desires are and get offended because they don't know what they are. Some get frustrated and over-eat or drink or do drugs or buy something to relieve the stress. We fold our arms and huff and puff, and usually the people around us don't even know how to deal with us. Thankfully,

God has an answer. It's found in the above verses. Here is a simplification.

"Don't worry. Let's talk about this. Tell Me exactly what it is that you want. Then give Me thanks. After you do this, I will give to you a peace that you can't even imagine, even before the answer comes."

When we seek God this way, we are expressing our faith in His grace toward us, (and I should add, greatly decrease the amount of pain we cause others). We are resting in His love. When He sees our faith, it pleases Him. Just as a parent rejoices when a frustrated child comes running to him for affection and help, so God rejoices when we run to Him for the same.

Great Faith Means Seeking God until He Answers

There are many examples of people seeking God to help them, but one in particular always blesses me. It is that of a Canaanite woman whose daughter was demon-possessed. Now, Jesus' ministry was to the Jews only, but this did not keep her from seeking the help she needed from God.

Matthew 15:21-28
Then Jesus went out from there and departed to the region of Tyre and Sidon. ²²And behold, a woman of Canaan came from that region and cried out to Him, saying, "Have mercy on me, O Lord, Son of David! My daughter is severely demon-possessed."
²³But He answered her not a word.
And His disciples came and urged Him, saying, "Send her away, for she cries out after us."
²⁴But He answered and said, "I was not sent except to the lost sheep of the house of Israel."
²⁵Then she came and worshiped Him, saying, "Lord, help me!"

> ²⁶But He answered and said, "It is not good to take the children's bread and throw it to the little dogs."
> ²⁷And she said, "Yes, Lord, yet even the little dogs eat the crumbs which fall from their masters' table."
> ²⁸Then Jesus answered and said to her, "O woman, **great is your faith!** Let it be to you as you desire." And her daughter was healed from that very hour.

I've often wondered how I would react if the only person who could possibly help my child said He wouldn't because He wasn't sent to help me. Wouldn't the comment about giving the children's bread to dogs cause most of us to mournfully walk away or perhaps mount a political protest? Not this woman. She obviously heard that Jesus was casting out demons. Her daughter needed what He had, and she was going to press for it until He gave it to her. She knew she was regarded as a Gentile dog by the Jews. Maybe she even already rehearsed what she would say if the comment came up. Or maybe she felt like a little dog begging at the table. We don't know, but whatever might have deterred her from asking and asking again until she received, she was able to set aside so that she would receive. Was Jesus offended that she pushed? Not at all. In fact, He expressed amazement and admiration at her faith calling it "great". She was determined to receive from Him, and He did not let her down.

Romans 10:11
For the Scripture says, "Whoever believes in Him will not be disappointed."

No one wants to be disappointed, so we often hesitate to ask, not wanting to be let down. Given the examples above, we see that seeking God implies that when we seek God, we believe (have faith) that not only does He exist (is able), and not only that He is willing, but also that He *will* reward us if we believe and do not give up. In this sense we can use the word "diligently", but if we are to translate "diligently" as a list of hoops through which we must jump in order "to earn" answered prayer, we are believing incorrectly.

Seeking God isn't a mere religious exercise that earns us bonus points for possibly answered prayer. We pray because we believe He will answer. This faith pleases Him, and nothing is more satisfying than knowing we please God.

Lord, I put my trust in You
When I don't know what to do
And I'm not sure of the way I should go.
I've had dreams, and I've made plans,
Now I place them in Your hands
And I know that You will lead by Your peace.

You're my God
And I trust that You are leading me always.
You're my God
And I know that You will show my heart the way.

Lord, I put my trust in You
When I don't know what to do
At all.

Lord, I put my trust in You
When I don't know what to do
And I'm not sure of the way I should go
I have thought this whole thing through,
Now, I leave it up to You
And I know that you will lead by Your peace.

You're my God
And I trust that You are leading me always
You're my God
And I know that You will show my heart the way.

Lord, I put my trust in You
When I don't know what to do
At all.[21]

---

[21] A song by C. D. Hildebrand

Day 19

CONFIDENCE AND PEACE

Confidence to Ask

Once we are convinced of God's power and good intentions toward us, and we believe the good news that pertains to our overwhelming circumstances, we will have the confidence to take steps of faith. Our first step is to ask. Let's look at this verse again.

> **1 John 5:14-15**
> Now this is the **confidence** that we have in Him, that if we **ask** anything according to His will, He hears us. [15]And if we know that He hears us, **whatever we ask**, we know that we have the petitions that we have **asked** of Him.

This scripture is marvelous because of all it so concisely includes. First of all, the word "confidence" is very strong. It means an "all out spokenness, that is frankness, bluntness, publicity; by implication assurance". In other words, this isn't just a quiet inner confidence that makes us feel warm and fuzzy inside. The confidence spoken of here is a boldness to speak without fear. (See also Heb. 4:16.)

How do we get this confidence? There are two main components: our relationship with God, and our knowledge of His good intentions toward us. These are so closely intertwined that they can't really be discussed separately.

A child raised in a normal loving home learns that there are certain things that are his parents' will. He feels confident that his parents will feed him when he is hungry, so he confidently asks for food. He knows his parents will comfort him when he is sad, so he boldly crawls into his parent's lap to receive affection. If his father or mother promises to do something for him, he has outspoken faith that they will do it. The child has a trusting relationship with his mom and dad that gives him every assurance to ask, knowing without any doubt that he will receive from his parents.

Children who have been abused don't have the same confidence and, therefore, hesitate to ask or simply don't. They've learned that asking for their basic necessities or for affection could actually result in punishment. When taken out of such an unhealthy environment and placed in a loving home, such a child will need to learn that his new parents will gladly respond to his needs and that it is OK to ask.

There are clear spiritual implications from this illustration. If one has a healthy view of God's love for him and His *desire* to give him the things he asks of Him, he will securely and fearlessly ask. If one has an abusive view of God's intentions toward him, he might be intimidated about making any request.

If someone has been spiritually abused or comes from an abusive family situation, it will be necessary to discover how deeply God loves him. As we begin to know and believe the love God has for us and that He is nothing like the abusive parents or spiritual authorities we've known in the past, we will begin to experience a new comfort and confidence when we pray.

Asking "according to His will" is exactly what one would think. It is what He wants. Once we know His will, we can have complete confidence to ask God for it. When we ask *anything* according to His will, we know that He hears us, and this means we have His audience. He is listening to our petitions. Since He hears our petitions, we know His answer will be yes.

The Peace that Surpasses Understanding

In Philippians 4:6-7 we read of a peace that surpasses understanding. This peace is precisely what God promises it will be—beyond comprehension. We can't work it up or try really hard to have it, and it would be ridiculous to pretend we have peace. When we do have it, we will not be able to figure out how it is we could have such peace. Our circumstances might dictate that we should be panicked or troubled or frightened, but instead we are perfectly calm. The peace that surpasses understanding is one of the most beautiful experiences we can encounter as we walk by faith and not by sight.

Everyone wants this peace, but there are some very simple steps of faith we need to take in order to obtain it. No, you won't need to live perfectly, give a large offering, or do good works, but we can see clearly that God does ask that we do certain things.

First of all, we are told not to be anxious about anything, but in everything—. The word for "anxious" in the Greek is interesting to me because it can be used either positively or negatively. Paul used this word when he said that the unmarried man or woman "cares" for the things of the Lord. This is a good thing. Jesus used it in the negative sense of worrying when He taught us not to worry about food or clothing. He told us that by taking thought (being anxious) we can't change anything.

When my head hits the pillow, my mind goes automatically into drive, and I can experience anxiety, not always about negative things, but good things, too. If someone has a long list of things to do in the upcoming days, his mind might jump here and there and everywhere. What good does this do? We can't change one thing by thinking about it. Jesus used this word when He asked who would be able to add a cubit to his stature just by *taking thought (being anxious)*.

I'm trying to paint a picture here. It's OK to care in the positive sense, but we are instructed here not to worry/be anxious—about anything, and this word means "not even one" thing or person, and where it says "in everything" it means "in everything". So, our initial step is to stop being anxious about anything.

"Yeah, right," or "Yeah, but," someone might be grumbling. Let me be clear here. If God tells us to do something, there is no other rational response than to do it, and if He tells us to do something, then it must be 100% possible for us to do. Otherwise, God is being unreasonable and unjust.

A loving and good father would never tell his child to do something that he can't do. When we say to a screaming child to stop yelling, no matter how diligently they might fight us, it is because we know they have the capability to stop hollering. If we tell them to wash their hands, brush their teeth, clean their room, eat their dinner, or go to bed, we are not unreasonable or unfair. We are giving them instructions that will help them.

When we are told not to be anxious about even one thing, we can choose to take this step of faith willfully. This can be in our hearts or aloud. "Father, You tell me not to be anxious about anything. So I refuse to be anxious about flying tomorrow. I will not worry about that bill I need to pay. I won't keep thinking about all I have to do this week. In Your name, I cast my cares upon You."

Next, we are told to do four more things that are so very closely linked that we often end up doing them simultaneously. We are told to pray which includes worship and making supplications (asking) and with thanksgiving to make our requests made known unto God. In other words,

**"Don't worry, tell God what you want
with worship and thanksgiving."**

We are instructed to cast our cares upon the Lord because He cares for us. Instead of worrying ourselves sick, we are to tell God what it is we want. When you catch yourself getting anxious, stop. If you don't, your body will begin to respond to your worry with all kinds of physical symptoms. After you take the step of not being anxious about anything, don't end there. Tell your loving Father what you want. Verbalize it.

"Father, I ask that You cause the mechanic and the pilot to be alert as to the soundness of the jet I'm taking tomorrow. I ask that You provide this need. I ask that You show me why I've been sick lately. I ask that You help me get organized," and the list goes on.

While we're choosing not to be anxious, and making our requests known to God, we should remember to thank Him. Thanksgiving here means "gratitude; actually grateful language (to God, as an act of worship)".

It might sound like this: "Thank-You, Father, for protecting me. Thank-You for providing for me. Thank-You for opening my eyes to see what is causing this problem. Thank-You for restoring this relationship. Thank-You for helping me to write this book."

After we do these very simple things, the miracle of peace happens. The word "peace" is defined as, "peace, by implication prosperity, quietness, rest, set at one again". Peace. Not just peace, but an exceeding abundant peace—the peace that goes beyond what our minds can comprehend.

"Surpasses" is a compound word, the first part of which is the word **huper** which is where we get our word hyper. The word **huper**, just like "hyper", magnifies a word. This peace doesn't just pass understanding; it hyper-passes it. It is over and above what we can imagine.

When we have this peace, we will be amazed that we have it. Perhaps our doctor wants to do a biopsy on something that could be life-threatening. "God, I refuse to be anxious about this. I ask You to heal me. I ask You to make this procedure go better than it ever has. I ask You that my body will tolerate it well. I ask that there will be no infection. I ask that there will be no excess bleeding." That's our part. God is faithful. Before we can imagine it happening, we will have peace. The thought of that upcoming medical procedure won't affect us in the same way it would have. The bill that is due that we currently can't pay will shrink in comparison to His amazing peace. It will be exactly the miracle it needs to be, and we will be in awe of His wonder and amazing grace.

This over-the-top peace will keep your heart and mind in Christ Jesus. The word "keep" in the Greek means "to be a watcher in advance, that is, to mount guard as a sentinel (post spies at gates), to hem in, protect, keep with a garrison." How powerful is peace like this! It guards our hearts (our thoughts and feelings) and minds (our perception, our intellect, thoughts)—protects them like an army in Jesus.

Let me say this one more time. We cannot make this peace ours any other way. Breathing exercises might calm our bodies down, but they can't give us this incomprehensible peace from within that protects our hearts and minds.

It is the perfect example of walking by faith. Our world all around us might give us legitimate reasons to fear, but we can live far above it. Yes, we have challenges ahead of us, but we can choose not to be anxious about them today. Jesus asked us why we worry about tomorrow when today has enough worries of its own. So, deal with each day. Do what He has asked you to do, and then sit back and watch His supernatural supply of peace.

Day 20

LIVING ABOVE THE FRAY

*C*hristians should never be hypocrites, but we do live a double life. On the one hand, we exist in this natural world. We experience what everyone else does. When we are overcome by life, our perceptions can be greatly magnified to the point of overloading them. We can't walk around with blinders on and simply ignore what our senses perceive; so, what are we to do?

Even Abraham, our great example of faith "contemplated his own body, now as good as dead since he was about a hundred years old, and the deadness of Sarah's womb" (Rom. 4:19 NASB). He wasn't unaware of the impossibilities of their situation. He couldn't pretend them away or ignore them. He was very old, and Sarah was far beyond the age to bear a child. These were the facts. His senses reminded him of them on a daily basis.

Even with these "truths" before him, Abraham walked by faith.

> **Romans 4:20-21**
> *Yet, with respect to the promise of God, he did not waver in unbelief but **grew strong in faith**, giving glory to God, 21and **being fully assured that what God had promised, He was able also to perform.***

As believers, we live a life on two planes: the natural plane which includes all we can perceive with our five senses, and the supernatural one which is based on our faith in the promises of God (His grace) which we perceive by His Spirit. Put simply, "We walk by faith, and not by sight," (2 Cor. 5:7). The Amplified Version of this well-known verse brings this truth to life.

For we walk by faith [we regulate our lives and conduct ourselves by our conviction or belief respecting man's relationship to God and divine things, with trust and holy fervor; thus we walk] not by sight or appearance.

Here is how I visualize this double life. We live a natural life of "sight" simply because we live on this earth, but because we are new creations, we also have the privilege of walking on the level of the supernatural life of faith. Another way to put this is we "live above the fray" (above the struggle or battle that might be raging).

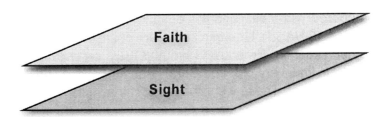

I adopted this term of living above the fray when I was a high school teacher. I adored my students but sometimes their drama was directed toward me, or I had to deal with it because it was disruptive. I had a choice how to respond when these storms would rise. I could get caught up in their adolescent emotional outbursts or live above them. While the storm was raging, I would tell myself, "Live above the fray." This helped me make compassionate and kind decisions.

As a parent, sometimes our children can put us to the test. They are too young to know how to walk by faith, so we must show them how. Our only other choice is to hurl insults in their direction and possibly cause psychological damage. No, we are the grownups. We must walk by faith not by sight patiently teaching them and giving them compassion and love. In marriage or any relationship, there are times when other people's storms threaten our own peace. Live above the fray! Walk by faith, not by sight. Someone needs to be clear-thinking. By faith, that person can be you.

Life can be so overwhelming at times. It is difficult to navigate the wind and waves that threaten us, but just as did Abraham, we can choose to esteem the promise of God as more valid than what we are forced to perceive with our senses. When we choose to walk by faith and not by sight, we discover an amazing joy and power that is beyond comprehension. We almost can't believe it ourselves when we experience it. We know we should be freaking out over all that is so disturbing, but instead we nearly fly on the wings of faith. This glorious blessing given to His children is meant to sustain us as we overcome the overwhelming.

I put my trust in the God
Who created everything
I put my faith in His Son, who died for me.
When no one else on earth can help or understand
I reach out to Him.
He takes my hand.[22]

Psalm 27: 1-3, 6
The Lord is my light and my salvation;
Whom shall I fear?
The Lord is the strength of my life;
Of whom shall I be afraid?
²When the wicked came against me

---

[22] I wrote this little song during a very scary experience many years ago. It helped me to focus on Jesus instead of the fears that loomed large in my life.

To eat up my flesh,
My enemies and foes,
They stumbled and fell.
³Though an army may encamp against me,
My heart shall not fear;
Though war may rise against me,
In this I will be confident.
⁶And now my head shall be lifted up above my
enemies all around me;
Therefore I will offer sacrifices of joy in His
tabernacle;
I will sing, yes, I will sing praises to the Lord.

Sometimes, God will help us as we walk by faith by giving us a practical way of remembering His promises. He did this for Abraham when he coupled His promise with two illustrations of its completion. He told him to look at the stars and to look at the grains of sand on the sea, and said, so shall your seed be. So, each day as he looked at the sand and each night as he glanced at the skies, he was reminded of God's promise to him.

How might this work in our lives? We have many resources. First of all, we can look at the lives of those recorded in Scripture who obtained great things from God. We can also look back to the many things God has done for us in the past. Sometimes, God speaks something into our hearts. For me, this was when He called me to preach the gospel to the saved. So many times when frustrations and obstacles have tried to hold us back, we've remembered this calling and then moved confidently forward.

The other idea is a bit more controversial, but I think it is acceptable, and that is to see with our spiritual eyes what the completed promise will look like. Some go astray here thinking that by visualizing they can make things come to pass. I don't endorse that at all. Yet, there is no harm in picturing our prayers being answered instead of focusing on the here and now, just as Abraham looked forward to the promises of God.

When we live the supernatural life of faith in God and His goodness and forsake living by sight, we actually experience joy and peace when we could reasonably be drowning in sadness and fear. This life of faith is so miraculous that words can never express it. It can only be known by living it. We walk by faith and not by sight.

Day 21

WHILE WE WAIT

Sometimes, God does an instantaneous miracle. Of course, we'd all prefer that, but sometimes the overwhelming situations we face involve other people. Other times, we are holding onto beliefs that we have no clue are inaccurate. Sometimes there are things we are doing that are working against us. Obviously, we can't control others, and if we don't know that we are believing something that's inaccurate or doing something counterproductive, we have some learning to do. It will take time for God to teach us, and it will take time for Him to teach those involved. Here are some helpful ideas that will help you while you wait.

Receive God's Discipline

If you've asked God to help you, expect that He will. One of the ways He moves us toward victory is by correcting our beliefs and our actions. This is also known as discipline. No one likes to be disciplined, but we should welcome it because it will help to set us free.

> **Hebrews 12:7-11**
> *If you endure chastening, God deals with you as with sons; for what son is there whom a father does not chasten? [8]But if you are without chastening, of which all have become*

*partakers, then you are illegitimate and not sons.⁹Furthermore, we have had human fathers who **corrected** us, and we paid them respect. Shall we not much more readily be in subjection to the Father of spirits and live? ¹⁰For they indeed for a few days chastened us as seemed best to them, but He for our profit, that we may be partakers of His holiness. ¹¹Now no chastening seems to be joyful for the present, but painful; nevertheless, afterward it yields the peaceable fruit of righteousness to those who have been trained by it.*

Many have struggled with what it means to be "chastened" by the Lord. Some sincerely think that God sends trials and struggles into our lives to purge us of sin. Others approach blasphemy as they blame God for deaths and destruction as a part of His correction. These things are not true. We need not fear the chastening of the Lord. As we read in the passage above, God disciplines us for our good, not by harming us. The end goal of all discipline is that we have "the peaceable fruit of righteousness".

So, if God's discipline doesn't include beating us up and thrusting calamity upon us, just what is it? Well, if we can read the passage above without those horrible fears in mind, we can see it as plain as day. Clearly, in context, chastening or discipline means to be *corrected*. How does our Father correct us? In two ways.

First of all, He teaches us by His grace about what it is we believe that is not correct and encourages us to change our beliefs. This is what true Biblical repentance is—changing our minds. Changing our minds is what leads to changing our behavior. We can't go at this backward, my friends. Yes, we have the power to change our behavior because if we do, we'll be rewarded, or if we don't, we'll be punished (as was true with the law system), but we can never truly be free until we change our minds.

The Jews who realized that they crucified their own Messiah were "cut to the heart". They asked Peter what they should do, and he told them to repent and believe. Repent of what—of sin? No—of unbelief. (See Acts 2.) This is the repentance that is required of every person who would be born again—change your mind about Jesus and believe in Him (Acts 20:20-21).

The second way God corrects His children is by revealing to us the things that we are *doing* that are incorrect or that are leading to our own defeat.

At one point in the healing of our marriage, God showed me that I expected David to show me grace, but when he didn't live up to my expectations in some way, I did not always extend grace to him. On the contrary, I would make sure he knew full well, that I was not pleased with something he said or did. In other words, grace for me, but no grace for you.

When God showed me this, I felt awful. I knew He was right. I didn't need my beliefs to be corrected because I already understood His grace. I was busy teaching it. I just wasn't applying it as I should. When the Lord showed me this, I remember being "cut to the heart". I was actually surprised because I obviously was always trying to practice what I preached. Yet, when I received this discipline, it led to more peace than ever in our relationship.

God is always teaching us by His grace, but sometimes we aren't listening for one reason or another. Perhaps it is primarily because we are too busy, overly frustrated, or it could also be because we don't want to hear. Let me encourage you, though, to open your heart and mind to God's correction. You don't have to be afraid of God. He won't hurt you in the process. He will gently correct you. Just ask Him, "Lord is there anything I believe that isn't correct? Is there something I'm doing that You want me to change?" Then keep your heart open. He will speak to you.

Believe that God Will Give You Wisdom

If you have asked God for wisdom, have confidence that He will give it to you. He might do that immediately when you ask, or it might take some time. He's not trying to test you to see if you can hear. He will generously give you the wisdom you need. You can trust Him. Even beyond knowing that God will give us wisdom when we ask, we can rejoice that Jesus Himself is our wisdom.

> ### *1 Corinthians 1:30 NASB*
> *By His doing you are in Christ Jesus, who became to us wisdom from God, and righteousness and sanctification, and redemption.*

Respond to His Spirit Leading You

A beautiful aspect of knowing that Jesus is our wisdom is the fact that His Spirit is leading us. As I said earlier in the book, this is a gift to us simply because we are His children. He is leading us right now. Ask Him to help you recognize His leading. When He nudges you in a certain direction, go. If you go and then realize you didn't hear right, that's OK. Little by little, you will become more aware of His voice speaking to you. As my grandfather said to me, "Get in the habit of saying, 'Yes,' to Jesus.

> ### *Romans 8:14*
> *For all who are led by the Spirit of God are sons of God.*

Worship

When our lives are upside down, and our struggles seem to go on forever, it is so easy to feel like giving up, but we must not. If we've done everything we can think to do, and we know we do believe in Him with all of our hearts, but nothing seems to be changing, or the storm continues to rage, we can take some time simply to worship Him. Express your frustrations and fears and hand them over to Him. Let Him know your requests with thanksgiving. Let Him know that you trust Him even though you feel you will surely fall apart any minute. "Father, I don't understand, but I trust You. You are worthy of my praise. You are my God. You are my Father. You are my Friend. I choose to keep my eyes on You."

At times like these, I can feel Your peace
Reaching out to comfort me.
In moments sweet I can feel Your love
Reaching out, reaching out to me.

So I lift up my heart, and I lift up my hands
To receive all that You want to give.
And I submit myself to all You want to do,
And say, Lord, that I love You, too.

Life gets hard sometimes.
It's hard to see things through.
Even at times like these, I feel Your peace.
So I reach out, reach out to You.
Reaching out, reaching we two.[23]

---

[23] A song written during a moment of peace in the midst of storms, C. D. Hildebrand

Day 22

SUDDEN AND GREAT STORMS

---

*M*any overwhelming situations we face are long-term—something with which we've struggled for months and maybe even years. Thankfully, as we put our faith in Jesus, things gradually begin to improve. We start to relax and breathe easier thinking the circumstances are finally going to change for the good. Then suddenly, without warning, an unexpected and great storm arises in that area. A check we were expecting to cover certain expenses doesn't arrive—in fact; it's not coming at all. A relationship that was on the mend takes an ugly turn, and we feel devastated. We have a setback with our health which we thought was improving. When these types of storms arise, we wonder if we are making any progress at all. We are blinded to the successes we've seen by the winds and waves that beset us.

Other times, we are just innocently going about our business with no particular problem at all, and without any warning, we are struck by a storm we hadn't anticipated. These storms can sometimes be actual, like an earthquake, tornado, fire, or flood which can alter our futures forever. Other times, the storms are more privately perceived. The doctor calls and is concerned about the results of one of your medical tests and it's one of those areas that could threaten not only your health but your life. Your mind begins to race, and your thoughts swirl with unanticipated emotions. Or per-haps your finances which have always been in control are put at risk by some whim of the financial market or a betrayal of trust. Others, thinking their marriage to be relatively solid discover that their spouse has been having an affair, maybe for a very long time—it seems to come out of nowhere.

All of these sudden storms are magnified by their abruptness and importunity. Life is demanding enough—who has extra time and energy to deal with these types of problems? You want the world to slow down so you can have a chance to catch-up, but does it? No, it just keeps turning seemingly uncaring about the shock you are experiencing.

You might find yourself devastated by the realization that the battle you've been facing is still not over, or if the storm was completely surprising, you might feel numb and unable to process it all fast enough to meet the decisions you have to make.

Sudden storms can be shocking, horrifying, and devastating. They can render us seemingly powerless by their perplexity. At the moment they hit, however, we can tap into a power that is higher than every wind or wave, one that will calm the storm within us and give us clarity to face any situation. We have a choice when the tempest arises. Will we have faith in Him or will we fear?

> **Matthew 8:23-27**
> *Now when He got into a boat, His disciples followed Him. ²⁴And **suddenly a great tempest arose** on the sea, so that the boat was covered with the waves. But He was asleep. ²⁵Then His disciples came to Him and awoke Him, saying, "Lord, save us! We are perishing!"*
> *²⁶But He said to them, "Why are you **fearful**, O you of little **faith**?" Then He arose and rebuked the winds and the sea, and there was a great calm. ²⁷So the men marveled, saying, "Who can this be, that even the winds and the sea obey Him?"*

Without a doubt, this event spoke to the disciples of Jesus' deity. Indeed, He calmed the winds and the sea, and they obeyed Him. Yet, when we take a closer look, we see a parable to help us when a sudden tempest arises in our lives. It might seem at first that Jesus was a bit harsh when He asked the disciples, "Why are you fearful, O you of little faith?" However, taking into consideration what they had just witnessed, the question becomes reasonable. Just prior to this storm, the disciples had seen amazing things. Jesus had given what we call His sermon on the mount. What amazing truths had proceeded from His lips! After that, a leper was completely healed, a centurion's servant was healed without Jesus even touching him. Peter's mother-in-law was healed of a fever. Many demon-possessed were set free. He healed "all who were sick".

Multitudes were following Him, so Jesus gave the command to go to the other side. Perhaps they were basking in the glory of all they witnessed. Maybe the boat ride even promised to be an enjoyable break from a very busy season of ministry. There likely wasn't a cloud in the sky about which they were concerned. The waters were calm. Jesus lay down His head and fell asleep in the boat. Maybe a couple others followed His lead as the rest navigated to the other side. Sounds idyllic, doesn't it—you and I, resting together in the boat of life obeying His command to go to the other side with not a care in the world except maybe to take a nap?

Then "suddenly a great tempest arose on the sea so that the boat was covered with the waves." Does this sound familiar? You are minding your own business, maybe even in rest mode, pursuing what you believe to be God's calling on your life, and enjoying His many blessings. Maybe you have also just recently witnessed His glorious miracles in your life, or you have been amazed by His great love for you. Then, whack! You are hit by a sudden and great storm. God didn't send it. You did nothing to deserve it. It just happened, and there you are being tossed by the wind and waves, and it looks like you are going under.

Will we freak out and ask God why He is asleep when we need Him most or will we instead express our trust in Him?

Recently, I had a sudden storm come into my life. When it hit, my world as I knew it began to come undone, my feelings were off kilter. I didn't know how to deal with it at all, but I saw at that moment **I had a choice to believe God or fold in despair.** I prayed, "God, I don't know how to process this. I don't know how to feel. How do I respond? What do I do?"

Now, it wasn't in words exactly that God immediately answered me, but if I could put it into words what came into my heart, it went something like this, **"It's OK to feel, but don't fear."** God understood how I felt. He wasn't in any way displeased with me for my immediate emotions. In fact, He was there to help and comfort me. It was perfectly normal for my whole being to respond to what had just happened, but **would I allow the winds and waves to overcome me or would I trust in God?**

Needing immediate encouragement, I printed out Day 9 of this book, the chapter I recommended that my readers bookmark to read when they might need some good news. With my personal storm raging, I began to preach good news to myself as I gave thanks to Him for His faithfulness.

"Father, I thank You that You are right here with me right now. I am one spirit with You. You see me in all this swirl of feelings that I don't know how to process. You hear my heart. You know I want to please You by my faith. You care about what I'm experiencing. You know the truth about my love for You, and You know exactly what the truth is about this situation. You are for me in this circumstance, not against me. Nothing is impossible for You, God, and nothing is impossible for me because I believe in You. You will take this awful situation and work it together for my good. You are not only able to help me but You are willing, and You will help me. You will not forsake me at my time of need. You love me, Father. I am Your child. You see the faith I have in You, Lord, and it pleases You."

Then, I fell asleep and rested in my boat as the storm subsided and His love rested upon me. When I woke, even though the threat of more storms was on the horizon, I felt peace. **I knew deep in my heart that my faith in Him had brought Him joy**, and I sensed that He would give me the strength to continue pleasing Him through it all.

We can speak to the storms that rage in our lives. No, we are not God, but we can speak with His authority. "Wind and waves, I command you in the name of Jesus, to be still." Sometimes, we are surprised by how quickly the storm subsides. That "person" who suddenly brought us too much drama just calms down. That threat of financial ruin amazingly turns out for our good. The doctor's report that seemed to threaten our very life turns out to be nothing at all.

Yet even if the storm continues, we can rest in His great love for us. It is like the cartoon I saw of my husband; we ride the waves of the storm instead of being pulled under by them. When we do this, He is pleased. He is proud of us as His child simply because we trust in Him. He isn't expecting us not to feel or to "be brave" or not to respond when more wind and waves arise, rather He will be there for us when they do, and each time we choose faith over fear, we put a smile on His glorious face because our faith pleases Him.

Baby Joey

When our second daughter, Joella, was born, we knew something was wrong when they didn't bring her in to see me. She was in an incubator gasping for each breath. Before they took her to a bigger hospital for evaluation, they rolled her into my room so I could see her. She was beautiful, and my arms ached to hold her. Her bushy red hair filled my heart with delight. Before she was two days old, the family started calling her Joey.

The next hospital decided to fly her to U.C. Davis Medical Center because she needed 100% oxygen.

I knew our church was praying for a miracle. This was so comforting as I was very weak right after my C-section. I only had just enough strength to say aloud, "Satan, you can't have my baby." A short while later, my husband who was with her called me, and he said, "Satan can't have our baby." I told him I had just said the same thing. We believed God's Word that the fruit of my womb was blessed (Deut. 28:4).

I could feel the support of the prayers of our church. I knew she would be fine, but it was serious. The valve between her lungs and heart that closes at birth had remained open.[24] We waited days to see if it would close naturally, but it didn't. We consented to experimental medicine to close it, but it didn't work. The next step would be surgery.

My understanding of Joella's medical condition was that it had to do with her breathing only. One day while on the phone with a nurse, she said something about her "heart" problem, and I said, "What about her heart? I haven't heard anything about her heart," which resulted in me being put on hold and the nurse immediately retrieving a doctor to explain.

It was like a storm in the midst of a storm, but David and I continued to believe that the fruit of my womb was blessed and that Satan could not have our baby. Shortly after this, the valve closed.

We asked the doctor about what happened. He told us plainly that the valve did not close because of the medicine because there were only a limited number of hours it could be effective, and they had long past. He said there was no explanation for it closing by itself. We said, "Then it was a miracle." He said that it would seem so.

Joella is an adult now with five, count them, five children of her own and perfectly healthy. She is a

---

[24] **(PDA)** is a congenital heart defect wherein the ductus arteriosus fails to close after birth.

long-distance runner, too. She loves God with all her heart and knows He saved her life. God was faithful to His Word, and now she lives to serve Him.

Psalm 46:1-5
God is our refuge and strength,
A very present help in trouble.
²Therefore we will not fear,
Even though the earth be removed,
And though the mountains be carried into the midst of the sea;
³Though its waters roar and be troubled,
Though the mountains shake with its swelling. Selah
⁴There is a river whose streams shall make glad the city of God,
The holy place of the tabernacle of the Most High.
⁵God is in the midst of her, she shall not be moved;
God shall help her, just at the break of dawn.
Psalm 5:11-12
Let all those who put their trust in You rejoice;
Let them ever shout for joy, because You defend them;
Let those also who love Your name Be joyful in You.
¹²For You, O Lord, will bless the righteous;
With favor You will surround them as with a shield.

Day 23

WALKING ON WATER

---

*Y*oung adult children can be really difficult. I say this because I was actually surprised by how hard it was to watch as they figured out adulthood for themselves. I had wisdom to give them, but for the most part, they weren't as interested in hearing it as I would have liked. Plus, my husband and I wanted them to become confident and independent, and we knew that if we intervened too often, we'd rob them of the joy of figuring things out. The only times we became insistent that they listen to us was when we felt their safety was at risk. Did they like this meddling? No, but as their friends and parents, we risked rejection to protect them from harm. For the most part, we stayed out of their ways and prayed for God's best.

Something I learned from "raising" young adult children and that my young adult children had to accept is that I cannot turn off "Mom" and that my heart would always care for their well-being. It was one storm after another during those years. My inclination in the face of each storm was to cast myself quite dramatically on my bed and begin to mourn and weep and wail and "intercede" for them. "Oh, God, speak to his heart. Keep her from danger." After my weeping session, I'd get up, but it seemed nothing ever changed.

It was during one of these praying sessions that I "heard" the Lord speak very clearly to me. "I want you to walk on water for your son." Suddenly, I saw clearly that I didn't need to go through all this drama.

"Okay, Jesus. I walk on water to You for my child. I trust You to take care of him. I will keep my eyes on You when the next storm comes up."

Many storms did come up after this time, but something rose up in me, and instead of freaking out, I would pray, "Jesus, I walk on water to You for my son." By doing this, my mind was freed up to think rationally and walk in grace.

One example stands out so wonderfully in my mind. Our son was planning to go with his friend to some weekend event. Of course, I felt uneasy about him going and, in fact, did not want him to go, but instead of voicing my objections, I chose to walk on water. So sweetly, the Lord spoke to my spirit, "Help him pack his ice chest." Again, without all the turmoil I usually put myself through, I was able to hear God more precisely.

"Okay, Lord," I said, and David and I helped him pack an ice chest. As he and his friend drove off for the festival and we waved our good-byes, my husband and I prayed, "Lord, we ask that they will not enjoy this weekend at all. Let them see how stupid this thing is."

What was supposed to be a weekend was just one night, for they returned the next day because, in their words, "It was really stupid." What I didn't learn about that night until years later was that both my son and his friend independently of each other had an experience which spoke to them of God in a miraculous way.

Some time later, as my son was driving one day, he prayed, "Jesus, I want You to come into my heart," and the Lord answered him, "I'm already here." From that day forward, he has never wavered in his faith.

I share this precious story with you because I know that we all face storms in this life, and many times the ones we face are caused by others. Yes, we can go to God in prayer, and He doesn't despise our tears or turn His back on us when we pour our hearts out to Him, but I want you to know there is a higher road, that of walking in faith keeping our eyes on Jesus.

When we focus on the storm that is fomenting about us, we will logically begin to fear. Our senses are feeding us information and our minds are translating this into emotions. The emotions then cause our bodies to respond with panic. Everything in us will scream that all is lost and that no one can help us.

The world will tell us, "When the going gets tough, the tough get going," but when our bodies are racing with fight and flight chemicals, we might be tempted to think we are all alone in the boat. "Going" isn't even an option when one feels paralyzed with fear. We see our only options as to sink or swim, but God has a higher road for us.

Matthew 14:22-29

Immediately Jesus made His disciples get into the boat and go before Him to the other side, while He sent the multitudes away. [23]And when He had sent the multitudes away, He went up on the mountain by Himself to pray. Now when evening came, He was alone there. [24]But the boat was now in the middle of the sea, tossed by the waves, for the wind was contrary.

[25]Now in the fourth watch of the night Jesus went to them, walking on the sea. [26]And when the disciples saw Him walking on the sea, they were troubled, saying, "It is a ghost!" And they cried out for fear.

[27]But immediately Jesus spoke to them, saying, "Be of good cheer! It is I; do not be afraid."

[28]And Peter answered Him and said, "Lord, if it is You, command me to come to You on the water."

²⁹*So He said, "Come." And when Peter had come down out of the boat, he walked on the water to go to Jesus.*

Imagine the thrill Peter experienced actually walking on water to Jesus. I wonder what it felt like to feel the cold water touching his toes. Did the water give way slightly like walking on the wet shore or did it feel like walking on air? The disciples must have had a variety of emotions and thoughts as they witnessed this miracle. Was Peter out of his mind? Would he sink? Why wasn't he sinking? "Oh, my Lord, he is walking on water!" Then something happened. He began to sink! But, why?

Matthew 14:30-33
But when he saw that the wind was boisterous, *he was* **afraid**; *and beginning to sink he cried out, saying, "Lord, save me!"*
³¹*And* **immediately** *Jesus stretched out His hand and caught him, and said to him, "O you of little* **faith**, *why did you* **doubt**?" ³²*And when they got into the boat, the wind ceased.*
³³*Then those who were in the boat came and worshiped Him, saying, "Truly You are the Son of God."*

When we walk on water to Jesus, whether it is for our own situation or for someone else, we are amazed at the peace we experience even while the storm blows on. What a miracle this is, but then for just a moment we get our eyes off of Jesus and begin to focus on the wind and waves. How can we not? The wind is cold, and the waves are wet; that is to say, what we are experiencing is *real*. If you are in the middle of a medical procedure to discover if you have a certain disease or your own child is cursing you to your face, or the bank is threatening to repossess your property, or you are in emotional or physical pain, you are going to feel these things. If you focus on the winds and waves, you will begin to sink, but you don't have to. Do as Peter did. Call out to Him, "Lord, save me," and then keep your eyes on Him and walk on water again with Him until the storm subsides.

This is a perfect illustration of walking by faith and not by sight. Let me walk you through this again. A sudden storm happens. You have a choice—will you have faith in Him or will you fear? Will you keep your eyes on Him or will you only focus on your circumstances? I hope you will choose faith over fear. Remember, God doesn't expect you to ignore your troubles. They are real. Putting a blinder on your eyes won't make them go away, but will you have faith and hope or will you fold in the face of this storm?

"God, I trust You right now. I'm in a storm. You know that. You are right here with me in my boat. You are not asleep. You do care. I choose to trust You. I choose to walk by faith and not by my senses which are currently being overloaded by the wind and waves. Thank-You for being here. Thank-You for caring. I choose to walk on water to You in this situation (or for this person I'm dealing with). I am keeping my eyes on You right now, Lord. In the name of Jesus, I speak to this storm to be still! I command any evil influencing this situation to be still. I know that my decision to have faith in You right now in this storm pleases You. You are smiling at me right now in this situation. You are taking this overwhelming situation. I cast this upon You knowing You care for me. You are my wisdom, Lord. Guide my words. Guide my steps. I refuse to be anxious. I am letting my requests be made known to You. You will bring peace. I praise You. I worship You. I will sing songs to You in my affliction because I know You will deliver me."

The sweetest name I know
Is Jesus.
The sweetest name I know
Is the Lord's.
The sweetest name I know
Can calm
A raging storm within
My heart.
The sweetest name I know,
Most awesome name I know,
The sweetest name I know
Is Jesus. [25]

---

[25] A song I wrote during a painful storm in my life, C. D. Hildebrand

Day 24

SPEAKING TO MOUNTAINS

I have observed that sometimes when it seems like God is silent about something, there is a very simple solution that He is working to bring to light. We might be battling a sickness that is being caused by something in the environment. Or we might be having financial woes without knowing someone is stealing from us. Sometimes strained relationships are caused by unknown misunderstandings. These situations can look like God is not answering our prayers, when actually, He is at work in our circumstances and our minds to help us see what is going on. Such was the case with me about 30 years ago.

Out of nowhere it seemed, I began to get a certain type of headache I didn't even know existed. Headaches were not unfamiliar to me, but this type was something that I'd never experienced before. People would describe what migraines were like in an effort to help me figure it out, but nothing matched the description. All I knew is that when they would hit, the pain was unbearable, and I thought I might die from their intensity. Many times I would be on the floor crying, even though I knew it frightened my children. I didn't know what else to do.

Along with occasional killer headaches, I was experiencing many other symptoms. We didn't have medical insurance at the time, so we paid what was an enormous sum for us, to see a doctor that was supposed to be a specialist.

After a lengthy exam and bloodwork, he could find nothing wrong with me. Fantastic news, right? Nothing was wrong with me, but then it hit me. Something was definitely wrong. The years went by. Through it all, I went back to college to work toward getting my teaching credential. Of course, I cried out to God during these episodes and about all the other maladies I was experiencing, but it seemed like there was no answer. There was an answer—a very simple one, but I was not yet aware of it.

Years later, as I was in the cafeteria line where I was teaching, the attendant there noticed that I was putting seven packets of sweetener into my extra-large iced tea, and casually commented about how many. It was just a little friendly comment, but it caused me to stop and think. I remembered that when I first started using the sweetener aspartame, I only needed two packets. This got my attention and even alarmed me. I wasn't a person to take medicines of any kind, and the fact that it took seven packets several years later to be as sweet to me as the two I used to take, rang some bell inside that I might be addicted. I doubt that I was addicted, but just the thought that I needed more and more caused me to decide to stop putting it in my iced tea.

Time went by, and I never thought a thing about it. It was a very busy time of life for us. About three months later, though, I noticed something. I was no longer getting those deadly headaches, and the other symptoms were also gone. It was curious and wonderful, but I didn't know why I was so much better. So I sat down one day and tried to figure out if I was doing anything differently, and the only thing that had changed was that I no longer used aspartame.

I share this because those headaches nearly destroyed my life, and I'm pretty convinced that I might have died one day because of the intense pain. There was such a simple answer that God knew about all along. He used a cafeteria attendant's comment and my own desire not to be dependent on drugs to bring a miraculous solution. He was answering my prayers all that time, bringing me to that moment that would set me free.

Remember when Paul wrote this to Timothy?

1 Timothy 5:23
No longer drink only water, but use a little wine for your stomach's sake and your frequent infirmities.

Keep in mind that God used Paul to do some amazing healings, so why didn't Paul just heal Timothy in Jesus' name? Certainly Timothy had taken this request before the Lord, perhaps even had others pray for him. Maybe he'd requested that Paul come and lay hands on him to be healed. Surely, he'd sought God's help, but God knew a very simple way for Timothy to be healed. We don't know if the water was of poor quality or if he had some disease that could be cured by drinking wine. We do know that drinking less water and a little wine was his cure. His situation didn't require a miracle. It had a very simple solution.

Sharing the story about my assassin headaches leads into this one. Headaches had been part of my life since puberty, but they were *normal* headaches caused by allergies, stress, and later an injury to my neck. It was not uncommon for me to have several a week, and waking up with a headache would never be surprising. Once in a while, I'd have what I called a perfect storm headache which was a combination of the above causes. Still, a good dose of over-the-counter medicine, and I'd be better within a half hour or so.

Probably the most painful headaches were the ones I'd have when I woke from sleep in the morning. My husband would patiently go get me some Excedrin and a glass of milk, and I'd lay down with a cold pack on my eyes until it subsided. I was so happy that I no longer had those assassin headaches caused by aspartame, that I more or less accepted the regular variety. They were part of my life, and I never went anywhere without some medicine "just in case".

One morning, I woke up with a particularly painful headache. I remember very distinctly that I was getting ready to pray this, "God why don't You heal me of these headaches?" The words were right there ready to come out, but something inside of me knew it wasn't right to blame God. Then came the thought, "Speak to your headache."

It wasn't my thought, and I had zero doubt that God had just spoken to me. I instantly remembered Mark 11:22-24—the verse about speaking to mountains to be removed. Inside I thought, "Well, duh!" Then I said aloud, "I speak to you, headache, in the name of Jesus to be removed and to be cast into the sea—and the cause of it." In less than a second, my rip roaring headache was completely gone. Being the great woman of faith that I was, I started to shake my head and move my neck to make sure it was truly gone and that I hadn't just temporarily done something to make it stop hurting. Nope. It was completely gone.

"Well, that's interesting," I thought and went about my day.

When the next headache came, I repeated my prayer. "Headache, I command you in the name of Jesus to be removed and cast into the sea—and the cause of it." Away went the headache. This happened again and again, and I remember thinking one day, "Wow, this is better than aspirin." When I got a headache, I commanded it and the cause of it to be removed. A couple times I forgot or got lazy and just took medicine, but it became normal for my headaches to take a hike.

Many months passed. Our daughter was getting married, and of course, I was in the middle of the preparations. On the day of her wedding, I spent multiple hours at the reception site setting up table decorations with the help of her sweet friends. By the end of it, my feet were *killing me.* I wondered if I'd be able to rest enough before the wedding. My husband gave me two Excedrin for the pain in my feet and for an energy boost before the big event, and suddenly it hit me. Why didn't I have a headache? I was exhausted. I was stressed. My feet were hurting like heck, but not my head.

Sitting down to stay off of my feet, I searched my memory for why it might be that I did not have at least a tension headache. Then I realized it! I'd been so busy preparing for the big day that I hadn't even noticed until just that moment that I hadn't suffered from a headache at all for weeks!

To say I was stunned about this does not do my realization justice. I had been speaking not only to my headaches but to the cause of them. I thought that they were temporarily removed each time, but as it turned out, the causes of my headaches were permanently removed also. Jesus did say they'd be cast into the sea, and that is mighty permanent, I concluded.

Our daughter was married nine years ago. Since then I would be surprised if I've had more than one morning headache a year. Having a headache during the day is also super rare—maybe two or three a year. Each time, I speak to them to be removed, and I would say that 99.9% of the time, they obey me. For the very rare time or two when they haven't, I simply took aspirin.

At my last physical, the doctor was looking over my chart which I'd filled out in advance. The questionnaire asked how frequently I got headaches. I wrote something like two to three per year. When she read that, she was shocked and had me affirm my answer. I asked her if she'd like to hear my story, and she listened as if she wished she could stop getting headaches, too. She was amazed, and I remain so blessed that my head is free of pain. By the way, my allergies are also gone. I haven't had an allergy symptom for nine years. Coincidence? I truly doubt that. Praise God!

Walking by faith and not by sight is how we live as Christians. It takes on many forms from living above difficulties that we are experiencing, walking on stormy seas, receiving a miracle from Him, to speaking to sickness in our bodies or problems to be removed. This entire life we live is *supernatural*. It's not that any of us are so holy or powerful, but because He has provided so many precious gifts for us. All we need to do is employ them in faith.

I'm convinced that in this lifetime, we will never fathom the depths of His grace and power toward us who believe, but I hope you will join me in my determination to ask, seek, and knock so that you may receive. Each time we choose to walk by faith and not by sight our faith brings pleasure to the heart of God.

Whoever says to this mountain,
"Be removed, and be carried into the sea,"
And does not doubt in his heart
But believes
Then the things that he says will be done.

For whatever you ask when you pray
Believe that you receive it
And you shall have it
Have faith in God.

Whosoever.
Whatsoever.
Whosoever means me.
Whatsoever.
Whosoever.
Whatsoever means anything.

I'm gonna say to this mountain,
"Be removed, and be carried into the sea."
I will not doubt in my heart
But believe
And the things that I say shall be done.

For whatever I ask when I pray
I believe that I receive it
And I shall have it.
I have faith in God.

Whosever
Whatsoever
Whosoever means me.
Whatsoever
Whosoever
Whatsoever
Means anything.[26]

---

[26] C.D. Hildebrand from Mark 11:22-24

PART 3

Enemies of Faith

Day 25

THE TRYING OF OUR FAITH

*T*here is a battle to be fought which involves our participation. We need to understand that our enemy doesn't ultimately care whether we live or die; his highest goal is to destroy our faith in Jesus and to keep us from sharing this faith with others. Curiously enough, it is through our faith that we resist the enemy when he comes against our faith. Remember, it is not just our faith standing alone, but our faith in Jesus as the Son of God.

> **1 John 5:4-5**
> *For whatever is born of God overcomes the world. **And this is the victory that has overcome the world—our faith.** ⁵Who is he who overcomes the world, but he who **believes** that Jesus is the Son of God?*

The enemy's ultimate end-goal is to get us to deny the faith we have in Jesus—to put Him to an open shame. He will throw a variety of things against us, but if we keep our eyes on Jesus, even the tribulations that come our way will end up working for our good. Let me be clear, God IS NOT sending evil to work good in our lives. That is blasphemous. However, God knows the enemy will come against us and that the trials of life will discourage us. That's why He has made it so that no matter what trouble or evil comes our way He will cause it to work for good.

To understand this battle better, let's first take a closer look at three passages that often are interpreted incorrectly.

James 1:2-3
My brethren, count it all joy when you fall into various trials, ³knowing that the testing of your faith produces patience.

The assumption many make with this verse is that God is sending trials to produce patience. This is not evident in this verse at all. We live in a corrupt world that is, for the most part, completely opposed to the gospel of Jesus Christ. "Fall into" means surrounded with. Every believer on earth is surrounded by trials, and they are various. "Various" means there are different types of trials, even complicated ones. (Multi-faceted is part of the definition of "various".) "Trial" is often translated "testing" which is why some assume it is referring to God, but this is *not* stated. In the context of James' letter, we know he was referring to the persecutions the Christian Jews were facing and the troubles their dispersion caused. This wasn't God's doing. The enemy and men opposed to the gospel were trying to silence them and snuff them out. The amazingly good news is that these trials (again, not sent by God), were working in them patience—cheerful, hopeful endurance.

Let's look at another similar example.

Romans 5:1-4
*Therefore, having been justified by faith, we have peace with God through our Lord Jesus Christ, ²through whom also we have access by faith into this grace in which we stand, and rejoice in hope of the glory of God. ³**And not only that**, but we also **glory** in tribulations, knowing that tribulation **produces***

perseverance; ⁴and perseverance, character; and character, hope.

I think we can all agree that verse one is a good thing that Paul is listing—we have peace with God because we are made righteous by faith. Then he says, "And not only that—". Paul gives us some more **good** news, another grace. What is this gift? The gift isn't the tribulations (troubles), but that we *glory* in them and *benefit* from them. God doesn't send troubles to produce these qualities in our lives. He doesn't send us troubles at all. The troubles are already here on earth. If we live here, we will experience them. If we are believers in Jesus Christ, we will be persecuted. This is part of the troubles we face.

For those who are not in Jesus, troubles are destructive. We all know people who have been beaten down by this life, those who are still suffering because of things that happened to them by people who should have loved them or by people who hated them. Some of them manage to survive, but remain damaged and harbor unforgiveness and even hatred toward their offenders.

This is not so for believers in Jesus Christ. When we experience the troubles of this life, an amazing miracle takes place which is the complete opposite of what others experience: perseverance, character, and hope are produced in us. This is why we can glory in tribulations. In this world troubles normally cause a person to be bitter, but for believers, tribulations cause us to be better. So, just as James wrote to the persecuted Jews to rejoice when they faced various trials, Paul teaches that believers have the gift of being able to glory in tribulation knowing that what is meant to destroy us will result in our good.

So, the next time you experience troubles, don't see them as from God or even "allowed" by God. See them as part of living on this fallen planet, and know that instead of them bringing you destruction, they will work perseverance, character, and hope in you. Only God can do something this amazing!

Finally, let's look at a well-known verse which also gets twisted.

> **Romans 8:28**
> And we know that **all things work together for good to those who love God,** to those who are the called according to His purpose.

This verse simply says that all things work together for good to us. Let me clarify. Believers are those who love God. This isn't saying that if we love God enough, all things will work together for good. John wrote, "We love God because He first loved us." A clear indicator of someone's faith in Jesus is that he loves Him. Secondly, some have blatantly said that if we aren't walking according to His calling in our lives, God can't work it together for our good. The verse doesn't say this. It is referring to Christians as "the called according to His purpose". That's who we are—the called. For all believers in Jesus Christ, all things work together for good to us.

What are these "all things"? This is made clear as we read on in the chapter.

> **Romans 8:31-34**
> What then shall we say to these things? If God is for us, who can be against us? [32]He who did not spare His own Son, but delivered Him up for us all, how shall He not with Him also freely give us all things? [33]Who shall bring a charge against God's elect? It is God who justifies. [34]Who is he who condemns? It is Christ who died, and furthermore is also risen, who is even at the right hand of God, who also makes intercession for us.

There are forces against us headed up by the enemy of our faith. They will bring false charges against us. They will condemn us, perhaps even sentencing us to punishment or death. Yet, what do we say to these things? "If God is for me, who can be against me?" God gave His own Son in death for us; how will He not now freely give us all things? He will take these attacks against us and supernaturally work them together for our good. He will even take our own missteps and work them together for good. That's our God. He isn't sending the troubles. **He is working those things that are seeking to destroy us for our benefit.**

> **Romans 8:35-39**
> *Who shall separate us from the love of Christ?*
> *Shall tribulation, or distress, or persecution, or famine, or nakedness, or peril, or sword? [36]As it is written:*
> *"For Your sake we are killed all day long;*
> *We are accounted as sheep for the slaughter."*
> *[37]Yet in all these things we are more than conquerors through Him who loved us. [38]For I am persuaded that neither death nor life, nor angels nor principalities nor powers, nor things present nor things to come, [39]nor height nor depth, nor any other created thing, shall be able to separate us from the love of God which is in Christ Jesus our Lord.*

Is God trying to separate us from His love? Of course not! Notice clearly here then that God isn't sending these things. He is making us conquerors against these things through Him. Otherwise, He would be fighting against Himself! No. He is taking these things and making us better, working the intended destruction which is against us for our advantage. This is why we are told to rejoice when tribulations come our way. They can't separate us from God's love for us, and God will even work them for our good.

All of this gives us confidence as we fight the **good** fight of faith. Paul instructed Timothy to fight this battle, and when Paul was nearing the end of his life, he declared that he had fought it and kept the faith.

> **1 Timothy 6:12**
> *Fight the good fight **of faith**, lay hold on eternal life, to which you were also called and have confessed the good confession in the presence of many witnesses.*
> **2 Timothy 4:7**
> *I have fought the **good fight**, I have finished the race, I have **kept the faith**.*

Let us also confidently fight this good fight of faith and finish our race. Let us overcome the overwhelming and not be crushed by it. All of the troubles we are right now facing, God is working together for our good. Our part is to believe in Jesus and what He has promised. Fight, my friends. Fight the good fight of faith.

> **1 Peter 1:3-9**
> *Blessed be the God and Father of our Lord Jesus Christ, who according to His abundant mercy has begotten us again to a living hope through the resurrection of Jesus Christ from the dead, ⁴to an inheritance incorruptible and undefiled and that does not fade away, reserved in heaven for you, ⁵who are kept by the power of God through faith for salvation ready to be revealed in the last time. ⁶In this you greatly rejoice, though now for a little while, if need be, you have been grieved by various trials, ⁷**that the genuineness of your faith, being much more precious than gold that perishes**, though it is tested by fire, may be found to praise, honor, and glory at the*

revelation of Jesus Christ, [8]whom having not seen you love. Though now you do not see Him, yet believing, you rejoice with joy inexpressible and full of glory, [9]receiving the end of your faith—the salvation of your souls.

Day 26

A DEFEATED FOE

*I*t is important that we have a proper perspective of the enemy. There are two improper extremes. Either we ascribe to Satan too much credit for what is happening in our lives, or we pretend that he barely exists.

Satan is not the evil equivalent of God. What I mean by that is we don't have the all-powerful, loving God on one side, and the all-powerful, evil god on the other. The enemy would like us to think this because he has always wanted to be God, but I assure you he simply is not.

There are many qualities of God which we could study, but let's look at just three of them to illustrate my point. First of all, Satan is not all-powerful (omnipotent) as is God. His authority and abilities are limited and cannot at all be compared to God's. He is an angelic being who was cast out of heaven because he wanted to exalt himself above God. So, any glory that he had in heaven was lost, and he was demoted. Imagine contrasting an angel with God. It is absurd at best. Then consider comparing a fallen angel with God. That is preposterous.

Nor is Satan everywhere present (omnipresent). He is a single being who can only be one place at one time. Some of you will need to get a cup of tea and take some time to think about this. The way some people talk, one would think that Satan is with them as much as Jesus is with them. Yes, he does have a demonic crew, but even they are limited in number. Demons don't procreate. The same number of angels who were cast out of heaven with Satan originally are the same number in existence today. Think about this, also, for every angel that fell, there are two angels who remained and were sent forth to minister to us (Rev. 12:3-9, Heb. 1:14). Let's look at a couple passages that give us a more accurate view of his mobility.

> **1 Peter 5:8**
> *Be sober, be vigilant; because your adversary the devil **walks about** like a roaring lion, seeking whom he may devour.*
> **Revelation 2:12-13**
> *"And to the angel of the church in Pergamos write, 'These things says He who has the sharp two-edged sword:* [13]*"I know your works, and where you dwell, **where Satan's throne is**. And you hold fast to My name, and did not deny My faith even in the days in which Antipas was My faithful martyr, who was killed among you, **where Satan dwells**."*

Our enemy dwells somewhere. Yes, he can walk about, but he isn't God. He is a being with limitations. I don't pretend to know exactly all this entails, but he is not everywhere present as is God. When I pray in California, God is here with me and everywhere else in the heavens and earth simultaneously. His presence is not limited to His throne. Our enemy, in contrast, can only be one place at one time.

Consider this also: Satan is not all-knowing (omniscient) as is our God. Whereas God knows our every thought, our enemy does not know any of our thoughts. God is aware of every single thing that is going on in the entirety of His creation. That's why it is futile to think we can hide from Him— and how blessed we are to know this as it allows us always to rest knowing He knows it all. In a similar sense, we don't need to worry about the enemy knowing anything about our thoughts. He is not privy to them.

Those are just three qualities of God which the enemy does not possess, and if we were to list all the qualities of God of which we human beings are aware, there would be not one which Satan possesses.

The above has always been true. Whatever authority Satan had prior to the cross was always greatly limited. However, when Jesus died, He destroyed him even further.

> ### Hebrews 2:14-15
> *Inasmuch then as the children have partaken of flesh and blood, He Himself likewise shared in the same, that **through death He might destroy him who had the power of death, that is, the devil,** ¹⁵ and release those who through fear of death were all their lifetime subject to bondage.*

The first time I read the above verses, my mind and heart nearly danced. Through Jesus' death, He destroyed him who had the power of death. Destroyed! In that same destruction, He released us from the bondage of the fear of death. Our present and future are eternal life.

> ### 1 Corinthians 15:51-57
> *Behold, I tell you a mystery; we will not all sleep, but we will all be changed, ⁵²in a moment, in the twinkling of an eye, at the last trumpet; for the trumpet will sound, and the dead will be raised imperishable, and we will be changed. ⁵³For this perishable must put on the imperishable, and this mortal must put on immortality. ⁵⁴But when this perishable will have put on the imperishable, and this mortal will have put on immortality, then will come about the saying that is written, "DEATH IS SWALLOWED UP*

IN VICTORY. *⁵⁵O DEATH, WHERE IS YOUR VICTORY? O DEATH, WHERE IS YOUR STING?" ⁵⁶The sting of death is sin, and the power of sin is the law; ⁵⁷but thanks be to God, who gives us the victory through our Lord Jesus Christ.*

Another amazing passage which paints for us a glorious picture of the defeat of Satan by the death of Jesus Christ is the following.

Colossians 2:13-15

*And you, being dead in your trespasses and the uncircumcision of your flesh, He has made alive together with Him, having forgiven you all trespasses, ¹⁴having wiped out the handwriting of requirements that was against us, which was contrary to us. And He has taken it out of the way, having nailed it to the cross. ¹⁵**Having disarmed principalities and powers, He made a public spectacle of them, triumphing over them in it.***

There are many fine commentaries on the above passage. I encourage you to read them.[27] This one stands out because it gives us a picture of what the original readers of this letter might have visualized.

The whole is an allusion to the victories, spoils, and triumphs, of the Roman emperors, who when they had obtained a victory, a triumph was decreed for them by the senate; in which the emperor was drawn in an open chariot, and the captives being stripped of their armour, and their hands tied behind them, were led before him and exposed to public

---

[27] Go to www.biblehub.com, select Comment, and then enter Colossian 2:13-15.

> *view and disgrace; while he was shouted and huzzaed through the city of Rome, and had all the marks of honour and respect given him (b): now all that is said in the preceding verses show how complete the saints are in and by Christ; and stand in no need of the philosophy of the Gentiles, or the ceremonies of the Jews;* **nor have anything to fear from their enemies, sin, Satan, and the law, for sin is pardoned, the law is abolished, and Satan conquered.**[28]

Whatever power or influence Satan might have had over us previously—that was removed when we put our faith in Jesus. Not only that, we are free from the power of sin and from the law.

---

[28] Gill's Exposition of the Entire Bible

Day 27

RESIST HIM

---

*L*et us now consider the other extreme view of our enemy, that of thinking that because he has been defeated, we need not consider him at all as if to imply that he no longer exists. Let us consider these two passages.

> **2 Corinthians 2:10-11**
> *Now whom you forgive anything, I also forgive. For if indeed I have forgiven anything, I have forgiven that one for your sakes in the presence of Christ,* **¹¹ lest Satan should take advantage of us; for we are not ignorant of his devices.**
> **1 Peter 5:8**
> *Be sober, be vigilant; because your adversary the devil walks about like a roaring lion, seeking whom he may devour.*

We see from these two verses that Satan is still roaming around seeking whom he may devour, and also that he has "devices". "Devices" has to do with his purpose, which as I've stated previously, is to get us to deny the faith. Again, we need not fear the devil. Jesus has stripped him of his power, but he will still try to stumble us. Here are some of his tactics.

Questioning God's Character

Not only will he roar like a lion to try and make us think he is more than he is (God's evil twin), Satan will bring into doubt God's true character, so much so that instead of us seeing Him as the loving, giving, and caring God that He is, who keeps His promises and abides with us forever, he will try and make us think that God punishes His children with sickness and even death, makes promises that He has no intention of keeping, and whose love is not consistent. If he can get us to doubt who God really is to us, we will be reluctant to trust in Him.

Questioning God's Directives

Thankfully, we are not under the law, but we have been given instructions for living. The enemy has been questioning God's will for us from the beginning of time, and he's still able to do this.

> ### Genesis 3:1
> *Now the serpent was more cunning than any beast of the field which the Lord God had made. And he said to the woman, **"Has God indeed said**, 'You shall not eat of every tree of the garden'?"*

This questioning sounds a bit like this: "Does God really want us to abstain from sexual immorality? Does it matter at all to Him if we dabble in other religions or the occult? When Paul told the believers to be sober, did he mean that for us also? Would it bother God if I cheated on my taxes? I mean they are unjust! God didn't mean to love *my* wife like Christ loves the church. She's intolerable. Surely submitting to one's husband is antiquated, isn't it? Is fellowshipping with other believers really required? God doesn't expect me to forgive *every* offense, does He?" God's grace teaches us to deny worldly lusts and to live godly lives in this earth. The enemy will challenge God's grace. **Grace isn't freedom to sin; it is freedom not to sin.**

The enemy will also challenge individual directives in our lives, and these can vary and change over time as our lives change. Whatever it is God is calling us to do, let us do it, but also understand that there will be opposition.

Not every person with whom David and I have tried to share the gospel of grace has listened. Some have ignored us; others have openly lied to defame us and then spoken ill of the message we preached once they had rid themselves of us. The temptation would be to preach a watered-down version of the message we've been called to share in order to be more acceptable. By God's grace, this is not going to happen.

Questioning God's Provisions and Promises

Clearly, questioning God's provisions and promises is the same thing as questioning His character, for if He provides for us and does not allow us to partake of it, or if He promises to do something, and then withholds what He has promised, He is not the God He claims to be. Yet He is who He claims to be. He will not keep us away from what He has provided. He will do what He has promised. We can rest in this, and when the enemy challenges these truths, we must resist his lies.

> *2 Corinthians 1:20*
> *For all the promises of God in Him are Yes, and in Him Amen, to the glory of God through us.*

This promise about His promises is faithful and true.

Accusations

We know that the enemy makes accusations against God, but one of his other tactics is to make them against believers.

> ### Revelation 12:10
> *Then I heard a loud voice saying in heaven, "Now salvation, and strength, and the kingdom of our God, and the power of His Christ have come, for **the accuser of our brethren, who accused them before our God day and night, has been cast down.***

Perhaps you've heard this before either in your mind or from the lips of those being used by Satan to destroy you. "You are a pitiful example of a human being. You are weak and worthless. No one loves you because there is nothing about you worth loving. You will never be successful. Your marriage will never be happy. You'll never be well. You failed again. This grace and faith message isn't working. Who would ever want to marry you? Nobody likes you. Everyone hates you." You know the rest of the song, don't you?

If all of these things were true, what would be the point of even trying or believing anything? Can you see that when we believe these lies about ourselves, the enemy has won? These ideas render us powerless. They put all the focus on us and our shortcomings, and get our eyes off of Jesus.

Resist Him!

My friends, don't be ignorant of how the enemy now fights against us. Recognize his thoughts against you and don't remain motionless while he accuses you before your God who loves you. Resist him! How do we resist him? Gloriously, "steadfast" is not an adverb describing how we resist. It is a noun referring to us. Resist him, steadfast (ones) in the faith.

It's not our steadfast efforts by which we resist, but by our position as being steadfast ones in the faith of Jesus Christ.

> **1 Peter 5:9**
> **Resist him, steadfast in the faith**, *knowing that the same sufferings are experienced by your brotherhood in the world.*
> **Ephesians 6:11-13**
> *Put on the whole armor of God, that you may be able to stand against the wiles of the devil. [12]For we do not wrestle against flesh and blood, but against principalities, against powers, against the rulers of the darkness of this age, against spiritual hosts of wickedness in the heavenly places. [13]Therefore take up the whole armor of God, that you may be able to withstand in the evil day, and having done all, to stand.*

Intimidation by False Prophets

Here is yet another tactic of the enemy. Sometimes he will use other human beings to do his dirty work—and I'm sorry to say that sometimes these people are misguided Christians.

This happens in two main arenas. The first is in the form of false doctrines. These are teachings about God and the gospel that are not true or which are a mixture of truth and error. Truth + Error = Error.

We aren't surprised that the world falsely accuses us, but it is most painful when our own brothers and sisters lash out against us. This is the second way false prophets will come against us. (Whether they are true believers or not—God knows.)

Verse 4 below has commonly been used to refer to Satan, and even though he is surely involved, it is actually speaking of false prophets.

1 John 4:1, 4-5
*Beloved, do not believe every spirit, but test
the spirits, whether they are of God; because
many false prophets have gone out into the
world. ⁴You are of God, little children, and
have overcome **them**, because He who is in
you is greater than he who is in the world.
⁵**They** are of the world. Therefore they speak
as of the world, and the world hears **them**.*

The good news is that we have overcome them because
the One living in us is greater than the ones living in the
world. While the enemy will use other human beings to try
and discredit the gospel of God's grace, we can continue
preaching it with confidence. Though false prophets abound
in the church today exalting themselves and their supposed
office, we need not fear. God in us is greater than the false
spirits guiding them.

Day 28

THE WEAPONS OF OUR WARFARE

There is a battle to be fought, but we must always remember that it is against a conquered foe. Along with this, we must keep in mind that even though we are in this body while we are fighting, we are not fighting against flesh and blood (even though flesh and blood might seem to be fighting against us).

> **2 Corinthians 10:3-6**
> For though we walk in the flesh, we do not war according to the flesh. ⁴For the weapons of our warfare are not carnal but mighty in God for pulling down strongholds, ⁵casting down **arguments** and every high thing that exalts itself against the **knowledge** of God, bringing every **thought** into captivity to the obedience of Christ, ⁶and being ready to punish all disobedience when your obedience is fulfilled.

Notice that part of our warfare is against thoughts that are contrary to the knowledge of God. We encounter this often in our ministry, and we have determined that we will not expose people who are teaching a mixed message of law and grace, but rather the wrong teachings themselves. Names of ministers and names of ministries are not discussed publicly. This is because we are not at war with our brothers and sisters in Christ.

The Armor of God

> ### Ephesians 6:14-18
> *Stand therefore, having girded your waist with truth, having put on the breastplate of **righteousness**, [15]and having shod your feet with the preparation of the gospel of **peace**; [16]above all, taking the shield of **faith** with which you will be able to quench all the fiery darts of the wicked one. [17]And take the helmet of **salvation**, and the sword of the **Spirit**, which is the word of God; [18]**praying** always with all prayer and supplication in the Spirit, being watchful to this end with all per-severance and supplication for all the saints.*

This is quite comical to me now, but the prayer I'd pray when "putting on my armor" went something like this. I would start at the top of my head and work my way down. "Lord, I put on the helmet of salvation. I have put my faith in You, Lord. I put on the breastplate of righteousness. You know how diligently I endeavor to be righteous before You. Now, I put on the belt of truth. Lord, I long to be truthful in every thought and word and deed, and Lord, I shod my feet with the gospel of peace which I am willing to share, Lord."

Then after being fully "dressed", I'd continue, "Now, I take up the shield of faith because I have faith in You, and my faith will protect me from the enemy's fiery darts. I pick up the sword of the Spirit, Your Bible, Lord. I know it's true, and it will protect me. I will pray in the Spirit, Lord and be watchful to the end."

God saw my heart. He understood the confusion, and patiently He showed me that I had most of it backward. I feel a little silly now because my idea of putting on the armor of God was totally centered on me.

The main reason I held these views about the armor of God was because of what we were taught and what we ourselves were teaching. What God has taught us is that the armor of God isn't about us and what we do. It is about Jesus and what He did and does. We stand in what He has accomplished. We wear what He has done as our armor, and thus we fight, not against flesh and blood, and not as flesh and blood, but in faith as a child of Almighty God.

The helmet of salvation has nothing to do with us. We simply believed in Jesus and were saved. He saved us. He is saving us. He will save us. When we put on this helmet, it is not in acknowledgment of our decision to be saved, but in the fact that He is our salvation.

The breastplate of righteousness can only be about the free gift of righteousness given to us when we put our faith in Him. How could we ever think we were good enough by what we did or didn't do? How could we have faith in ourselves? No, we have faith in the fact that we are righteous with God by faith apart from works.

How could the belt of truth be about how truthfully we live when Jesus said that He is the way, the truth, and the life? The belt held the other armor in place. He is the One that keeps our armor sure. He is the One who overcame the enemy. It is in His victory we stand.

Our feet are not shod with our efforts to spread the gospel, but with the gospel itself. The glad tidings of good things about Jesus bless our feet, making us able ministers of the good news.

The shield of faith isn't about doing our best to believe in Jesus. It is Jesus Himself and our faith in Him.

The sword of the Spirit, which this passage calls "the word of God" isn't the Bible. The term "word of God" in the New Testament most frequently refers to the gospel of Jesus. The word of God is the good news to the lost and to the saved—the gospel. When we take up that sword, we aren't wielding scripture verses, we are sharing the good news of Jesus Christ.

When we get the focus off of us and wear the true armor of God, we will boldly and confidently stand, for we will not need to rely on our own discipline and efforts, but simply rest in the accomplishments and power of God. We will be fighting in His name based on His victories and not on our feeble efforts.

We pray, not because we have to or in order to demonstrate our great discipline, but because prayer will be effective when offered in faith in Jesus. We know that our prayers for the saints will be heard and answered.

This battle we fight is all about Jesus, not all about us and how mighty and diligent we are. Once we have put on His armor once and for all, let us stand with our faith fully in Him. He authored our faith, and He will finish it.

Hebrews 12:1-2
Therefore we also, since we are surrounded by so great a cloud of witnesses, let us lay aside every weight, and the sin which so easily ensnares us, and let us run with endurance the race that is set before us, [2]**looking unto Jesus, the author and finisher of our faith,** *who for the joy that was set before Him endured the cross, despising the shame, and has sat down at the right hand of the throne of God.*

Day 29

UNDERESTIMATING GOD'S POWER

*I*t is not uncommon for us, even as believers, to need a revelation of His great power toward us. Paul prayed that the eyes of the Ephesians, whom he'd personally taught for two years, would be enlightened to see the greatness of His power toward them.

> **Ephesians 1:15-20**
> *Therefore I also, after I heard of your faith in the Lord Jesus and your love for all the saints, ¹⁶do not cease to give thanks for you, making mention of you in my prayers: ¹⁷that the God of our Lord Jesus Christ, the Father of glory, may give to you the spirit of wisdom and revelation in the knowledge of Him, ¹⁸the eyes of your understanding being enlightened; that you may know (see, perceive, understand) what is the hope of His calling, what are the riches of the glory of His inheritance in the saints, ¹⁹***and what is the exceeding greatness of His power toward us who believe***, according to the working of His mighty power ²⁰which He worked in Christ when He **raised Him from the dead** and seated Him at His right hand in the heavenly places.*

The exceeding greatness of His power is toward us who believe in Him!

Colossians 1:9, 11
For this reason we also, since the day we heard it, do not cease to pray for you, and to ask that you may be filled with the knowledge of His will in all wisdom and spiritual under-standing...[11]strengthened with all might, according to His glorious power for all patience and longsuffering with joy.

This power strengthens us—with all might. "'All' might?" my brain asks? "Yes, 'all' might," the Spirit answers. Wow. Is it because we fast and pray and read our Bibles? No! It is according to His glorious power through His Spirit who dwells in us.

Psalm 8:3-4
When I consider Your heavens, the work of Your fingers,
The moon and the stars, which You have ordained,
[4]What is man that You are mindful of him, And the son of man that You visit him?

As many times as we have personally experienced His power working in our lives, I still cannot completely wrap my head around this idea of God's power in me. When praying, I believe God will answer me, yet sometimes when He does, I am completely in shock that He did because the situation looked so impossible.

Let me give a recent example. Recently, I faced a sudden and great storm in my life. A doctor told me I needed a certain medical test that horrified me. He made it sound as if it was absolutely necessary, so I set an appointment, even though I felt very uneasy about it. As is my custom, I did some research on the procedure and ended up nearly frightening myself out of undergoing it. Something inside of me was cringing about it, but because the winds and waves of concern for my health were raging, I had a hard time hearing God speak to me. Employing Philippians 4:6-7 I prayed, "God I ask that before they do this test, they will discover they don't need to do it."

I did amazingly well the days before the test, and was living in the peace that passes understanding, but as I went to my appointment, I felt like a sheep heading toward the slaughter. I kept focusing on Him through the storm. As I was in the waiting room, I sang songs about putting my trust in Him to keep my body calm, but the winds and waves were pressing in. "Jesus, I walk to You on these waves," I said.

Please don't think, "Oh, she's such a woman of faith," because I was on the very edge of going under! The technician was wonderful at keeping me calm, but I was ready to lose it, and she could see that. The doctor who entered the examination room, was not the doctor who'd prescribed the procedure, and when he asked if I had any questions I said, "Can I change my mind about this?" He said that of course I could, but not wanting to be unwise, I signed the consent form. If I really did have a problem, it would be better to get it diagnosed and deal with it than to ignore it. Still, I remained unsettled and unable to think clearly.

They couldn't sedate me for this because I had to be consciously perfectly still. The technician kept coaching me, and I kept praying, "God don't let them see anything." She did a couple images and was strangely silent.

I asked, "Can you see anything?" She said that she couldn't see anything yet. Then she took more images.

"Can you see anything?" I asked again.

Her response gave me a ray of hope, "Let me go ask the doctor what he thinks."

The doctor came in and looked at the images. He said something to the technician and then came to the examination table to talk to me. "We will not be able to do this test," he seemed to apologize. I don't see anything, and we don't do tests just to do them."

"Oh," I said, "I am so happy to hear you say that." Now, he wasn't saying that there was nothing there because a former image showed there was, just that he could not see it with the instruments he would have used for the test. He gave me my options and said, "If you were my mother, I would tell you to take this option." I asked him if these abnormalities ever go away, and he said no, but that they can either remain the same (a good thing), change in characteristic (another good thing) or grow (not good). Since he said that they don't go away, that is what we later decided to ask God to do—to ask for the impossible.

It was probably the first time a technician in that office got such a happy hug from a patient. I felt like the damsel in distress whose Knight in shining armor had galloped in and saved her from certain doom! I was so happy when I told my husband and children about this that I sobbed with joy. God answered my prayer. Oh, my goodness. God rescued me. I was thrilled beyond words.

Psalm 18:1-3
I will love You, O Lord, my strength.
²The LORD is my rock and my fortress and my deliverer;
My God, my strength, in whom I will trust;
My shield and the horn of my salvation, my stronghold.
³I will call upon the LORD, who is worthy to be praised;
So shall I be saved from my enemies.

I don't mean this in a negative sense, but why was I so surprised? It is what I asked, and it turned out that God had done exceedingly above all I'd asked or thought by saving me from an unnecessary procedure. With all of this glorious good news, why wasn't my response more like, "I knew it"?

It seems every time God answers a prayer we are amazed by it. All I can figure is that in the presence of a miracle, we can't do anything less than be amazed at His grace.

May God help us all to trust more and more in His power, and to never underestimate what His power can do for us.

> **1 Corinthians 2:9-12, 16**
> *But as it is written:*
> *"Eye has not seen, nor ear heard,*
> *Nor have entered into the heart of man*
> *The things which God has prepared for those*
> *who love Him."*
> *¹⁰***But God has revealed them to us through His Spirit.** *For the Spirit searches all things, yes, the deep things of God. ¹¹For what man knows the things of a man except the spirit of the man which is in him? Even so no one knows the things of God except the Spirit of God. ¹²Now we have received, not the spirit of the world, but the Spirit who is from God,* ***that we might know the things that have been freely given to us by God.***
> *¹⁶For "who has known the mind of the Lord that he may instruct Him?"* ***But we have the mind of Christ.***

God has great things prepared for us. We might not be able to comprehend them with our natural minds, but we have the mind of Christ and have received the Spirit who is from God so that we can know the things that God has freely given to us. May our eyes be enlightened to understand and believe in the exceeding greatness of His power toward us who believe in Him.

Day 30

IGNORANCE

---

*M*ost of us have heard it said, "What you don't know can't hurt you," which is ridiculous. Of course, what we don't know can hurt us. In the negative sense, if our water is contaminated, and we don't know it, we can still be hurt by it. If our spouse is having an affair, it is going to hurt our relationship. If we have a disease that is silently progressing in our body, not knowing about it could kill us.

There are also many good things that we don't know. We aren't necessarily damaged by not knowing them, but surely we are not benefited by them. One common sermon illustration is that of not knowing we've inherited a small fortune. On paper, we'd be rich, but we wouldn't be enjoying what was left to us because we simply wouldn't know about it.

So it is with many provisions and promises of God. Why is it that so little is known about them? Yes, we are all experiencing salvation, and some of us believe God still heals today, and there are even those who believe God will make them successful, but for the most part, the church remains largely ignorant of His graces toward us. Why is this?

My observation is that the church today spends more time teaching about what God requires *from* us than it ever does in teaching what God has done *for* us.

The subtle idea behind this is we shouldn't be concerned about what we can get as believers, but in what we can give. Jesus did say that it is more blessed to give than to receive. On the other hand, Jesus paid a very high price to give us an abundance of blessings.

Doesn't *He* deserve that we have what He *died* to give us?

Go ahead. Read that last sentence again. Jesus deserves that we receive what He purchased for us with His blood. Usually, however, when a minister does venture to share the glorious things God has provided for us, there is often an "if you will only" or a "but you need to" added in a vain effort to somehow "balance" the glories of His generosity.

Ignorance of His Provisions

The main things about which Christians are ignorant are of His provisions and promises. Now, promises are technically provisions, and provisions are promises, but I will distinguish between them slightly. From my perspective, a provision is something we already have in Christ such as forgiveness, righteousness, and wholeness, and a promise is something we have but might not yet possess such as answers to prayer. When we learn about something that is provided for us, we need not ask. It's ours already. We simply begin to reap its benefits. A promise, while also a provision, is something God has pledged to do for us if we will believe and ask without doubting. If you would like to begin a topical study of Scripture, this would be a good one to pursue. What are the many things God has already provided for us in Christ? What are His promises to us?

If I only listed without expounding, it would take many pages to catalog the many things God has freely given us, but my goal here is to bring attention to the fact that ignorance of His provisions and promises for us will diminish our abilities to benefit from them.

For example, if someone doesn't know that he has, right now, eternal life, he will live his whole Christian life wishing he will "make it" in the end by perhaps living right or doing good works, but never have complete confidence. Since I use this as an example, let me clear it up before we continue.

We already have eternal life. Notice in the verses that follow that God wants us to know that we already have eternal life, and this knowledge is to those who believe in Jesus.

> ### 1 John 5:13
> *These things I have written to you who **believe** in the name of the Son of God, that you **may know** that you have eternal life, and that you may **continue to believe** in the name of the Son of God.*
>
> ### John 3:16
> *For God so loved the world that He gave His only begotten Son, that whoever **believes** in Him should **not** perish but have **everlasting** life.*

In fact, we have everything we need to live this life of faith.

> ### Ephesians 1:3
> *Blessed be the God and Father of our Lord Jesus Christ, who has blessed us with **every spiritual blessing** in the heavenly places in Christ*
>
> ### 2 Peter 1:2-4
> *Grace and peace be multiplied to you in the knowledge of God and of Jesus our Lord, ³as His divine power has given to us **all things that pertain to life and godliness**, through the knowledge of Him who called us by glory and virtue, ⁴by which have been given to us exceedingly great and precious promises,*

*that through these you may be partakers of
the divine nature, having escaped the corruption that is in the world through lust.*

We already have or have been promised everything we
need to overcome the overwhelming in our lives, but we
might not know yet what these promises and provisions are.
This is part of the process we discussed concerning hearing
good news. When we hear the good news about what we
already have in Christ, faith will come to us, and we will
begin to live as the person He has made us and benefit from
what He has given us. Notice that these are not only "spiritual" blessings that we have received, but all that we need
for this life.

Peter not only speaks of His power giving us all we
need but of "exceedingly great and precious promises". It is
through these promises that we are partakers of the divine
nature. Notice, we have already been given these promises.
Our part is only to believe and receive them.

These promises aren't for sale. They are free.

Romans 8:32
*He who did not spare His own Son, but deliv-
ered Him up for us all, how shall He not with
Him also **freely give** us all things?*
1 Corinthians 2:12
*Now we have received, not the spirit of the
world, but the Spirit who is from God, that we
might **know** the things that have been **freely
given** to us by God.*

The term "freely give" is a perfect translation of the Greek
word **charizomai**. Notice the first part of that word is the
word in Greek for "grace". This act of freely giving to us has
everything to do with His grace toward us. Grace isn't only
how we are saved by faith. It isn't only the power to not sin.
Nor is grace only the ability to go through difficult situations

such as persecutions and the troubles in life. It is also everything that we've been given in Him. We can know of this grace by the Scriptures and also through His Spirit opening our eyes.

We aren't born again knowing everything. Even if we read the whole New Testament, it is unlikely we will grasp all the glories of what is written there the first or even second time through. This is why Paul prayed for those to whom he ministered that they might know who they'd been made in Christ and what they possessed in Him (Eph. 1:15-20).

Ignorance of His Promises

Discovering the exceeding great and precious promises is a glorious journey. We can begin it by recognizing that the promises of the New Covenant are better than those of the Old.

Hebrews 8:6
*But now He has obtained a **more excellent** ministry, inasmuch as He is also Mediator of a **better** covenant, which was established on **better** promises.*

This is when reading the Old Testament can take on new meaning. When we read the blessings promised under the Old Covenant, we can rejoice that our blessings are not only better, but they are based on our faith in Jesus and not on us keeping the law. Not only that but the New Covenant promises, since they are based on faith, have no curses attached to them.

Here is another amazing passage that was perceived as benefits to Old Covenant believers. Shall not our benefits be at least this marvelous and even better?

Psalm 103: 1-5
Bless the Lord, O my soul;
And all that is within me, bless His holy name!
²Bless the Lord, O my soul,
*And **forget not all His benefits:***
*³Who **forgives** all your iniquities,*
*Who **heals** all your diseases,*
*⁴Who **redeems** your life from destruction,*
*Who crowns you with **lovingkindness** and **tender** *
mercies,*
*⁵Who **satisfies** your mouth with good things,*
*So that your **youth is renewed** like the eagle's.*

After contemplating that the New Covenant promises are even better than the Old Covenant promises, we can begin our search for His many specific promises of the New as we read Matthew through Revelation. Though this is beyond the scope of this book, it does make studying the Bible a wonderful adventure. Enjoy it!

Ignorance of the Specific Good News for Our Situation

As we tackle the overwhelming in our lives, we need new faith in the specific areas we are facing, but how can we have faith if we don't know the specific good news that pertains to our situations? In many ways.

We have the Scripture to teach us what this good news is, but we also have His Spirit guiding us into all truth. He will show us things we do not yet know that will bring us victory in our time of trouble. Remember, Jesus said, "Everyone who seeks will find."

There might be things we are doing or not doing that are causing our situation, and finding this out will change everything for the good. We might lack understanding about many things God has done and wants to do, but when we discover them, we will see how they might apply to help us in our distress.

We need to consider too that when we feel all tied in knots about something, there is likely law in operation somewhere. Even if we read the Bible again and again, we might not see it, but because we have asked God for wisdom and because we know that Jesus is our wisdom, God will show us something that is holding us back—either a belief or a practice.

The very good news is, God wants us to be free and to live freely. He sent His Son to die for us so that we could freely have all that He wants to give us. Think about it. Jesus suffered greatly so that we could not only have Him but "all things". We may not think we are worthy to have them, or we might have been taught that it's wrong to think about what we can receive from God, but the truth is Jesus wants us to both know and receive His abundance to us.

2 Corinthians 8:9
For you know the grace of our Lord Jesus Christ, that though He was rich, yet for your sakes He became poor, that you through His poverty might become rich.

Day 31

DISOBEDIENCE

$\mathcal{T}$he topic of obedience is grossly misunderstood to the point where many blood-purchased beloved saints of God are rendered nearly immobile in their relationship with God and the ability to have faith when they pray by the fear that they have committed some unpardonable sin or that God will not answer their prayers because they are falling short in some way.

The truth is that all born again believers want to obey God. We are new creations who have been changed from rebellious haters of God to adoring children of His. Will we have a bad day and make a mistake in thought or word or deed? Probably. However, a true child of God will feel uncomfortable about being disobedient and long to please Him.

This topic of obedience can be one of the most restraining when it comes to our faith. That's why I discuss it as an enemy of faith. How can we have faith in God if we think perfect performance is required to receive from Him—that we have to earn His grace? So, let's tackle verses commonly used to say that if we do not obey, God will not only ignore our prayers but that our relationships with Him will be tainted, or even our salvation will be in jeopardy (which is not true).

Your Sins Have Separated You from God

This misunderstanding is overwhelmingly present in teachings in the church today—that our sins separate us from God, and thus, our prayers are not heard and will not be answered. This is not true. This is the verse used to "prove" the point.

Isaiah 59:2
But your iniquities have separated you from your God;
And your sins have hidden His face from you,
So that He will not hear.

To whom was God speaking in this verse? It was to the children of Israel who had sinned by not keeping the covenant they made with God. Under the Old Covenant obedience was rewarded with blessings and disobedience was punished with curses.

Are we under the Old Covenant? Absolutely not! We are under the New Covenant only (Heb. 8:13). Under the New Covenant God is not holding our sins against us (2 Cor. 5:19). He remembers them no more (Heb. 8:12). Nothing can separate us from His love, no, not even our sin (Rom. 8:37-39). To top all of that off, He has promised never to leave us or forsake us, no, not ever for any reason (Heb. 13:5).

If we don't know this amazingly good news of the New Covenant, that we have uninterrupted fellowship with God not dependent on us being perfect, how could we ever pray in faith about anything?

Willful Sin

This verse is often used to imply that if we willfully sin, there is no forgiveness for us (or that we will not be saved). We hear this interpreted to mean that after we are saved, any sin we commit on purpose will be brought up at the judgment

seat of Christ—some have even said God is making record-
ings of these sins to demonstrate them to all.

Hebrews 10:26
*For if we sin willfully after we have received
the knowledge of the truth, there no longer
remains a sacrifice for sins*

Before I discuss the context of this verse, let me state
the obvious. **All sin is on purpose.** Think about this for a
second. No one forces us to sin. We *decide* to do it, and
then we do it. That process might take two seconds or several days, but sin is always willful. If this verse is saying that
there is no sacrifice for willful sin, then we are all condemned
to judgment, and this is not a possibility.

John 5:24
*"Most assuredly, I say to you, he who hears
My word and **believes** in Him who sent Me
has everlasting life, and **shall not come into
judgment**, but has passed from death into life."*

We need to be thoroughly convinced of this: God is not
taking down a record of our sins—He is not holding our sins
against us. He doesn't bring them to remembrance now,
and He won't bring them up when we stand before Him. He
took away our sins, all of them! He took away our past sins,
the ones we might choose to commit today, and any sin in
the future.

So, then, what did the author of Hebrews mean when
he spoke of willful sin? Let's look further into the context of
this verse.

Hebrews 10:26-29
*For if we sin willfully after we have received
the knowledge of the truth, there no longer
remains a sacrifice for sins, [27]but a certain*

fearful expectation of judgment, and fiery indignation which will devour the adversaries. ²⁸*Anyone who has rejected Moses' law dies without mercy on the testimony of two or three witnesses.* ²⁹*Of how much worse punishment, do you suppose, will he be thought worthy **who has trampled the Son of God underfoot, counted the blood of the covenant by which he was sanctified a common thing, and insulted the Spirit of grace?***

The book of Hebrews was written to the Jews to show the superiority of Jesus and the New Covenant over Moses and the Old Covenant. Many of them were living in two worlds —still clinging to the law and temple worship while also confessing to believe in Jesus. Paul, who many believe to be the author of Hebrews, and who we believe wrote it in response to what he witnessed in the account given in Acts 21, is reasoning with them strongly against this. It was Jesus or nothing. Everything he wrote in the preceding chapters was reinforcing this truth. In context, to "sin willfully" is to willfully and knowingly reject the New Covenant. It is to regard His blood as a common thing. It is a rejection of Jesus.

He isn't talking about Christians who are confused and wounded by false teachings and teachers, and not even about Christians, who for whatever reason, are willfully living the life of a prodigal child. It is speaking of those who knowingly and willfully reject Christ—specifically those Christian Jews who were tempted to turn their back on Christ.

You Are My Friends If

Recently, I heard this verse used to mean that if we want to be Jesus' friend, we must do all that He commands.

John 15:14
You are My friends if you do whatever I command you.

Perhaps we should stop singing that we are friends of God because we don't always do what He commands. Or perhaps we're His friends only when we are good and His enemies when we aren't (when we need His friendship most). No, of course not!

It would seem very important for us to know what Jesus meant when He said, "whatever I command you". The best way to do this is to include the surrounding verses.

John 15:11-17
*"These things I have spoken to you, **that My joy may remain in you, and that your joy may be full.** [12]**THIS** is My commandment, **that you love one another as I have loved you.** [13]Greater love has no one than this, than to lay down one's life for his friends. [14]**You are My friends if you do whatever I command you.** [15]No longer do I call you servants, for a servant does not know what his master is doing; **but I have called you friends**, for all things that I heard from My Father I have made known to you. [16]You did not choose Me, but I chose you and appointed you that you should go and bear fruit, and that your fruit should remain, that whatever you ask the Father in My name He may give you. [17]**These things I command you, that you love one another.***

These words weren't meant to bring uncertainty about our friendship with Jesus, rather joy—a joy that would *remain* in us and a joy that would be full. How are we supposed to have joy if Jesus is sometimes our friend and sometimes not?

Would you (or do you) have a "friend" or maybe a spouse who is sometimes your friend and sometimes not based on how well you obey him? What kind of relationship is that? Jesus is referring to one commandment and that is to love each other as Jesus loved us. This is His commandment of the New Covenant. We know this because this is all part of what He said at the last supper as He was preparing for the cross which would inaugurate the New Covenant in His blood. Two chapters prior Jesus said, "A new commandment I give to you, that you love one another; as I have loved you, that you also love one another. [35]By this all will know that you are My disciples, if you have love for one another," (Jn. 13:34-35). Jesus was speaking to His disciples who were all Jews. They had the Ten Commandments, but now Jesus wanted them to have a new commandment. The Ten Commandments were the Old Covenant (Deut. 4:13). The commandments of the New Covenant are to believe in Jesus and to love each other as He loved us (1 Jn. 3:23).

When we love each other, we are His friends, which translates to me that He is always my Friend since He has put it in our hearts to love each other.

Hindered Prayer

Now for the verse often used to attempt to control unruly husbands by threatening them that God won't answer their prayers if they aren't the perfect spouse.

> *1 Peter 3:7*
> *Husbands, likewise, dwell with them with understanding, giving honor to the wife, as to the weaker vessel, and as being heirs together of the grace of life, **that your prayers may not be hindered.***

What is God asking husbands to do here? He is encouraging them to honor their wives, keeping in mind that they are not as physically strong as men. He also reminds them that they are heirs together of the grace of God. Isn't that beautiful? So many people say that Christianity is sexist because it encourages women to submit to their husbands, but here we have the lovely truth that men and women are equal in Christ. (See also Gal. 3:28.) Although it is true within the "Christian" church that women are sometimes sidelined in ministry, it is not true that this is God's doing.

The assumption made at this point is that when Peter writes "your" prayers that he means the husbands, but most commentators agree, and it makes more sense that he is referring to the prayers of the husband and the wife. How on earth can two people agree in prayer if they are living in strife? They simply can't. This has nothing to do with God punishing a husband by not answering his prayers if he doesn't honor his wife and treat her as a joint heir. It has everything to do with unity.

> **Matthew 18:19**
> *"Again I say to you that if **two of you agree on earth concerning anything** that they ask, it will be done for them by My Father in heaven."*

"Can two walk together unless they agree?" (Amos 3:3) Let us stop threatening husbands with the doom of God ignoring their prayers! Instead, let's encourage them as did Peter, to honor their wives and see them as joint heirs so that their prayers will be answered.

> **Ecclesiastes 4:9-12**
> *Two are better than one,*
> *Because they have a good reward for their labor.*
> *¹⁰For if they fall, one will lift up his companion.*
> *But woe to him who is alone when he falls,*
> *For he has no one to help him up.*
> *¹¹Again, if two lie down together, they will keep warm;*
> *But how can one be warm alone?*

¹²Though one may be overpowered by another, two can withstand him.
And a threefold cord is not quickly broken.

If You Love Me

Jesus said in John 14:15, "If you love Me, keep My commandments." What commandments? Notice that this statement is sandwiched between John 13 and 15 in which Jesus made clear that His commandment is to love each other. John, who wrote the Gospel of John, also wrote in his letter repeatedly about loving one another. He speaks of Christ's message being that of loving each other. He declares that those who do not love the brethren, do not know God. He appeals to them to love each other because they are loved by God. He says that if God abides in us, if we have this fruit of loving each other, we can ask what we will, and it will be done for us. This commandment to love each other was from the beginning of the church. When we love each other, we are keeping His commandments.[29]

1 John 3:11
For this is the message that you heard from the beginning, that we should love one another.
1 John 4:7-8
Beloved, let us love one another, for love is of God; and everyone who loves is born of God and knows God. ⁸He who does not love does not know God, for God is love.
1 John 4:11
Beloved, if God so loved us, we also ought to love one another.
1 John 4:12
No one has seen God at any time. If we love one another, God abides in us, and His love has been perfected in us.

---

[29] If you would like to study this topic at length, I recommend a book by Gaylord Enns entitled <u>Love Revolution: Rediscovering the Lost Command of Jesus</u>.

2 John 1:5
And now I plead with you, lady, not as though I wrote a new commandment to you, but that which we have had from the beginning: that we love one another.

Confidence toward God

I love the passage below because of what it reveals to us about the will of God. It says that there are two things that God is asking of us. The first is to believe in Jesus. This is a call not only to the lost but also to the saved. Believe in Him. Believe in Him in order to be saved, and believe in Him as we go through this life. Remember that faith pleases God. It brings joy to His heart. It also brings Him pleasure when we love each other, and it is clear here that this is referring to loving our brothers and sisters in Christ, not just mankind in general.[30] Jesus isn't only speaking about the emotion of loving someone, but the love that causes us to demonstrate our love.

How do we know this? It is because Jesus commands us to love "as I have loved you" and then He said, "Greater love has no one than this than to lay down one's life for his friends." True love is giving ourselves for the benefit of another.

Have faith in God and love each other—when we do these two things, our hearts will not condemn us, and whatever we ask we will receive from Him because we are doing those things which are pleasing in His sight.

1 John 3:21-23
Beloved, if our heart does not condemn us, we have confidence toward God. ²²And whatever we ask we receive from Him, because we keep His commandments and do those

---

[30] Of course, we are to love all people.

things that are pleasing in His sight. **²³And this is His commandment: that we should believe on the name of His Son Jesus Christ and love one another, as He gave us commandment.**

Day 32

FALSE TEACHING

---

*M*any years ago, as I sat in a funeral chapel mourning the death of a 13-year-old girl who lost a very long battle with cancer, I couldn't help but hear the two ladies sitting behind me. They were trying to make sense of it all. Obviously, when someone dies we wonder why, but when a child or younger person dies, we can't make sense of it. At first, I didn't pay much attention to these ladies, but then one of them said, "She was such a strong Christian. Perhaps God knew that when she grew up, she would rebel against Him, so He took her to heaven beforehand," (so she wouldn't go to hell).

If I had been then the person I am now, I would have turned around and said, "That's an awful thing to say," but I was young myself. I'd never heard such a horrible accusation against God before, and my doctrinal foundation was in its beginning stages. I had no way of knowing how to tackle such a ridiculous thought, and of course, I didn't want to make a scene either. So, I tuned them out and continued to mourn with those who had gathered.

The first false assumption was that God had killed the girl with cancer. Can someone please give me just one example in the life of Christ where Jesus prayed for anyone to make them sick or cause them to die? Since Jesus is the visible image of the invisible God (Col. 1:15), and He Himself declared, "If you have seen Me, you have seen the Father,"

(Jn. 14:9), shouldn't there be at least one example in the four gospels where Jesus saved someone, then killed them because He knew they would later reject Him? Shouldn't there be a story about Him praying for someone who believed in Him to get sick and die before they had a chance to change their minds? Shouldn't we, after someone confesses faith in Jesus, drown them during their baptism? These examples simply do not exist, my friends. They are absurd.

Christians, let us stop saying things that are not true about our loving and giving God in order to explain something we don't understand. The life of Christ demonstrates to us the will of God. Jesus came to bring us life—abundant life. Let us be honest. Sometimes it is better just to say, "I don't *know* why," when something so tragic happens.

I present the following false teachings because these errors have robbed many a believer from receiving good from God. They are so commonly held as truth that someone might find himself resisting as he reads as if the thought is a treasured tradition. Let us carefully consider what is written here because these false teachings discredit God and His promises. If we hold to them, they will destroy our faith and keep us from receiving from Him.

Believing that God Does Miracles Based on Our Power or Holiness

For many years, my husband and I sought God for revival. This involved more than praying. Seeing revival had much to do with how *holy* and *sincere* our lives were and how *hard* we prayed. Sometimes, during "revival services" we would have repentance sessions in our church where people would get up and confess some flaw in their lives. We did this because we believed if we did, revival would come—but it didn't. We were clearly taught that if we would live holy lives and pray and fast and repent that God would begin to do mighty works through us as in the book of Acts. We would walk by someone on the street, and they would fall under the power of God or be instantly healed—oh, and of course, the whole city where we lived would be saved.

Don't get me wrong. God is perfectly capable of doing just what I've described, but David and I had it all backward. To make matters worse, we were fed the idea that our parents hadn't sought God and brought about this "mighty move of God", but we were the chosen generation whom God would use if we would just sanctify ourselves.

I'm 61 years old, and we still haven't seen this happen. The pity is, the same message is being fed to today's young people. These are the days of the mighty prophets of old they sing. They are a new generation who will replace the previous generations. What previous generations? Well, who else but we, their parents and grandparents, who obviously weren't dedicated and diligent enough to make it happen.

This is madness. Can't you hear the pride swelling within these words? Younger Generation, I believe God will move through you, but please don't make the mistake we did by allowing teachers to separate you from the wisdom of your parents and grandparents. Don't receive this yoke of bondage that it is up to you to bring revival. Don't repeat the same errors we made in believing this recycled lie that you are the special chosen generation superior to those who have gone before you.

Paul was very clear about who it was and how it was that miracles happen among us.

Galatians 3:1-5

O foolish Galatians! Who has bewitched you that you should not obey the truth, before whose eyes Jesus Christ was clearly portrayed among you as crucified? ²This only I want to learn from you: Did you receive the Spirit by the works of the law, or by the hearing of faith? ³Are you so foolish? Having begun in the Spirit, are you now being made perfect by the flesh? ⁴Have you suffered so

many things in vain—if indeed it was in vain?
⁵Therefore He who supplies the Spirit to
you and works miracles among you, does
He do it by the works of the law, or by the
hearing of faith?

It isn't by our human efforts. It isn't by the works of the law. It is by the hearing of faith that miracles take place. People hear that God is able and willing to heal them or to help them. Faith comes to them by hearing this good news. Who is doing the miracles? Are we performing them? No, the Spirit of God works them among us.

When God worked miracles among the believers, did they ever once attribute it to their own efforts in prayer or to how godly they lived? Of course, they prayed, and yes they lived holy lives, but they denied that the miracles that occurred had anything to do with these things. Here we see a miracle, one very much like the kind our generation was praying and fasting and living holy lives to see.

Acts 3:1-12
Now Peter and John went up together to the temple at the hour of prayer, the ninth hour. ²And a certain man lame from his mother's womb was carried, whom they laid daily at the gate of the temple which is called Beautiful, to ask alms from those who entered the temple; ³who, seeing Peter and John about to go into the temple, asked for alms. ⁴And fixing his eyes on him, with John, Peter said, "Look at us." ⁵So he gave them his attention, expecting to receive something from them. ⁶Then Peter said, "Silver and gold I do not have, but what I do have I give you: In the name of Jesus Christ of Nazareth, rise up and walk." ⁷And he took him by the right hand and lifted him up, and immediately his

feet and ankle bones received strength. ⁸So he, leaping up, stood and walked and entered the temple with them—walking, leaping, and praising God. ⁹And all the people saw him walking and praising God. ¹⁰Then they knew that it was he who sat begging alms at the Beautiful Gate of the temple; and they were filled with wonder and amazement at what had happened to him.

*¹¹Now as the lame man who was healed held on to Peter and John, all the people ran together to them in the porch which is called Solomon's, greatly amazed. ¹²So when Peter saw it, he responded to the people: "Men of Israel, why do you marvel at this? Or **why look so intently at us, as though by our own power or godliness we had made this man walk?***

Peter knew what the people were thinking. They were looking to him and to John as those who healed the lame man. They put a stop to this immediately. It wasn't because of their own power. It wasn't because of how godly they were. It was because of Jesus! John and Peter might have been considered the chief leaders in the Jesus movement of those days, but this had nothing to do with why the man was healed.

Sadly, we know that this exaltation of man is allowed in the body of Christ today. Believers will stand in lines to "get a word from God" from some supposed prophet when the truth is, they can hear from God just as easily as any other believer. We all know God. We all hear His voice. He is leading us all. We set up these people to be higher than ourselves (and often these people set themselves up as higher). Thousands will gather at a meeting in hope of receiving healing through the hands of someone who somehow has more power in him than the normal Christian, when the same power that raised Jesus Christ from the dead dwells in us all.

Friends, God does give callings and gifts in the body of Christ today, but no one who is called is better or more powerful than the rest of us who believe in Him. If we ask someone for prayer, it should not be because we think he has a special power or because he is more holy than we are. It should be a matter of joining our faith with another's to believe God together for our needs.

We were saved by grace through faith. We live by grace through faith. Miracles happen by grace through faith. As soon as we insert ourselves into the equation beyond that of believing, we wander from His grace.

False Understanding of the Sovereignty of God

The word "sovereignty" is one that is difficult to encounter in Scripture, and when we do find it, there is no resemblance to how the concept is perceived in the body of Christ today. Usually, when someone says that God is sovereign, what they mean is "God can do whatever He wants whenever He wants." Let me ask this: Is our God as the mythical gods randomly doing something good and then next minute doing something mischievous?

> *The Greeks associated Poseidon with calamities like tidal waves and earthquakes. A spiteful god, Poseidon's moodiness manifested itself through shipwrecks and drownings. The Greeks associated Ares with bloodshed and pillaging, and considered him the god of warfare, rebellions, banditry and rage. Ares's vengeful nature becomes apparent from his murder of innocent Adonis, whom he saw as a rival for Aphrodite's affections.*[31]

---

[31] http://www.ehow.com/info_8463040_character-traits-greek-gods.html

Is not God accused of such among the church today? Every time there is a weather tragedy, God gets the blame. On 9-11, many Christian groups accused God of sending judgment on the United States of America for whatever that group's cause might have been: for making abortion legal, for not being a true friend of Israel, for not allowing prayer in public schools, or for legalizing sin. Do we really believe God killed thousands of innocent people, including believers in Jesus Christ to punish the nation? Does God punish the innocent with the guilty?

On a personal level, if we believe that it is God's doing when destruction enters our lives, how will we have faith to stand against it? Won't we be more inclined to accept it? If "everything that happens is God's will", then we must accept everything that comes our way. Why speak to mountains? Why ask for anything? We can start to adopt the false belief that God's will happens no matter what we believe or do.

Listen, God is sovereign, but don't define sovereignty beyond what is revealed about God in Scripture. God is King over His kingdom, and He has established His kingdom upon Jesus. His kingdom is based on who He has revealed Himself to be in Scripture and who we can see Him to be in the life of Christ. His kingdom is founded on what He has provided and promised through His Son. He didn't send Jesus to give us disease or to kill us. We might have a disease. We will likely one day see someone we know die too young. However, God is not to blame. Many of the injustices we suffer in this life have more to do with the depraved world in which we live.

God, in His Sovereignty, has given men on earth free wills, but that doesn't mean, as some have said, that God is "allowing" men to do evil. Billions of times a day, human beings choose to disobey their own consciences, and evil happens. A loved one dies in a car accident because the driver was intoxicated or because someone was driving care-lessly, not because God "took them". When the Twin Towers came down that horrifying day in New York City and terrorism rocked Paris, France, God was not sending these events or "allowing" them. Evil men filled with hate and driven by evil planned and executed what happened. Innocents died and Christians who should have known better blamed God.

We need to understand what God's will is and base our beliefs about Him on what is **written**. For example, we know that it is not God's will that any individual perish and that all come to know Him, but do people go to their grave cursing Him and refusing to believe in His Son? Yes, very sadly they do. Things that are not God's will happen every day. We must be wise. Let us study the Scriptures so that we may know His noble character and receive His grace.

> ### Ephesians 5:15-17
> *See then that you walk circumspectly, not as fools but as wise, ¹⁶redeeming the time, because the days are evil. ¹⁷Therefore do not be unwise, but **understand what the will of the Lord is**.*
> ### 2 Peter 3:9
> *The Lord is not slack concerning His promise, as some count slackness, but is longsuffering toward us, **not willing that any should perish** but that all should come to repentance.*
> ### Romans 8:31
> *What then shall we say to these things? If God is for us, who can be against us?*

God is for us, not against us. He does not send tragedy upon His people. He sent His Son to die for us so that we could live abundantly.

Dying to Sin

Some very sincere Christians believe that God is on a mission to break them instead of build them and that He does this through sending them hard times. If we believe that our overwhelming circumstances are God's way of breaking us down, our faith in Him will not be able to survive because we will end up accepting those circumstances as God's will instead of resisting them.

I wrote of this in my first book, but I feel I must touch on this again. When we come to Jesus Christ, we die and are resurrected in Him. As this happened once to Jesus, it also happens once to us.

> ### Romans 6:5-11
> *For if we have been united together in the likeness of His death, certainly we also shall be in the likeness of His resurrection, ⁶knowing this, that our old man was crucified with Him, that the body of sin might be done away with, that we should no longer be slaves of sin. ⁷For he who has died has been freed from sin. ⁸Now if we died with Christ, we believe that we shall also live with Him, ⁹knowing that Christ, having been raised from the dead, dies no more. Death no longer has dominion over Him. ¹⁰For the death that He died, He died to sin once for all; but the life that He lives, He lives to God. ¹¹**Likewise you also**, reckon yourselves to be dead indeed to sin, but alive to God in Christ Jesus our Lord.*

God does not need to kill us so that we will die to sin. We already died to sin (Rom. 6). Praise God. This is such good news. This sets us free to live in Him and through Him.

Dying Daily

I know what some are thinking. Aren't we supposed to die daily? Didn't Jesus say to pick up our cross daily and follow Him? Is my overwhelming circumstance a tool of God to help me die daily? No. Let me explain.

There are three accounts of a precise moment when Jesus told the disciples to pick up their cross and follow Him. Only one of these uses the word "daily". What many Christians don't know is that in that passage (Luke 9:23), the word "daily" does not actually appear in the Greek New Testament According to the Majority Text.[32]

Matthew 16:24
Then Jesus said to His disciples, "If anyone desires to come after Me, let him deny himself, and take up his cross, and follow Me.
Mark 8:34
When He had called the people to Himself, with His disciples also, He said to them, "Whoever desires to come after Me, let him deny himself, and take up his cross, and follow Me.

Jesus was getting ready to die, and yet we know that the disciples did not pick up a cross and follow Him to His death at this time. Jesus wasn't talking about following Him to the cross. He was asking them to follow Him in identification with His death as we read in the passage of Romans 6 above.When we put our faith in Jesus, we died with Him. This is what Jesus was telling them to do. Deny themselves, take up their cross and follow Him. Then, just as Jesus died once and rose once from the grave, so do we. Jesus did not go through all of this to give us everlasting death. He came to give us everlasting life.

Then what did Paul mean when he said that he died daily? Did he intend to say that he daily died to his flesh as some have taught we should do? To discover the answer to this question, let us include the surrounding verses. It is so obvious when we do this that Paul was referring to the sufferings and persecutions he suffered in the ministry.

---

[32] The Greek New Testament According to the Majority Text is believed to be one of the most accurate representations of Scripture. Though very expensive, we recommend the Majority Text Greek New Testament Interlinear published by Thomas Nelson.

1 Corinthians 15:30-32
And why do we stand in jeopardy every hour? [31] I affirm, by the boasting in you which I have in Christ Jesus our Lord, I die daily. [32] If, in the manner of men, I have fought with beasts at Ephesus, what advantage is it to me?

If we have been called to minister, we will die daily in the sense that we will give up the pleasures of this world more than most in order to share the gospel of God's grace with others. We will likely make less money than the average person if we are in ministry full-time even though we might be working more than most top executives. We will be persecuted. Our care for the body of Christ will take our time and our prayers. In some countries we could be jailed for our beliefs, tortured for our faith, and even suffer martyrdom. This is what Paul meant when he said he died daily. Yet even in that daily process of giving himself for his calling, he lived. He wrote eloquently of the treasures we have in Christ while he was imprisoned. He worshiped God in song. He did this for His Lord and the people not because God was trying to make him more like Jesus.

The reason for bringing this up is that many believers today think that everything bad that comes their way is God's way of causing them to "die daily" so He can root out sin in their lives. If we believe this, we will accept what comes against us. The truth is, when evil comes our way, it is not from God, and we can resist it.

Paul's Thorn in the Flesh

This brings us to Paul's thorn in the flesh. This has been interpreted to mean many things from being a certain person in our lives who is always a bother, to a disease that persists. Often when we can't explain why a trouble won't go away, we shrug our shoulders and say, "Oh, well. This must be my thorn in the flesh." (You might enjoy reading that sentence again using Eeyore's voice.)

This is not true. Paul's thorn in the flesh was not a disease (though people go to great lengths to "prove" it was). It was not the punishment of God for some ongoing sin in his life. It wasn't his annoying partners in ministry. Paul's thorn in the flesh was the trouble and persecutions he faced. He asked the Lord to deliver him from them, but He would not; for all who desire to live godly in Jesus will face them.

> **2 Corinthians 12:7-10**
> *And lest I should be exalted above measure by the abundance of the revelations, a thorn in the flesh was given to me, a messenger of Satan to buffet me, lest I be exalted above measure. ⁸Concerning this thing I pleaded with the Lord three times that it might depart from me. ⁹And He said to me, "My grace is sufficient for you, for My strength is made perfect in weakness." Therefore most gladly I will rather boast in my infirmities, that the power of Christ may rest upon me. ¹⁰Therefore I take pleasure in infirmities, in reproaches, in needs, in persecutions, in distresses, for Christ's sake. For when I am weak, then I am strong.*

Understanding this truth can set us free to believe for good from God. Here is a perfect example of that. One of our Sunday Bible class students from many years ago was told that her constant back pain was her thorn in the flesh— the assumption being that all of us have at least one. She was basing her belief on what others had told her. When we talked about Paul's thorn in the flesh in class, she could see from the passages surrounding Paul's mention of it that it was not referring to sickness. Unknown to us, that week she asked God to heal her back, and she returned the next

Sunday to declare excitedly that her back pain was going away day by day. Can you see how this false teaching was hindering her from even *asking* God to heal her? She thought her back pain was God's will for her personally. Once she was set free from this false teaching and embraced the good news, she had faith to ask and receive.

He Gives and Takes Away

We need to ask ourselves, what is the lesson we as New Covenant believers are to gain from Job's experience? What does it say in the New Testament that we are to gather from his faith? First of all, we are to follow his example of being patient during hard times, and the only example of this given in Scripture is in this verse below which was written to the Jews who were suffering for Christ.

> **James 5:11** *WEB*
> *Behold, we call them blessed who endured. You have heard of the patience of Job, and have seen the Lord in the outcome, and how the Lord is full of compassion and mercy.*

We also see God's character revealed. He is full of compassion and mercy. Finally, we are to remember the outcome of Job's story. His suffering lasted months, not years, and in the end, he was not only healed of his affliction but abundantly blessed.

However, the comparisons some teachers make in the church today with Job's experience and ours are not justified. There are, however, some important contrasts to be made. To begin with, Job lived before the Old Covenant was instituted. If he had at least been under the Old Covenant, Job would have been promised nothing but blessings and protections from destruction if he obeyed the law. Job had no covenant to protect him at all.

Secondly, Jesus had not yet died and destroyed the devil. Today, Satan cannot demand that God test us as Job was tested. Jesus stripped him of this authority. Any such request of his would be denied based on the victory Jesus won over "him who had the power of death; that is, the devil" (Heb. 2:14-15). **The only power Satan has in our lives right now is to lie to us, and we don't have to believe his lies.** As long as our faith is in Jesus, we are protected. This is our covenant, and Job did not have what we have.

When we think of Job, we can admire him. Even though he lost everything, he continued to believe in God. When all looks lost, will we still believe in Him? Will we keep on asking and giving thanks when things look impossible? This is what pleases God—our faith in His goodness.

When the enemy threatens "to steal, kill, and destroy" in our lives, resist Him in the faith knowing that he has been defeated through the death of Jesus. This verse bears repeating. This time, let's read it in the Amplified Version.

Hebrews 2:14-15 AMP
*Therefore, since [these His] children share in flesh and blood [the physical nature of mankind], He Himself in a similar manner also shared in the same [physical nature, but without sin], so that through [experiencing] death He might make powerless (ineffective, impotent) him who **had** the power of death— that is, the devil— ¹⁵and [that He] might free all those who through [the haunting] fear of death were held in slavery throughout their lives.*

God doesn't want us to be in bondage to the haunting fear of death, not fear of our own deaths, nor the death of someone we love. Jesus Christ experienced death in order to make the devil powerless. Resist Him.

John 10:10
*The **thief** does not come except to steal, and to kill, and to destroy. I have come that they may have **life**, and that they may have it more abundantly.*

Furthermore, can we find one example in the life of Christ in which He gave and took away? No. We can't. Did Paul, Peter, John, Jude or even James teach that God gives and takes away? Did any of them quote Job? No. None of them taught this.

What they taught is that God gives. We do not need to fear that God will "take away" what He has given us, and when the enemy does seek to "steal, kill, and destroy", we can resist him in Jesus' name.

Romans 11:29
For the gifts and the calling of God are irrevocable.
1 Corinthians 2:12
Now we have received, not the spirit of the world, but the Spirit who is from God, that we might know the things that have been freely given to us by God.
Romans 8:32
He who did not spare His own Son, but delivered Him up for us all, how shall He not with Him also freely give us all things?

While we can learn from Job's perseverance, we need to understand that in multiple ways, our lives under the New Covenant have nothing to do with his experiences. As far as we know, Job had no covenant with God—no promised protection. Though we might not fully comprehend it, whatever power Satan had then, he no longer has. He has been defeated, and we have been set free.

Into Each Life, a Little Rain Must Fall

Most people have heard the expression, "Into each life, a little rain must fall." This is usually used to mean that each person faces difficulties in this life. While this is true, it isn't Scripture. In fact, rain in the Bible often refers to a blessing from God rather than hard times.

When Jesus told His disciples to love their enemies, and to pray for those who persecuted them, He said that in doing this, they would be like their Father in heaven, because, "He makes His sun rise on the evil and on the good, and sends rain on the just and the unjust," (Mt. 5:45).

In other words, the sun and the rain are given by God as a BLESSING to those who deserve it and to those who don't. He didn't say He sends trouble to the just and unjust, but *blessings*.

This is important to know so that we do not mistake troubles as coming from God and are thus able to resist them in His name.

Disappointments and Set-Backs

When I was a young woman, I experienced a painful break-up from someone I thought I might marry one day. This may seem like a small trial to those who have endured things so much more severe, but at my age then, it was very painful. I was so consumed by my loss the weeks after the break-up happened that I hadn't even noticed that winter had passed, and the evidence of spring was everywhere surrounding me.

As I was driving down a beautiful tree-lined street, the thought came to me to look up. When I did, I saw the lovely new lacy green leaves were already dancing in the trees. The skies were clear blue, and the air seemed so fresh. A sense of joy came over me, and I wrote this song.

Look up, and see what God has done.
Get your face up off the ground now.
Look up and see what God has done.
Tell your face to smile awhile.
Tell your soul that things are under control.

That old devil will try to fool you
Telling you that he can rule you.
Well, just remind him that Jesus is in your heart,
And then start to praise the Lord.

Look up and see above your problems.
Rest assured that God can solve them.
Look up and see into His face.
Tell your heart that all is done.
The Bible says the battle has been won.

Sometimes it seems pretty hopeless,
But I'm telling you, we can know this:
God's word is absolutely true.
So, it's up to you (to look up and see what God has done).
His word is true.
He loves you.

When I got my mind off the past and the pain, and purposely chose to focus on Jesus and all that He did for me, I was able to receive healing. In less than one month, I was engaged to be married— not to the person who had broken my heart, but to someone who had been my dear friend and partner in ministry for over a year. Eight months later, we were married, and in December 2015 David and I celebrated our 40th anniversary.

273

Day 33

"CHRISTIAN" SUPERSTITIONS

Superstitions are false teachings in the extreme. I separate them not to distinguish them acutely from each other, but to spare you from what would have been a very long Day 32. I placed the more absurd false teachings in this category of superstitions. There are many more superstitions than these, of course. I hope this chapter will serve to get you thinking about it: are we basing our beliefs about God on what is written or on something else?

"God Willing"

Many Christians today have been taught that they cannot be sure of anything, so it is wrong to make plans. So, when they are talking about the future, whether it has to do with plans they are making or whether or not they should eat a piece of pie after dinner, they tag on the expression, "God willing." The problem with this thinking is it gives us a sense of insecurity—perhaps we won't live until tomorrow, or some other calamity will take place, or we might be going against His will. It can result in us heading nowhere and without any direction because we think it is evil to make plans beyond today. This superstition comes primarily from a misunderstanding of this verse.

> **James 4:13-16**
> *Come now, you who say, "Today or tomorrow we will go to such and such a city, spend a year there, buy and sell, and make a profit"; ¹⁴whereas you do not know what will happen tomorrow. For what is your life? It is even a vapor that appears for a little time and then vanishes away. ¹⁵Instead you ought to say, "If the Lord wills, we shall live and do this or that." ¹⁶**But now you boast in your arrogance. All such boasting is evil.***

When we read the entire chapter of James 4, we can see that he is addressing a very arrogant group of people. He called them lustful murderers, covetous, pleasure-seekers, adulterers, friends of the world, enemies of God, proud, sinners, with impure hearts, double-minded, those who spoke evil of each other, law-breakers, and arrogant boasters. My friend, if these words describe you, either you need to be born again, or get out from under law-based teachings which are giving strength to sin, and certainly, don't make any extensive plans until you take care of what is causing you to behave like an unbeliever.

There are many examples of godly people making plans. Jesus had a mission. He knew where he was going. He knew what He was going to do. He moved steadily toward that goal. Paul and the other apostles made plans in ministry. Paul believed that he would live to fulfill the ministry God called him to do. He was determined to go to Jerusalem, and let nothing deter his plans. The truth is, we need to make plans and prepare for the future. When a couple finds out they are going to have a baby, they need to make plans. If someone is going to buy a house, they need to plan ahead, gather the needed funds, fill out contracts, call a moving company, pack, and then move. Older people need to make sure their finances are in order, so they don't have to be dependent on their children during their retirement years. Churches have annual planning meetings, and so does every business in the world. God doesn't see planning as evil, but planning based on greed by people as he described in James 4 is unwise. Think about it. Certain things are God's will. Let us read the Bible to learn of His provisions and promises to us, and let us seek Him concerning His will for us as individuals. Once we know what His will is, we can confidently move forward, and He will be encouraging us as we go without the need to tag on a "God willing" to everything we hope to do because we already know He is willing. However, if we have the attitude that we are going "to make things happen" by pushing forward without any regard for God's will in the matter, we need to take a step back and discover what His will is.

Ephesians 5:17
Therefore do not be unwise, but understand what the will of the Lord is.

Kristian Karma

Karma is defined as "the sum of a person's actions in this and previous states of existence, viewed as deciding their fate in future existences".[33] My friends, this is not a Christian concept. Yet, it is everywhere.

I don't know of any true Christian who believes that individuals have a prior life on earth or that they will have another life on earth after they die—in reincarnation, but this idea of being rewarded or punished for our past or even our parent's past is clearly present. What if we haven't done anything right our whole life? What if we raised our children with oppression, messed up our finances, and our marriage is more "worse" than "better"? What if we've been an unkind human being most of our life? Will we only be able to receive from God according to our past actions?

---

[33] Oxford University Press

Please, let's stop this. The whole glorious truth of Christianity is that Jesus took the penalty for our sins, and gave us His righteousness. We are completely forgiven for our past[34]—for everything.

Now, there will likely be people in our lives who refuse to forgive us for the pain we have caused them, and we might need to seek to make amends with them (whether they accept our attempts, we cannot control), but God forgave us in Christ, and He is not counting our sins against us.

God is not seeing to it that we suffer because of mistakes we have made in the past. He is not holding our sins against us. Period. It is equally important to recognize that He is also not keeping a record of how good we are and making sure we are equally blessed according to our goodness. This is a safeguard against us thinking that God "owes" us. He doesn't. He has chosen to give to us because of our faith in Jesus.

Sometimes things happen that are not fair. If we believe that things go well for us *because* we are living up to whatever standards we believe we should, we might be tempted to wonder how this could happen to *us*—that because we've been "good", we should get good. Can you see how this is a function of the law? It is the belief that when difficulties come, God is punishing us, and when blessings come, He is rewarding us.

Grace is *undeserved* favor from God. If we earn His blessings as some sort of cosmic reward, then it is no longer grace. If we are punished for our sins, as we deserve, then the penalty that Jesus paid for our sins was not enough (Gal. 2:21).

If we are focusing on how well or how poorly we live and think that God will bless us or punish us based on our accumulation of right or wrong living, it will be nearly impossible to receive from God. God's gifts to us are by grace which by definition means, we do not deserve them. We are

---

[34] Past, present, and future sins

made right before God by faith in Jesus, not by how perfectly we live.

Generational Curses

Even more extreme than Kristian Karma is the belief that we can be cursed and affected by demonic activity based on the sins of our ancestors. This false belief is derived from what God said when He revealed Himself to Moses.

> *Exodus 34:6-7*
> *And the Lord passed before him and proclaimed, "The Lord, the Lord God, merciful and gracious, longsuffering, and abounding in goodness and truth, ⁷keeping mercy for thousands, forgiving iniquity and transgression and sin, by no means clearing the guilty, visiting the iniquity of the fathers upon the children and the children's children to the third and the fourth generation."*

The false teaching is that if someone's great-grandfather was involved in cultic activity or some gross sin, this would still be cursing him today and that in order to be free from this curse, he must be exorcised from it or be set free from it by a greatly disciplined spiritual life. If one only took the above verse into consideration, perhaps the conclusion would have some basis, but under the same Old Covenant, God said this through the prophet Ezekiel.

> *Ezekiel 18:20*
> *The soul who sins shall die. **The son shall not bear the guilt of the father, nor the father bear the guilt of the son.** The righteousness of the righteous shall be upon himself, and the wickedness of the wicked shall be upon himself."*

This is God speaking, my friends. The only sins that were held against us were our own, and those sins were taken away in Christ. God will absolutely not hold us responsible for anything our relatives did in the past. Furthermore, we aren't under any curse—not our ancestors' and not the curses of not obeying the law, because we are not under the law, but under grace. Glory to God. We are free indeed!

> ***Galatians 3:13-14***
> ***Christ has redeemed us from the curse*** *of the law, having become a curse for us (for it is written, "**Cursed** is everyone who hangs on a tree"), ¹⁴that the **blessing** of Abraham might come upon the Gentiles in Christ Jesus, that we might receive the promise of the Spirit through **faith**.*

More Curses

There are "ministries" out there that teach that we need to be delivered from a variety of curses. Let me say it again. Christians are under no curse whatsoever. When we came to Christ, we became free indeed.

We have a friend who was taught that a particular type of curse existed. Since he had experienced repeated and substantial financial losses in two particular months, he started to believe that he had this type of curse and needed to be delivered. Each time these months would roll around, he would suffer a financial blow.

Then he began to learn the good news about the finished work of Christ on the cross, and that Jesus became a curse for us so that we could be free from the curse of the law. So, he began to put his faith in what Jesus provided and rejected the lie that he had a financial curse. When the following supposedly cursed month arrived, instead of a financial loss, he was blessed financially.

Dearly beloved I plead with you to forsake the idea that you are cursed **in any way for anything**. Your sins are forgiven, and God is not cursing you. Jesus became a curse for you so that you could be free. This verse bears repeating.

> **Galatians 3:13-14**
> *Christ has redeemed us from the curse of the law, having become a curse for us (for it is written, "Cursed is everyone who hangs on a tree"), ¹⁴that the blessing of Abraham might come upon the Gentiles in Christ Jesus, that we might receive the promise of the Spirit through faith.*

Basing Our Doctrines on Experience

It is very important that we base our beliefs on what is written in Scripture and not on what we or someone we know has gone through. Experience can teach us many things, but we must not allow it to override the truth of God's promises.

Thirty-one years ago, three days after my thirtieth birthday, my mother passed away from breast cancer. By the time she was diagnosed, it had spread to her bones, internal organs, and brain. After the pain of a double mastectomy, chemotherapy, and radiation, she was only weakened further, and much too slowly she withered away before our devastated eyes. Thankfully, my mother was a true believer in Jesus.

We'd seen God do miracles before, so we prayed that God would heal my mom. When she died, I was overwhelmingly distraught beyond words because she was my life-long best friend.

I determined when she passed that I would never engage in the folly of blaming God in the slightest for my mom's death in order to explain it. I knew that it was not God's will that she die. I knew that He would never "take her". I disregarded completely, ignorant comments from others which tried to explain her early death. Instead, I praised God through my tears. I didn't understand why she wasn't healed, but I knew that in time, God would help me recover and eventually give me an understanding.

In view of the prevailing belief at that time that breast cancer was hereditary, I knew I was at a crossroads: would I base my beliefs about the grace of divine healing on what my mother experienced or on what the Bible had to say? That is to say, would I live my life in fear of inheriting breast cancer, expecting it to hit me eventually, or would I believe God that I would be free from it? The only option viable for me was to turn to what is written.

Years later, I started a journey to learn all I could about divine healing from Scripture. I read slowly through the Bible writing down every verse that shed light on the topic. After two years of study, I wrote my first book (unpublished) entitled <u>Healing Verses</u>. (Much of the content of that book is included in this work.) During that study, I discovered that I not only didn't fully understand healing at the time of my mother's illness but that I was also confused about God answering any prayer.

I know now that when I was praying for my mom to live, my prayers were not from faith, but from desperation. I was begging and pleading with God to please heal her, thinking the more I cried and the "harder" I prayed, the more likely she would be healed. There were many misconceptions I had in those days about faith in God partly caused by false teachings about it.

As my pain subsided, and I was able to think more clearly, I was able to understand many things about why she died. The number one factor, I believe, was that my mother did not seek medical attention when she first found a lump in her breast. Prior to that her Labrador Retriever had accidentally bumped into her breast. At first she thought the lump was from that blow, so she thought it would gradually heal. Also, though she did not exactly say so, I got the impression that she believed God would take away the lump based on a recorded testimony of a minister who claimed God removed a tumor from his chest. Although I did plea with her to see a doctor, I also was hesitant to stand in the way of her "faith". The truth remains, however; if my mom had gone in immediately when she found a small lump, she might still be alive today. She waited two years before seeing a doctor even though she could tell the lump was increasing in size.

The Christmas before she went to see a doctor, I could see that her breast was much larger. When I said something to her about it, she put her fingers on her lips asking me not to say anything to anyone, including my brother who was there for the holidays. True to form, she wanted everyone to have a great Christmas without worrying about her. I felt I needed to respect her request. I remember thinking then that I was too young to lose my mother.

A month later, she gathered her brother and sisters and parents together to share with them that she was going to a doctor and why. That was the night her mom passed away. The next day, my mom was admitted to the hospital; the cancer was everywhere. Was God to blame for this? My conclusion is that He was not.

Almost everyone knows someone who "believed God" for something, but it seemed nothing happened, and some of us also had experiences where it looked like God disappointed us, **but we must not base our faith on our experiences or those of others**. We don't know what someone else was thinking or what they were believing, and it could be that we ourselves still have some misconceptions.

My best advice is to research for *yourself* so that you may be fully confident of God's provisions and promises to you because ultimately it is each of our own responsibilities to "prove all things and hold fast to that which is good". Once convinced that God has promised something, whether it be physical, emotional, financial, or relational, you will be able to receive it based on His benevolent character and love toward you. God cannot lie. He keeps His promises.

Numbers 23:19
God is not a man, that He should lie,
Nor a son of man, that He should repent.
Has He said, and will He not do?
Or has He spoken, and will He not make it good?

Still numb from the news of my Grandmother's passing
and the confusing pain I felt about my mother, I penned this
song about my Grandmother, which I sang at her funeral. As
I wrote, I couldn't help but think of my own mom.

We're gonna miss you.
There will always be a special place in our hearts
No one else can fill
We're gonna miss you, Grandma.
We can still recall the loving arms that held us
When we were young.

Your soft brown eyes,
Your loving smile
Still warm us;
The love you gave
The life you lived for your Jesus.
We're gonna miss you.
We're gonna miss you, Grandma.

"If you could see me now,
I know a smile would come upon your faces
Through all the tears.
For I am singing, 'Hallelujah,'
Before the throne of God
And the Christ who died for me.

"And I'm still hoping
That all of you will come and join me
On that day,
For I never, ever want to say

To any of you
That I'm gonna miss you."

We're gonna miss you, Grandma.
We're gonna miss you, Mom.

Being "Authentic"

A few years ago, a young minister stood up among a group of mature ministers and shared how important it is for us as ministers to be "authentic". Perhaps she didn't mean for it to sound this way, but it was as if she was authentic, but older people were not. If it hadn't been so offensive, I might have laughed right then and there. I couldn't help but think that it was *my* generation that majored in being authentic, but we called it being real.

Should we be real? Yes, of course, but this idea of trying to be sincere can become an interference in the process of believing if we focus forever on our weaknesses, and in some bent way, glory in them in an attempt to appear to be "authentic" instead of standing up against them.

Being real is just being who you are. It doesn't mean we must share our past or present intimate difficulties with the whole world. It may be that it is enough simply to share them with Jesus. Authenticity does not negate privacy.

Suffering and Sacrificing to Obtain Favor

God *wants* to meet our needs. He loves to answer our prayers, but His gifts to us cannot be purchased. Still there are many people in the world who think that if they will make some sort of sacrifice or do a good work; in short, bargain with God, then He will repay them with a favor. Crawling on our knees to the church through rocks and broken glass has no effect on God at all except that it breaks His heart that someone would think he needs to do this.

Titus 3:4-7
*But when the kindness and the love of God our Savior toward man appeared, ⁵**not by works of righteousness which we have done**, but according to His mercy He saved us, through the washing of regeneration and renewing of the Holy Spirit, ⁶whom He poured out on us abundantly through Jesus Christ our Savior, ⁷that having been justified by His grace we should become heirs according to the hope of eternal life.*

Begging God and Prayer Chains

It's OK to ask for prayer, but our prayers are not more likely to be answered based on the number of people praying. The bowl in heaven with our prayers isn't waiting to be filled with **enough** prayers until it tips and the prayers are finally answered. God isn't waiting to answer until we've prayed enough. We don't need to set up 24-hour prayer and worship chains to get God's attention as if we are signing a petition to get Him to act. How absurd. These things were not practiced in the early church. People prayed together, but they prayed in faith that God would answer, not because they thought if they could just get enough people praying, God would finally be moved. Remember this: God is already *for* us, not against us. We simply ask in faith.

Matthew 6:7-8
*And when you pray, do not use vain repetitions as the heathen do. **For they think that they will be heard for their many words.** ⁸"Therefore do not be like them. For your Father knows the things you have need of before you ask Him.*

Everything Happens for a Divine Purpose

We have already discussed that God causes all things to work together for our good, but this is not to say that "everything happens for a divine purpose". Please consider what that implies before you allow this accusation to come through your lips. First of all, to say this is to say that God causes everything including all the evil and destruction that takes place on the earth. Did God send His only Son out of the love He had for mankind because of His desire that none would perish and that all would come to know Him and then turn around and slay them? This is simply not logical in the slightest. Does He steal, kill, and destroy to bring about good? What good is it then if people who don't know Him end up dying before they have heard of Him?

Who is this monster god that many in the church have invented who is supposedly behind every tragedy that happens? It is not our God. We can rest assured. God can take devastating events that happen in the lives of His children and work them together for good, but He is not harming and killing the ones for whom He died.

When hard times come into our lives, let us not automatically assume that the things that are happening are from God. Let us use our brains and pick up and read our Bibles and be careful about falsely accusing God of evil.

Shelley's Sudden Storm

One day, a friend of ours was on her way to work when suddenly a truck going 50-60 mph in a 35 mph zone ran directly into her on the driver's side as she was beginning to turn left. So severe was the crash that the rescue workers had to remove her car door and remove her using the Jaws of Life. She suffered a head injury, two fractures in her leg, one in her arm, and injuries to her neck and back, and went into shock.

She remembers that as she was in the emergency room, she raised her hands and said, "Thank-You Lord," because she knew that God was taking care of her and that she would be OK.

Her rehabilitation and recovery were long and often painful, but now, almost three years later she is almost completely healed. She writes, "Through all of this trauma I never questioned God about 'why' this happened or asked Him if I'd done anything wrong or what He wanted to teach me. I knew He was working all things together for good. I am continually growing in grace, learning of who I am in Christ and who He is in me. I know it's a miracle I'm alive. My heart is full of gratefulness for His amazing love and grace."

This is such a lovely example of the difference it can make in our lives when we stop thinking that God sends evil to teach us lessons and begin to understand that He is for us not against us. Instead of blaming Him for tragedy, we can turn to Him in times of need knowing He will help us.

Attributing Everything to God

This superstition is very similar to the one above, but even more ridiculous. It is the thought that every single thing that happens is God "teaching me something". If a friend is driving us crazy, we say God is teaching us patience. If we trip over the shoes we left in the hallway, we say that God is trying to teach us to be organized. If we are rushing around to get out the door and then spill our coffee all over our things, we frustratingly yell, "God! Why?"

I'm laughing aloud right now; hopefully, you are, too. Let's not be ridiculous. God has better things to do than spoil our day.

God Needs Her in Heaven

We say some pretty ridiculous things when we see people suffering the loss of a loved one, especially when the person who died was too young to die. We mean well, but we need to be careful about what we say. My opinion is that it is not possible to make sense of someone dying when they are young, especially a baby. It makes no sense at all, and really, there is nothing anyone can say that will make up for the loss that is felt. Usually, it is best to tell the person that we are sorry for their loss and mourn with them.

Perhaps you've been at a funeral of someone who died too young, and someone said, "God needed her in heaven," or even more bizarre, "God needed more angels in heaven."

First of all, God doesn't have a shortage of help in heaven. Secondly, human beings cannot ever turn into angels. When Christians die, God gladly welcomes them home, but He doesn't "take" people by killing them. If He really wanted us in heaven, He is completely capable of simply snatching us off the earth without killing us. There are only two records of this happening in Scripture. One was when Elijah was taken up in a chariot of fire (2 Kings 2), and the other was Enoch. In both cases, they did not die.

> **Genesis 5:23-24**
> *So all the days of Enoch were three hundred and sixty-five years. [24] And Enoch walked with God; and he was not, for God took him.*
> **Hebrews 11:5**
> *By faith Enoch was taken away so that **he did not see death**, "and was not found, because God had taken him"; for before he was taken he had this testimony, that he pleased God.*

If we as believers live long enough, we too will be snatched off of the earth without experiencing death. In the meantime, let us live with the confident expectation of being satisfied with a long life so that we may share the glad tidings of good things from our great God.

> **1 Corinthians 15:51-54**
> *Behold, I tell you a mystery: We shall not all sleep (die), but we shall all be changed— ⁵²in a moment, in the twinkling of an eye, at the last trumpet. For the trumpet will sound, and the dead will be raised incorruptible, and we (those who are still alive) shall be changed. ⁵³For this corruptible must put on incorruption, and this mortal must put on immortality. ⁵⁴So when this corruptible has put on incorruption, and this mortal has put on immortality, then shall be brought to pass the saying that is written: "Death is swallowed up in victory."*

My Time to Go

Does God know our lives from beginning to end? Does He see the day we will die? More importantly, has He planned the day you will die? Well, you might not know this, but the topic is highly debated.

Since God is all-knowing, it makes sense that He also knows the future. Yet, there is a turn people take from this point that is inaccurate. We call it "my time to go", and we use it falsely to mean that there is a certain date and time set by God when we are appointed to die, and that when that moment comes, we are going to die—no matter what. Thankfully, this thought cannot be substantiated in Scripture.

The horrible implication of this line of thinking is that every murder and premature death is God's will and plan. Every sickness that ends in death was known and preordained by God. Every person who died in a weather tragedy—this was also ordained of God. This is simply not true.

First of all, let's agree that if we are not removed from the earth at Jesus' second coming while we are still alive, we will one day die. I think most people agree with this, and more importantly, so does Scripture.

>**Hebrews 9:27-28**
>*And as it is **appointed for men to die once**, but after this the judgment, [28]so Christ was offered once to bear the sins of many. To those who eagerly wait for Him He will appear a second time, apart from sin, for salvation.*

This verse does not say or mean that we are each individually assigned a specific day to die by God. It means that all people die once. It's just the way it is. There is no reincarnation or second chance. Each of us has one life to live, and then we face our Maker. There's no middle place we can go to make amends after death. What's done is done.

Over the years, I've heard people quote from Psalm 90:12 with the thought that no one knows how long he or she will live. Any of us could die at any moment; it is incorrectly argued; so, we should learn to "number our days". When studying for this little section, I was delighted to discover the context of this verse.

>**Psalm 90:10-12**
>**The days of our lives are seventy years;**
>**And if by reason of strength they are eighty years,**
>*Yet their boast is only labor and sorrow;*
>*For it is soon cut off, and we fly away.*
>*[11] Who knows the power of Your anger?*
>*For as the fear of You, so is Your wrath.[35]*
>*[12] So teach us to number our days,*
>*That we may gain a heart of wisdom.*

This above verse is not implying at all that we could die "any day". It is telling us that we won't live forever, perhaps

---

[35] Though not a part of this lesson, Christians need not fear the wrath of God. We are forgiven forever.

70 or 80 years or more and that we need to take this into account as we spend our days. In actuality, God's desire is to give us long lives. What a beautiful truth.

Psalm 91:14-16
Because he has set his love upon Me, therefore I will deliver him;
I will set him on high, because he has known My name.
¹⁵He shall call upon Me, and I will answer him;
I will be with him in trouble;
I will deliver him and honor him.
*¹⁶**With long life I will satisfy him**,*
And show him My salvation.

Paul had the following to say about dying. He actually would have preferred to pass away and be with Jesus, but knowing that he was called to preach the gospel of grace, he chose to stay. Do you know that there are people who need you, who would suffer deeply if you died? Your life matters. You can make a difference in the kingdom of God. Determine to be satisfied with a long life so that you may glorify Him while on this earth.

Philippians 1:21-26
For to me, to live is Christ, and to die is gain.
*²²But if I live on in the flesh, this will mean fruit from my labor; yet what I shall **choose** I cannot tell. ²³For I am hard-pressed between the two, having a desire to depart and be with Christ, which is far better. ²⁴Nevertheless to remain in the flesh is more needful for you.*
*²⁵**And being confident of this, I know that I shall remain and continue with you all for your progress and joy of faith**, ²⁶that your rejoicing for me may be more abundant in Jesus Christ by my coming to you again.*

291

A dear friend of ours with whom I lived when I was single who was getting on in years told me about an experience she had when she'd been very sick for an extended period of time. She explained to me that she had a dream, and Jesus appeared to her as a lamb and bid her come telling her it was "her time to go". At first, she welcomed this, but as she looked closer in her dream, she noticed that underneath the sheep's clothing was a wolf, and that it wasn't Jesus bidding her to die, but the enemy. So, of course, she refused. She was old when she had this dream, but she continued to live on many more years to minister to the body of Christ.

What an amazing illustration to us all. Don't be deceived by this idea that it might be "your time to go." Remember, God wants to give us a long productive life so that we can be a blessing to others and bring honor to His name.

Why Live?

Giving in and giving up seems like the easiest path sometimes, especially when we have been beaten down for a long time. Knowing that death will bring us directly into the arms of Christ makes it appear to be a better alternative than fighting an illness. We might look at this awful world or our own undesirable circumstances and be tempted to think heaven would be so much better. Of course, it would, but there are many important reasons for us to live.

David wrote in Psalm 6:4-5:

"Return, O Lord, deliver me!
Oh, save me for Your mercies' sake!
For in death there is no remembrance of You;
In the grave who will give You thanks?"

The number one reason why we should live is so that our lives can go on giving praise to God. Alive we can be a light to a lost world and proclaim His greatness. There are still people to whom we can minister, people who need us. Our families need us. Our friends need us. Our future family and friends need us. Their lives will never be the same without us in them.[36]

---

[36] From Healing Verses, an unpublished book by C. D. Hildebrand

Day 34

THINGS WE ACCEPT

---

1 Corinthians 2:12
Now we have received, not the spirit of the world, but the Spirit who is from God, that we might know the things that have been freely given to us by God.

Sometimes we have the tendency to fall into the thinking that because we live on this earth, we will necessarily experience life the same as those who do not have Jesus. We tend to accept that just because it is "allergy season" or some disease "runs in the family" or because "these are hard financial times for everyone" that these things have to be true for us also. My perspective on this topic radically shifted about twenty years ago.

It happened when I was teaching in high school. It isn't hard to imagine how many sicknesses are present in one school on any given day. Between children coughing and sneezing and teachers sharing equipment, a person is exposed to illness all day long. It was normal to assume that eventually, I'd get sick, and I did about twice a year.

When the symptoms started coming on, I requested a substitute teacher and started making lesson plans because when I got sick, it was usually in the extreme. I'd make arrangements for someone else to transport my kids to and from school, and my husband would make a trip to the grocery store for foods and meds that would help in my recovery. I would then crawl into bed, and my husband would pray for me to be healed. I always felt so defeated about being sick, but I still believed I'd recover.

Now, teaching is a very demanding profession. The ignorant ones who say, "Those who can do, and those who can't, teach," have never taught adolescents or small children while keeping everyone alive by the end of the day and then doing that five days a week for an entire school year. So, getting sick, though it made me feel miserable, represented some sort of warped form of vacation in my mind. I did nothing for several days; well, because I was too sick to do anything, but being sick was not only accepted because "everyone gets sick", but because I needed the "rest". I know, it's a bit distorted, but I'm just being honest here, and I don't think I'm the first person on earth to accept sickness because of the perceived benefits.

On one of my "vacations", I was reading a pamphlet on healing, and it was basically saying that when we get sick, we can trust God to heal us. I already believed that, so I was just trying to encourage myself that I'd be OK.

It is what happened while I was reading it that changed my viewpoint forever. Like a gift from heaven, the thought came into my thinking, "If I can believe that God will heal me when I get sick, can't I believe God not to get sick in the first place?" I shared this thought with my husband and let the idea roll around in my heart for a couple days. This thought was like hearing good news, and I came to the conclusion that yes, God could keep me from getting sick in the first place, but how would this happen? I didn't have any teaching on the topic—didn't know anyone who was teaching this, so I began a journey which, quite frankly, was a wonderful surprise.

First of all, I changed my mind (repented) of the idea that just because I was surrounded all day by germs that I was necessarily going to get sick. When thoughts about the inevitability of getting sick would come into my mind or someone at work would start moaning about "flu season", inside my heart I would say, "I reject that thought in the name of Jesus." When I'd be in line for the copy machine at work, and the teacher right before me was sneezing and sniffling so much that he should have been home not at school infecting others, instead of subtly thinking, "Oh, great. Thanks a lot for sharing your germs," I'd say in my heart, "I refuse to accept this illness in Jesus' name." When children would sit in my class red-nosed and listless, I would not only pray for them under my breath but declare, "I do not accept that I will be sick because this child is sick."

The temptation to give into illness in order to have a mini vacation was replaced with this thought: If I need a break, I can take one. I'd rather relax being well than sick. So, when the stress of my job became overwhelming, I would take a mental health day off.

For the next two years, I did not get sick at all ever. Mind over matter? Let's not be ridiculous. That was twenty years ago. Have I been sick since then? Yes, I have, but significantly less. When I have been sick, my faith has been that "by His wounds I was healed", and I have been healed. Still, now I try to watch myself for merely accepting sickness, and for the most part, enjoy a healthy life. Although, I do take the normal precautions against getting sick such as washing my hands, etc., I don't live in a bubble. I travel on planes, babysit grandchildren, and work among the people in our ministry. I visit stores, eat in restaurants, and visit friends in hospitals. When someone around me is sick, I don't allow myself to worry or get freaked out. In my heart, I simply say, "I don't accept that I will get that illness. By Your wounds, I am healed."

When "allergy season" comes around, and I feel that first tickle and have a little sneeze attack, I have a conversation with my body. I say, "OK, Body, it is OK for you to sneeze and respond to the junk that's in the air, but you will not overreact. You will respond appropriately like normal people's bodies." When a sneeze or two happens, I say, "By Your wounds I am healed." Instead of thinking, "Oh, no! It's not working," I insist on being well in Jesus' name.

Christina's Faith

Our daughter, Christina, began showing allergies to food at a very young age. She was allergic to eggs, milk products, red apples, mandarin oranges, and especially to corn. Even though we made sure she didn't eat these things, sometimes we'd forget, or someone wouldn't know and feed one of these foods to her. She would get horrible stomach aches followed by a rash. I figured this was just how it would be for her, but I started to notice that it was affecting her personality by making her irritable. Her little three-year-old eyes would look at me as if to say, "Help me, Mommy." When I began to see how miserable she was and that it was altering her personality, I got mad. Why was I allowing this to go on?

Around that time (in 1980), during a prayer service, I went into the nursery and got her to have the elders anoint her with oil and pray for her. I told her that Jesus was going to heal her of her allergies. In my heart, there was a holy anger at these allergies. I felt like somewhere in my spirit I was putting my foot down. I was not going to take this anymore! The man who prayed for her did just as I asked. He prayed that she would be completely healed.

A day or two later, we were having dinner at a friend's house. As they passed around the whole kernel corn, the worst possible food for her, she put some on her plate. I looked at her and was going to remind her of her allergy to corn, but before I had a chance, she said, "It's OK, Mommy. Jesus healed me." I was not about to get in the way of her faith, and I said, "OK." From that moment on, Christina had no food allergies of any kind. One day, she was allergic to almost everything. The next day, after our prayer and her confession of faith, she was allergic to nothing.

I know that sometimes children grow out of food allergies, but not overnight. God honored His promise and her faith. The most wonderful part was that this made a tremendous difference in her personality. She was finally free from pain and able to enjoy life and all the good foods God created.

We told my mom about this miracle by asking her to make us some popcorn. She, at first, looked at me as if I'd forgotten that Tina couldn't have it recalling how sick Tina got when my mom made popcorn for her a few months before that. With both Tina and I smiling at her, we explained that Tina had been healed. My mom's eyes just about popped out of her head, and then she sat down on her kitchen floor and cried like a baby. How full of joy we all were at God's faithfulness.

Sickness seeks to destroy and even kill. We can't afford to accept it. Remember just because others are sick does not mean we must be. Should we become sick, then we can believe God to be healed. If we aren't "there" yet, then we can believe that the medical care we are receiving will heal us. God will meet us where our faith currently is, and He will continue to encourage and teach us to believe Him for greater things, but let us consider if we are "accepting" things we could conquer in His name.

Isaiah 54:17
No weapon formed against you (me) shall prosper,
And every tongue which rises against you (me) in judgment
You (I) shall condemn.
This is the heritage of the servants of the Lord (is my heritage),

And their (my) righteousness is from Me (God),"
Says the Lord.

Psalm 91

He who dwells in the secret place of the Most High
Shall abide under the shadow of the Almighty.
²I will say of the Lord, "He is my refuge and my fortress;
My God, in Him I will trust."
³Surely He shall deliver you from the snare of the fowler
And from **the perilous pestilence**.
⁴He shall cover you with His feathers,
And under His wings you shall take refuge;
His truth shall be your shield and buckler.
⁵You shall not be afraid of the terror by night
Nor of the arrow that flies by day,
⁶**Nor of the pestilence that walks in darkness**,
Nor of the destruction that lays waste at noonday.
⁷**A thousand may fall at your side,**
And ten thousand at your right hand;
But it shall not come near you.
⁸Only with your eyes shall you look,
And see the reward of the wicked.
⁹Because you have made the Lord, who is my refuge,
Even the Most High, your dwelling place,
¹⁰**No evil shall befall you,**
Nor shall any plague come near your dwelling;
¹¹For He shall give His angels charge over you,
To keep you in all your ways.
¹²In their hands they shall bear you up,
Lest you dash your foot against a stone.
¹³You shall tread upon the lion and the cobra,
The young lion and the serpent you shall trample
underfoot.
¹⁴"Because he has set his love upon Me, therefore I
will deliver him;
I will set him on high, because he has known My name.
¹⁵He shall call upon Me, and I will answer him;
I will be with him in trouble;

I will deliver him and honor him.
¹⁶With long life I will satisfy him,
And show him My salvation."

Day 35

WHEN WE ARE OUR OWN WORST ENEMIES

---

*T*here are many things we as Christians do that actually work against our own faith. We can't blame the devil, and of course, it is folly to see God as the culprit. In many situations, we are, as they say, our own worst enemies. This is not meant to condemn anyone, but to point out common ways of thinking that undermine our own success as we seek to overcome.

Faith is what comes when we hear of His grace—His benevolent character, His provisions, and His promises to us. However, faith isn't just something we are given; it is something that causes us to act. It is futile to act in order to produce faith. Don't think for one second that I am suggesting that if we say or do something enough, we will finally believe. What I am saying is that when we come to a place of faith, we should take hold of it and not let go. Let's bring what we've learned from previous challenges into new ones.

Philippians 3:12-16
Not that I have already attained, or am already perfected; but I press on, that I may lay hold of that for which Christ Jesus has also laid hold of me. ¹³Brethren, I do not count myself to have apprehended; but one thing I do, forgetting those things which are behind and

> *reaching forward to those things which are ahead, ¹⁴I press toward the goal for the prize of the upward call of God in Christ Jesus. ¹⁵Therefore let us, as many as are mature, have this mind; and if in anything you think otherwise, God will reveal even this to you. ¹⁶**Nevertheless, to the degree that we have already attained, let us walk by the same rule, let us be of the same mind.***

Following are several things that are common to us all. I've participated in some of these and regretted it, and am learning that we don't have to fall into these traps that we set for ourselves. May the Lord give us grace to identify these enemies and the strength to reject them.

Dictating to God How He Will Work

If someone lives in a country where he is given an amazing set of freedoms to live as he chooses and accomplish what he sets out to achieve or if the opposite is true and someone is used to having other people do things for him, one might fall prey to this way of thinking.

Remember, God is the King of His kingdom. He is the One who sets up the principles that guide it. While He clearly gives us free will, wisdom teaches us that when it comes to how He chooses to run His kingdom, our wisest choice is to say, "Yes, Lord."

For example, if He says, "Ask believing and it will be given to you," then our part is to ask believing, and His part is to give. Yet, sometimes we get it in our minds that we are the kings of His kingdom. We think, "Well, if God wants to do a certain thing in my life, He will do it." Yes, this sounds very noble and even as if we have faith, but if we have it in our minds that "because God is sovereign" we don't need to ask, then we have set ourselves up for failure.

Another example is that of following God's instructions. He tells us not to be anxious about anything, but someone might say, "Oh, I can't help it. I'm a worrier by nature." You may very well be a natural worrier, but if God tells us not to be anxious about anything, then we are perfectly capable of obeying Him. He's the King. If He gives instructions, it only makes sense to follow them.

God gives us simple instructions to follow, but we often think they don't apply to our situations. God will "understand" if we ignore the clear instruction to abstain from sexual immorality. He won't mind if we knowingly eat foods sacrificed to idols. Really? We can't afford to think like this.

Faith causes us to act. As we discover God's kingdom principles and live according to them, then we can have confidence that God will do what He's promised.

Gathering Sympathy Instead of Seeking Solutions

We all know that there are people who either exaggerate weaknesses or use their troubles to garner sympathy and attention from others. This is very unhealthy. Yes, the people who love us in our lives should care about us when we are suffering, but we mustn't use our trials to feed our emotions that need healing. Perhaps no one reading this book has ever done this before, but at least, most of us have been tempted.

When I face difficulties, I don't want anyone's sympathy because sympathy won't help me one bit. Yes, of course, we should express concern for each other, but not as if we are preparing for their memorial service. This is why I usually don't widely share my struggles with others. I don't want to open my personal life to a public discussion. If someone gets a call from me when I am having a hard time, it is because I need prayer and someone to stand with me to see victory, not to have a pity party.

Recently, I went through a health scare (previously mentioned). The only people who heard about this were our children and a couple close friends. I didn't want others to know because I didn't want to get advice or hear anyone's fears about it. I needed to focus my faith on Jesus, and I didn't want to have to battle other people's unbelief or worries about me. It's OK to do this, by the way—to protect your heart. Even Jesus sometimes limited the ones surrounding a need to only those who would believe.

> ### Mark 5:21-24, 35-42
> *Now when Jesus had crossed over again by boat to the other side, a great multitude gathered to Him; and He was by the sea. ²² And behold, one of the rulers of the synagogue came, Jairus by name. And when he saw Him, he fell at His feet ²³and begged Him earnestly, saying, "My little daughter lies at the point of death. Come and lay Your hands on her, that she may be healed, and she will live." ²⁴So Jesus went with him, and a great multitude followed Him and thronged Him.*
> *³⁵While He was still speaking, some came from the ruler of the synagogue's house who said, "Your daughter is dead. Why trouble the Teacher any further?"*
> *³⁶As soon as Jesus heard the word that was spoken, He said to the ruler of the synagogue,* **"Do not be afraid; only believe."** *³⁷And He permitted no one to follow Him except Peter, James, and John the brother of James. ³⁸Then He came to the house of the ruler of the synagogue, and saw a tumult and those who wept and wailed loudly. ³⁹When He came in, He said to them, "Why make this commotion and weep? The child is not dead, but sleeping."* **⁴⁰And they ridiculed Him. But when He had put them all outside,** *He took the father and the mother of the child, and those who*

were with Him, and entered where the child was lying. ⁴¹Then He took the child by the hand, and said to her, "Talitha, cumi," which is translated, "Little girl, I say to you, arise." ⁴²Immediately the girl arose and walked, for she was twelve years of age. And they were overcome with great amazement.

Responding to Life Based Only on Our Five Senses

We can't afford to let our faith to be weakened by focusing only on what we can perceive with our senses. When our bodies are screaming with pain, it is impossible to ignore, or if we are receiving threatening letters from creditors or a relationship is causing us too much grief, we will be tempted to get our eyes off of Jesus and put them on ourselves. Take a moment to refocus your heart on Jesus. He is with you, and He will not forsake you in your time of need.

Folding Instead of Having Faith When Sudden Storms Arise

We have a choice when sudden storms arise. Will we freak out accusing God of being asleep or will we choose to trust in Him? (See Day 22.) Remember, it pleases God when we choose to have faith in Him instead of panicking. The next time your ship is tossed, turn to your Father and see Him smiling back at you.

Ignoring the Power of Our Words

We have a choice of what comes out of our mouths, and one of the principles in God's kingdom is that our words have power both to give life and to bring death.

Proverbs 18:21
Death and life are in the power of the tongue,
and those who love it will eat its fruit.

Our words do matter, and they are a reflection of what is in our hearts. How we speak to our children is a prime example. Children who are belittled can grow up angry and insecure. Those who are encouraged and spoken to with kindness tend to be more confident and content.

How do we speak to ourselves? How do we speak to our problems? There is no need here to get all tied in knots about this, but we still need to acknowledge that our words are powerful and use them to build and not tear down.

We might find the following passage shocking at first, but keep in mind, it was directed to the hypocrites challenging Jesus, not to those who believed in Him. Even so, we see here again the importance that God places on words.

Matthew 12:33-37
"Either make the tree good and its fruit good, or else make the tree bad and its fruit bad; for a tree is known by its fruit. ³⁴Brood of vipers! How can you, being evil, speak good things? For out of the abundance of the heart the mouth speaks. ³⁵A good man out of the good treasure of his heart brings forth good things, and an evil man out of the evil treasure brings forth evil things. ³⁶But I say to you that for every idle word men may speak, they will give account of it in the day of judgment. ³⁷ For by your words you will be justified, and by your words you will be condemned."

How might these words instruct us? We are the "good man". Out of the good treasure of our hearts, we bring forth good things. Allow your lips to speak the good things that are in your heart. Instead of raising our fists to the heavens, let us lift our voices in praise.

Sluggishness

Sometimes we just get lazy about believing God to do big things. I experienced this at first with my journey of speaking to my headaches to be removed and cast into the sea and the cause of them. Sometimes, it just seemed easier to take aspirin instead. Expressing our faith in Him is really so easy. He asks so little of us: "Believe in Me and speak your faith in Me," but then we just don't.

Sometimes it seems easier at the moment to just whine and complain or get mad or feel depressed about our situation than to express our trust, gratitude, and love toward Him, but really they both take about the same amount of time, and what a difference our tiny efforts make. Let us ponder the examples of those who boldly believed in their God and imitate their faith.

> **Hebrews 6:11-12**
> *And we desire that each one of you show the same diligence to the full assurance of hope until the end, [12]that you **do not become sluggish**, but **imitate those who through faith and patience inherit the promises.***

Doubting

Doubting is not the temptation not to believe. It isn't the fears we face. It isn't the emotions that swirl about us as a storm is raging. Doubt isn't the reality we face when we are made aware of the facts about our situations. It isn't the insecurities we feel when standing in faith. All of these things are normal human emotions. **God is not asking us not to feel or to ignore the facts of our circumstances. He's asking us to choose to believe in Him in the midst of them.**

Doubting is much more sinister than our reasonable responses to trouble. It is a purposeful choice not to believe. The word for "doubt" in the Greek is **diakrino**. It means "to withdraw, to desert, to separate oneself in a hostile spirit, to oppose, strive with, dispute, contend, to be at variance with oneself".[37] When we doubt God, we are deserting faith in Him. We are separating from Him in a hostile manner. We are opposing Him, striving against Him, and disputing faith in Him. We are doing these things deliberately and knowingly. Doubt says, "I won't believe."

Faith comes by hearing the good news of what God has provided and promised in Christ. After we hear the good news, faith will come to us, but we have the choice to embrace faith or to doubt. Doubt nullifies faith.

Notice in the verses below the use of the word **diakrino** (doubt).

Romans 4:19-22
And not being weak (diseased, feeble, impotent) in faith (pistis), he did not consider his own body, already dead (since he was about a hundred years old), and the deadness of Sarah's womb. [20]He did not waver (diakrinō) at the promise of God through unbelief (apistia), but was strengthened in faith, giving glory to God, [21]and being fully convinced that what He had promised He was also able to perform.[22]And therefore "it was accounted to him for righteousness."

James 1:6-8
But let him ask in faith (pistis), with no doubting (diakrinō), for he who doubts (diakrinō) is like a wave of the sea driven and tossed by the wind. [7]For let not that man suppose that he

---

[37] Thayer

will receive anything from the Lord; ⁸he is a double-minded man, unstable in all his ways.
Mark 11:22-23
*So Jesus answered and said to them, "Have faith in God. ²³For assuredly, I say to you, whoever says to this mountain, 'Be removed and be cast into the sea,' and **does not doubt (diakrinō) in his heart, but believes** that those things he says will be done, he will have whatever he says.*

Giving Up Hope

When our struggles are long, lasting perhaps many years, we will be tempted to give up hope (joyful anticipation of good from God). We've heard everything. We've tried everything. We don't know what else we can do. We become unwilling to keep on fighting the good fight of faith.

When the doctors give someone a limited time to live, that person will be more inclined to prepare for death than to continue believing for life. Giving up seems the only rational option, and we might even have family and friends who will encourage us to let go, or who might even be "praying" that we pass away so we won't suffer any longer. In today's climate, there might be those who are inconvenienced by our illnesses who might try to coerce us to "go peacefully". These are very private moments indeed, but we have to ask ourselves, am I going to give up hope or continue believing?

This applies to every difficulty we face, not just to sickness or dying—and some of the circumstances we face, like divorce and financial ruin, feel like death, one that just goes on and on. It might seem like we can't afford to keep believing, but actually, we simply cannot afford to give up hope.

Romans 4:17-18
(As it is written, "I have made you a father of many nations") in the presence of Him

whom he believed—God, who gives life to the dead and calls those things which do not exist as though they did; [18]***who, contrary to hope, in hope believed***, *so that he became the father of many nations, according to what was spoken, "So shall your descendants be."*

How different the story would have been if Abraham had chosen to doubt. He had every possible reason to do so. His wife was too old to conceive. Period. Maybe you are facing death, or maybe you are experiencing a living death due to your situation. Don't give up hope in God. He is deserving of our hope in Him.

The Cares of This World and the Deceitfulness of Riches

Mark 4:18-20
Now these are the ones sown among thorns; they are the ones who hear the word, [19]*and the cares of this world, the deceitfulness of riches, and the desires for other things entering in choke the word, and it becomes unfruitful.* [20]*But these are the ones sown on good ground, those who hear the word, accept it, and bear fruit: some thirtyfold, some sixty, and some a hundred."*

The "cares of this world" refers to the cares/anxiety/distractions of life. Much is required of us on a daily basis. If we are not careful, these responsibilities become our entire focus, and we forget that our lives here are temporary.

Riches are deceitful. They promise us that if we have them, we will be at last content, but they do not live up to their promise. The constant pursuit of increased wealth for the purpose of self-realization can be a snare.

The desire/lust for other things can become an endless urge to accomplish. Just as riches are not evil, but the love of them, it is not always true that the desire to accomplish is necessarily wrong. God knows each of our hearts. What might be a benign bucket list for one could be a constant obsession and object of pride for another. Still, it is worth our time to consider how much energy and time we put into achievements and riches.

Whenever our focus is off of the good news of Jesus and our emphasis becomes this life and its pleasures of this world, we can't experience the glories He longs to give. We have no time to believe God for great things when we are concentrating on this life only.

This does not mean that 24 hours of each day must be filled with some religious pursuit. Even this way of thinking can choke the good news in our lives.

Here and Now Perspective

Nothing we go through on earth comes anywhere near to being worthy to be compared with the glorious future we have in Christ. It's so easy to forget this and allow ourselves to feel burdened down. Our Blessed Hope could happen at any time. Being focused on His imminent return as we navigate through this life is a powerful weapon against the enemies of our faith.

Romans 8:18-25

For I consider that the sufferings of this present time are not worthy to be compared with the glory which shall be revealed in us. [19]For the earnest expectation of the creation eagerly waits for the revealing of the sons of God. [20]For the creation was subjected to futility, not willingly, but because of Him who subjected it in hope; [21]because the creation itself also will be delivered from the bondage of corruption into the glorious liberty of the children of God. [22]*For we know that the whole creation groans and labors with birth pangs together until now.* [23]*Not only that, but we also who have the firstfruits of the Spirit, even we ourselves groan within ourselves, eagerly waiting for the adoption, the redemption of our body.* [24]*For we were saved in this hope, but hope that is seen is not hope; for why does one still hope for what he sees?* [25]*But if we hope for what we do not see, we eagerly wait for it with perseverance.*

1 Corinthians 15:51-54

Behold, I tell you a mystery: We shall not all sleep, but we shall all be changed— [52]*in a moment, in the twinkling of an eye, at the last trumpet. For the trumpet will sound, and the dead will be raised incorruptible, and we shall be changed.* [53]*For this corruptible must put on incorruption, and this mortal must put on immortality.* [54]*So when this corruptible has put on incorruption, and this mortal has put on immortality, then shall be brought to pass the saying that is written: "Death is swallowed up in victory."*

Isaiah 25:8

He will swallow up death forever,
And the Lord God will wipe away tears from all faces;
The rebuke of His people
He will take away from all the earth;
For the Lord has spoken.

Forgetting About the Bread and the Fish

Mark 6:44-52

*Now those who had eaten the loaves were about five thousand men. [45]Immediately He made His disciples get into the boat and go before Him to the other side, to Bethsaida, while He sent the multitude away. [46]And when He had sent them away, He departed to the mountain to pray. [47]Now when evening came, the boat was in the middle of the sea; and He was alone on the land. [48]Then He saw them straining at rowing, for the wind was against them. Now about the fourth watch of the night He came to them, walking on the sea, and would have passed them by. [49]And when they saw Him walking on the sea, they supposed it was a ghost, and cried out; [50]for they all saw Him and were troubled. But immediately He talked with them and said to them, "Be of good cheer! It is I; do not be afraid." [51]Then He went up into the boat to them, and the wind ceased. And they were greatly amazed in themselves beyond measure, and marveled. [52]**For they had not understood about the loaves, because their heart was hardened.***

Most of us have experienced many miracles in our lives. First of all, He saves us making us new creations. He provides for "all things pertaining to life and godliness". For many, God has opened the door for a better job and place to live. We are blessed with family and friends. He heals us. He lifts us up when we are weak. He sends people along to encourage us. He does big things for us that bring us to our knees in gratitude and praise.

Then something goes wrong, and we somehow totally forget how faithful He has been to us, and instead, panic and fear. We focus only on the trouble at hand. **We forget about the loaves and the fish.**

Faith expresses itself in praise. We praise because we believe in HIM. We praise because we believe in His goodness. We give thanks because we know He will do what He promises. We express our gratitude to Him because we trust in His love. We remember all the wonderful things He has done, and lift our praise to Him for all He will do. He is worthy of this.

When God hears us praising Him, He sees our faith in Him. Our faith in Him pleases Him and makes nothing impossible for us.

Day 36

FEAR INSTEAD OF FAITH

---

*M*any of the enemies listed in this section involve fear. It can be subtle in the form of nervousness about something, and it can be overwhelming as in feeling threatened or having extreme anxiety. It's important to keep in mind that once we begin to fear, our physical bodies will respond in some way which only complicates and confuses the situation. Once these chemicals get running around in our bodies, it takes quite some time for them to dissipate. It's important to recognize fear and cut it off before it overtakes us.

Here is a perfect example of this principle. Many years ago, we were camping with our young children who had each brought along a friend, in a state park which has bears in the area. Although the park itself has never had a problem with bears (since they stay away), it still causes one to be aware while hiking nearby.

However, while we were all snuggled in our tent one night and after the kids had settled down and were falling asleep, I heard bones being crushed outside as a bear was eating away at the garbage we foolishly had not put in the designated receptacle. I was HORRIFIED. Here we were in our tent with our three sweet children and three of their friends, and outside there was a bear probably only ten feet from our tent. I have NEVER been so afraid in my life, and there was nothing we could do. To make matters worse, there had been a case reported recently in another state that a boy had been mauled by a bear in his tent!

No one had cell phones in those days, so we couldn't call for help without notifying the bear that we were there. I was paralyzed with fear. How could I protect them? It would be all my fault if something happened to them. David, being a little braver and level-headed than I at that moment, unzipped the window of our tent and looked toward the noise. What did he see? Raccoons and skunks. No bears.

When he told me, I believed him, but my body was already full of those chemicals that one gets when faced with the impending doom of being eaten alive by bears. In my brain, I knew those bears were not there. I even peaked out myself. Still, I lay there horrified for several hours, not because I had reason to fear, but because the chemicals were still raging in my body—the ones that were preparing me to defend six children against a pack of bears!

Sometimes the fears we face are imagined, and other times they are real. In both scenarios, fear will cause our bodies to respond. **The best way to stop fear from progressing to this physical response is faith.** When fear arises, even legitimate fear, we can immediately express our trust in Jesus. Confessing aloud that He loves us, that He is with us, that He will help us—asking Him for wisdom and guidance, then praising Him for it—all of these counteract fear. This isn't a formula. It's just a fact. When we forget to fight fear with faith, and those chemicals begin raging, we can simply ask God to help us calm down so we can respond more rationally.

Remember Jairus who came to Jesus so that his dying daughter could be healed? It was only a matter of minutes before she would die. Jesus agreed to go with him to heal her, but on the way, the woman with an issue of blood touched the hem of his garment and was healed. By the time they were ready to continue their journey to heal his daughter, people from his house came and informed Jairus that he no longer needed to trouble Jesus for his daughter had died.

How would we feel if we had our hopes up that Jesus would heal our child, but then she died? Jesus knew exactly how he felt and immediately responded.

Mark 5:35-36
While He was still speaking, some came from the ruler of the synagogue's house who said, "Your daughter is dead. Why trouble the Teacher any further?"
[36] As soon as Jesus heard the word that was spoken, He said to the ruler of the synagogue, "Do not be afraid; only believe."

Here is another example, a more positive one of how powerful it is to "only believe". On one occasion, our son had a severe allergic reaction. He called me to tell me the symptoms he was experiencing. He was parked on a street, but he didn't know where he was. He said that everything around him looked like cartoonish figures framed by darkness. He was, at least, an hour from us, and I knew we couldn't get to him in time to help. I told him to hang up and call 911, and to let us know right away where he was.

My friend was visiting at the time. She'd come to see my gardens, so I quickly showed her around before my husband and I took off. Of course, we were concerned about him, but we were determined not to fear. On the drive to intercept our son, my husband and I prayed and rebuked the spirit of death. We confessed that our son would live and not die.

We got a call from him along the way. He was in the ambulance now, and they were taking him to a hospital even further away. He'd found his way to a street sign and could barely read it to tell the ambulance service where he was. God gave us faith to continue to trust in Him and not allow fear to overtake our hearts. We refused to entertain the idea that he might die. We both felt an amazing calm.

Unknown to us, his condition became very serious. His heart rate dropped to a life-threatening level. He was surrounded in the ER by several medical professionals trying to save his life. Tim said the impression he got from looking at them was that they feared they would lose him.

He then realized that he was going to die, but instead of being afraid, he felt joy knowing he would be able to leave this earth and be with Jesus. He had the sensation that he would pass through his skin and "go immediately into wonder and beauty with Jesus."

He said he could perceive Jesus right there with Him beyond a barrier that kept him in his body. There was, at some point, a moment when he felt he had left his body, but couldn't identify when. He said it seemed Jesus was just inches from him, and he wanted to go to Him.

But Jesus said to him, "No, you will not die. I still have work for you to do." At His word, Tim began to come back into his body as if he could not resist the reality that he would not die. He said that when he slipped back into his body, he felt happy because he had been with Jesus, but disappointed because he wanted to be there and not here.

When we arrived at the hospital, all of this had already transpired. Our son was on a stretcher extremely swollen and yellowish and obviously weak, but he was able to communicate with us. We comforted him, and he comforted us. We didn't know at that moment that we almost lost our beloved son. How we praise God for medical care, and how we praise God for calling and saving our son. Don't be afraid. Only believe.

PART 4

Exceeding Great and Precious Promises

Day 37

BETTER PROMISES
BASED ON A BETTER COVENANT

---

2 Peter 1:2-4

Grace and peace be multiplied to you in the knowledge of God and of Jesus our Lord, ³ as His divine power has given to us all things that pertain to life and godliness, through the knowledge of Him who called us by glory and virtue, ⁴ by which have been given to us exceedingly great and precious promises, that through these you may be partakers of the divine nature, having escaped the corruption that is in the world through lust.

When Peter wrote of "exceeding great and precious promises" he was likely referring to all the promises of God—the ones that have already been fulfilled in us through Christ, the promises that we need to live out this life, and those that we have concerning the life that will one day come when we put on immortality and live with Him forever.

Where he says that by these promises we become partakers of the divine nature, most of us remain in awe. Surely there will forever be only one God, so what does this mean? I believe the answer is found in understanding the word "partake". It is **koinonos**. The first part of this word is similar to the word **koinonia** which many believers associate with our fellowship with each other. The definition of **koinonos** is "a sharer, that is, associate: -companion, partaker, and partner".

This is beautiful even without further definition, but let me elaborate a bit more. The Holy Spirit lives inside of us, and we are one spirit with the Lord. In this way, we partake of His divine nature on earth. We also share in His power which has given us all that pertains to life and godliness. God's power dwells in us, and it also has given us exceedingly great and precious promises. Through these promises we were saved, are being saved, and will be saved. Oh, it's all too beautiful for my meager words. To be a partner with God, His associate, and His friend is amazing grace indeed.

Oh, the love that drew salvation's plan.
Oh, the grace that brought it down to man.
Oh, the mighty gulf that God did span at Calvary.

Mercy there was great and grace was free
Pardon there was multiplied to me
There my burdened soul found liberty
At Calvary.[38]

This book was written with one main goal, to help the body of Christ rediscover faith in God so that we will be equipped to overcome the overwhelming in our lives. Faith in God comes from hearing of His goodness and grace toward us. So, it seems fitting that this book come to a close by focusing on more of His provisions and promises. Though it is impossible to cover every promise here, let the treasure hunt continue!

Let us begin with the amazing promises given by God and foretold by Jeremiah of our relationship with God under the New Covenant.

---

[38] "At Calvary", words by William Reed Newell, 1895, ©Public Domain

Hebrews 8:6-12

But now He has obtained a more excellent ministry, inasmuch as He is also Mediator of a better covenant, which was established on better promises. ⁷For if that first covenant had been faultless, then no place would have been sought for a second. ⁸Because finding fault with them, He says: "Behold, the days are coming, says the Lord, when I will make a new covenant with the house of Israel and with the house of Judah— ⁹not according to the covenant that I made with their fathers in the day when I took them by the hand to lead them out of the land of Egypt; because they did not continue in My covenant, and I disregarded them, says the Lord. ¹⁰For this is the covenant that I will make with the house of Israel after those days, says the Lord: I will put My laws in their mind and write them on their hearts; and I will be their God, and they shall be My people. ¹¹None of them shall teach his neighbor, and none his brother, saying, 'Know the Lord,' for all shall know Me, from the least of them to the greatest of them. ¹²For I will be merciful to their unrighteousness, and their sins and their lawless deeds I will remember no more."

A Covenant for Us Not by Us

The Covenant God the Father made with God the Son is permanent. He didn't ask us to offer a sacrifice, or promise anything in order to receive it[39], so even if we aren't the

---

[39] Sadly, there are prayers presented to those desiring to be saved based on one's willingness to forsake sin or to make Jesus the Lord of every area of one's life. These formulas for salvation expressly contradict the pattern we see in Scripture. "Believe in the Lord Jesus Christ, and you will be saved." Salvation is by grace through faith—not of works (Rom. 10:9-10).

perfect recipient of His covenant, He will still keep His promises to us. This should be good news for us all, for since the New Covenant is between the Father and the Son, then we cannot break His Covenant.

Remember, that under the Old Covenant, the **people** swore, "All that the Lord has spoken we will do." Again and again, we hear the heart of God lamenting that the people had broken the Covenant. However, the Lord spoke through Jeremiah of the coming of a New Covenant which would not be like the Old Covenant, saying that the New Covenant would not be "according to the covenant that I made with their fathers in the day that I took them by the hand to lead them out of the land of Egypt, **My covenant which they broke**, though I was a husband to them, says the Lord," (Jer. 31:32). As we continue to read this passage, it becomes very clear Who would be doing the work in this covenant.

> **Hebrews 8:10-12**
> For this is the covenant that **I will make** with the house of Israel after those days, says the Lord: **I will put** My laws in their mind and write them on their hearts; and **I will be** their God, and they shall be My people. ¹¹None of them shall teach his neighbor, and none his brother, saying, 'Know the Lord,' for all shall know Me, from the least of them to the greatest of them. ¹²For **I will be** merciful to their unrighteousness, and their sins and their lawless deeds **I will remember** no more (oume)."

The Old Covenant consisted of "Thou shalt," and "Thou shalt not." In this New Covenant God says, "I will," and "I will not," (Isa. 54:9-10). He knew full well that He would remove forever any barriers between us and make us new creations who would be internally guided by His law of love.

A New Covenant Not Like the Old

Another glorious promise of the New and Better Covenant is that The New Covenant is not like the Old. It is completely different. Yet the impression received by most Christians today is that we are under both covenants, and this is clearly not the case, for as the writer of Hebrews proclaims in just a few verses after these, the old is obsolete (Heb. 8:13). Jesus is now our Mediator, not angels or prophets or priests. He Himself is the Mediator of a better covenant based on better promises.

All of those who believe in Jesus become full partakers of this New Covenant. Under the Old, there was a separation between Jew and Gentile (non-Jews), male and female, and slave and free. Now there is no difference. We are all sons of Abraham by faith in Jesus.

Galatians 3:21-29
*Is the law then against the promises of God? Certainly not! For if there had been a law given which could have given life, truly righteousness would have been by the law. ²²But the Scripture has confined all under sin, that the promise by faith in Jesus Christ might be given to those who believe. ²³But before faith came, we were kept under guard by the law, kept for the faith which would afterward be revealed. ²⁴Therefore the law was our tutor to bring us to Christ, that we might be justified by faith. ²⁵But after faith has come, we are no longer under a tutor. ²⁶For you are all sons of God through faith in Christ Jesus. ²⁷For as many of you as were baptized into Christ have put on Christ. ²⁸**There is neither Jew nor Greek, there is neither slave nor free, there is neither male nor female; for you are all one in Christ Jesus.** ²⁹And if you*

are Christ's, then you are Abraham's seed, and heirs according to the promise.

Although the prophecy concerning the New Covenant is addressed to the house of Israel and Judah, those who receive the New Covenant by faith in Jesus become one. Thus, by faith, we partake of the New Covenant.

Romans 2:28-29
For he is not a Jew who is one outwardly, nor is circumcision that which is outward in the flesh; [29] ***but he is a Jew who is one inwardly; and circumcision is that of the heart***, *in the Spirit, not in the letter; whose praise is not from men but from God.*

Ephesians 2:11-22
Therefore remember that you, once Gentiles in the flesh—who are called Uncircumcision by what is called the Circumcision made in the flesh by hands— [12]*that at that time you were without Christ, being aliens from the commonwealth of Israel and strangers from the covenants of promise, having no hope and without God in the world.* [13]***But now in Christ Jesus you who once were far off have been brought near by the blood of Christ.*** [14]***For He Himself is our peace, who has made both one, and has broken down the middle wall of separation,*** [15]***having abolished in His flesh the enmity, that is, the law of commandments contained in ordinances, so as to create in Himself one new man from the two, thus making peace***, [16]*and that He might reconcile them both to God in one body through the cross, thereby putting to death the enmity.* [17]*And He came and preached peace to you who were afar off*

and to those who were near. [18]For through Him we both have access by one Spirit to the Father. [19]Now, therefore, you are no longer strangers and foreigners, but fellow citizens with the saints and members of the household of God, [20]having been built on the foundation of the apostles and prophets, Jesus Christ Himself being the chief cornerstone, [21] in whom the whole building, being fitted together, grows into a holy temple in the Lord, [22] in whom you also are being built together for a dwelling place of God in the Spirit.

I Will Put My Laws in Their Mind and Write Them on Their Hearts

We used to assume that this meant that God writes the Ten Commandments in our minds and hearts. If ministers in the church today believed even that much, they would not feel the need to teach them so incessantly, would they—since God already wrote them in our hearts? Yet the Ten Commandments are routinely taught, vehemently defended, and monumentalized by the church.

The good news is that He is not speaking of the Ten Commandments. How could He when He just said that the New Covenant was NOT like the Old Covenant, and the Ten Commandments **are** the Old Covenant?

> ### Deuteronomy 4:13
> *So He declared to you **His covenant** which He commanded you to perform, the **Ten Commandments**; and He wrote them on two tablets of stone.*

Paul wrote that the law was our tutor to bring us to Christ, but now that faith has come, we are no longer under a tutor

(Gal. 3:24-25). Since this is the case, why would God write the law of Moses on our hearts?

Paul called the Ten Commandments the ministry of condemnation and the ministry of death (2 Cor. 3:7-11). Surely God would not write condemnation and death in our hearts and minds. Paul stated clearly that the law arouses sinful passions (Rom. 7:5) and strengthens sin (1 Cor. 15:56). If He were to write the law in our hearts, wouldn't that be counterproductive—stirring sinful desires and empowering sin?

So then, the question remains, what law exactly does God write in our hearts? It is the very law that sets us free.

> **Romans 8:2-4**
> For the **law of the Spirit of life in Christ Jesus has made me free from the law of sin and death**. *³ For what the law could not do in that it was weak through the flesh, God did by sending His own Son in the likeness of sinful flesh, on account of sin: He condemned sin in the flesh, ⁴ that the righteous requirement of the law might be fulfilled in us who do not walk according to the flesh but according to the Spirit.[40]*

That being said then, the good news and larger point to be made is that we no longer have an external commandment teaching and condemning us as did the Old Covenant. We are new creations with new hearts who are guided from within by the Spirit of God (Rom. 8:14) and taught by His grace (Titus 2:11-14).

Recently, a friend asked, "What is the difference between writing them on our minds or our hearts."

The answer rose up in me with complete simplicity as if I'd studied the question for quite some time. I said, "By

---

[40] Those "who do not walk according to the flesh but according to the Spirit" are Christians.

writing them in our minds, we *know* what is right. By writing them on our hearts, we *want* to do what is right."

I Will Be Their God and They Shall Be My People

It is tempting to skip over this promise of the New Covenant, yet when we begin to ponder it deeply, it can make us wonder, for certainly God was called "the God of Israel". How will what He is saying here be a "better" promise? Perhaps the answer can be found in the following verses.

> ### Hebrews 8:8-9
> *Because finding fault with them, He says: "Behold, the days are coming, says the Lord, when I will make a new covenant with the house of Israel and with the house of Judah— ⁹not according to the covenant that I made with their fathers in the day when I took them by the hand to lead them out of the land of Egypt; because they did not continue in My covenant ("My covenant which they broke" Jer. 31:32), and I disregarded them, says the Lord.*

God did not break His covenant with Israel in order to make a new one. He made a New Covenant because Israel broke the Old. This is in no way to imply that God was making things up as He went along. The Old Covenant wasn't God's Plan A with the New Covenant being Plan B. It was always God's intention to send His Son to redeem us (Rev.13:8). God desired to be their God, but they refused Him.

> ### Matthew 23:37-39
> *"O Jerusalem, Jerusalem, the one who kills the prophets and stones those who are sent to her! How often I wanted to gather your children together, as a hen gathers her chicks*

> *under her wings, but you were not **willing!***
> [38] *See! Your house is left to you desolate;*
> [39] *for I say to you, you shall see Me no more till you say, 'Blessed is He who comes in the name of the Lord!'"*

Under the New Covenant, God is forever our God, and because the New Covenant is not contingent on us obeying it, and because He makes us new creations who are led by His Spirit and taught by His grace, there is no danger that He will "disregard" us. God is now what He has always wanted to be. He is our God and all that this implies.

> *And I will be to them a God; not in such sense as he is the God of all mankind, or as he was the God of Israel in a distinguishing manner, but as he is the God of Christ, and of all the elect in him; and he is their God, not merely as the God of nature and providence, but as the God of all grace; he is so in a covenant way, and as in Christ... and as such, he has set his heart on them, and set them apart for himself; he saves them by his Son, adopts and regenerates them, justifies and sanctifies them, provides for them, protects and preserves them; and happy are they that are interested in this blessing of the covenant, which is preferable to everything else; they have everything, and can want no good thing; they need fear no enemy; all things work together for their good; and God continues to be their God in life and in death; so that they may depend on his love, be secure of his power, expect every needful supply of grace, and to be carried through every duty and trial, and to share in the first resurrection, and to enjoy eternal happiness.[41]*

---

[41] Gill's Exposition of the Entire Bible

His promise to be a God to us includes all that He provides and promises under the New Covenant. Everything is ours because He is God permanently to those who believe in His Son—both Jew and Gentile.

> **Romans 9:25-26**
> *"I will call them My people, who were not My people,*
> *And her beloved, who was not beloved."*
> *[26]"And it shall come to pass in the place where it was said to them,*
> *'You are not My people,'*
> *There they shall be called sons of the living God."*

This verse equates God's people as "sons of the living God". Under the New Covenant, we are His very children, and He is our Father.

> **1 John 3:1**
> *Behold what manner of love the Father has bestowed on us, that we should be called children of God!*
> **Galatians 4:4-7**
> *But when the fullness of the time had come, God sent forth His Son, born of a woman, born under the law, [5] to redeem those who were under the law, that we might receive the adoption as sons. [6] And because you are sons, God has sent forth the Spirit of His Son into your hearts, crying out, "Abba, Father!" [7] Therefore you are no longer a slave but a son, and if a son, then an heir of God through Christ.*

They Shall All Know Me

Consider how many sermons have been preached and how many songs have been sung which express the desire to know God or to know Him more. So needlessly we long and weep for this glorious provision which we have already been given in this New Covenant. We know God.

> **Hebrews 8:11 KJV**
> *And they shall not teach every man his neighbor, and every man his brother, saying, Know the Lord: for all shall know me, from the least to the greatest.*

It is entirely delightful to me that the word for "not" is our dear friend **oume**. Remember that **oume** is a double negative which strengthens the denial. We will not, will not ever again teach each other to "know the Lord". Why not? Because we already know Him.

The wording in Jeremiah (Hebrew), from which this passage is quoted is also very revealing.

> **Jeremiah 31:34 KJV**
> *And they shall teach no more every man his neighbour, and every man his brother, saying, Know the Lord: for they shall all know me, from the least of them unto the greatest of them, saith the Lord.*

The Hebrew word for "more" is **"ode, ode"** and means "again, repeatedly, still, more: - again, all life long, at all, besides, but, else, further (-more), henceforth, (any) longer, (any) more." Under the New Covenant, His promise is that we will not (and thus, need not) repeatedly (all our lives long) teach each other to know the Lord.

During our early adult Christian education, we were continually taught to not only know the Lord but to know Him more. This left us with an unsatisfied longing for something that we already had. Please consider the psychological conflict this engenders.

Beyond the unnecessarily taught need to know the Lord were the endless things we needed to do in order to know Him and to know Him more—a very long and ever-expanding list.

When we stop *trying* to know the Lord or to know Him more, and we recognize that we already know God, we can begin to enjoy this promised grace. We know God, and I should add that the idea that some of us know God more than others is also off-kilter for He adds, "from the least of them to the greatest." Yes, it is entirely possible that someone who has walked with the Lord long and studied the Bible more years will know more about God and clearly have more experience with God, but we are all on an equal plane when it comes to knowing God. Glory to His name. What a glorious blessing to know the living God. What rest!

Paul wrote about knowing God, but the church has mostly misinterpreted what he said. You have likely heard this passage used to show that we still need to know God or know him "more", but read it again, and notice what it was that Paul said he did (in the past before he was a Christian) to know God.

Philippians 3:4-11

If anyone else thinks he may have confidence in the flesh, I more so: ⁵circumcised the eighth day, of the stock of Israel, of the tribe of Benjamin, a Hebrew of the Hebrews; concerning the law, a Pharisee; ⁶concerning zeal, persecuting the church; concerning the righteousness which is in the law, blameless. ⁷But what things were gain to me, these I have counted loss for Christ. ⁸Yet indeed I also count all things loss for the excellence of the knowledge of Christ Jesus my Lord, for

> *whom I have suffered the loss of all things,*
> *and count them as rubbish, that I may gain*
> *Christ ⁹and be found in Him,* **not having my**
> **own righteousness, which is from the law,**
> **but that which is through faith in Christ,**
> **the righteousness which is from God by**
> **faith; ¹⁰that I may know Him** *and the power*
> *of His resurrection, and the fellowship of His*
> *sufferings, being conformed to His death, ¹¹if,*
> *by any means, I may attain to the resurrection*
> *from the dead.*

Paul gave up his self-righteousness which he derived from obeying the law for the righteousness which is only by faith in Christ—in other words, he put his faith in Jesus (was saved) so that he could know Christ. It's perfectly clear here. When we believe in Jesus, we know God.

For

The word "for" connects what has been previously said to the reason stated that follows. In other words, "because" He is merciful to our righteousness and He remembers our sins no more: God writes His law in our hearts; He is our God; we are His people, and we know Him. None of these things would be possible if we were not permanently forgiven.

I Will Be Merciful to Their Unrighteousness

The word for "merciful" used here is not the normal word used for "merciful" elsewhere in the New Testament. The only other time this word is used, it is in the sentence, "*Far be it* from you." The concept of our sins being moved away from us is not uncommon in Scripture, but the author could have simply put it in those terms if that's what he meant. Perhaps we would do best to go back to Jeremiah, who first gave this prophecy. He wrote, "I will forgive their iniquity", and this is a fair interpretation.

Yet, surely, if He was merciful to our unrighteousness when we were His enemies, He will be merciful to us now that we are His children.

> **Romans 5:19**
> *For as by one man's disobedience many were made sinners, so also by one Man's obedience many will be made righteous.*

Their Sins and Lawless Deeds I Will Remember No More

What a beautiful thing it is to know that He not only forgives our iniquities but that He will never ever again bring them to his remembrance. Believers in Jesus want to please God. We don't desire to sin. If we do sin, though, we are already forgiven, and God, who is our God, will never turn His back on us.

The reason this promise is so powerful and how it applies to overcoming the overwhelming is this. Often when we are suffering trials or sudden storms arrive, the enemy will bring to our remembrance some area in our lives where we are falling short. Because we've had it drummed into us that God sends hard times to purge us of our sins or that He ignores our prayers when we fall short, we are tempted to think these hard times are from God. This can cause us to accept them instead of fighting. When we finally fully see the truth that God is not keeping a record of our sins and that He is not bringing them to His remembrance, we can confidently fight against the lies and accusations of the enemy and stand in the time of trouble.

> **Romans 4:5-8**
> *But to him who does not work but **believes** on Him who justifies the ungodly, his **faith** is*

accounted for righteousness, ⁶just as David also describes the blessedness of the man to whom God imputes righteousness apart from works:
⁷"Blessed are those whose lawless deeds are forgiven,
And whose sins are covered;
⁸**Blessed is the man to whom the Lord shall not (oume) impute sin.**"

Day 38

ALL SUFFICIENCY IN ALL THINGS

*T*he Scriptures have much to say about money including multiple warnings about becoming obsessed with the love of it. Jesus clearly stated that we cannot serve God and money and warned that the deceitfulness of riches chokes the word, and we become unfruitful (Mk. 4:19). Paul wrote to Timothy telling him to instruct the rich to not be haughty or trust in uncertain riches but in the living God—to do good so that they would be rich in good works, ready to give, and willing to share (1Tim 6:17-18). This chapter is written assuming that the reader knows these warnings and will heed them.

When we speak of "prosperity", it should be in terms of our whole well-being, and not only about finances. God's will for us is "to prosper and be in health" even as our souls prosper (3 John 1:2). All the money and good health in the world can't make up for a suffering soul.

Without denying these important truths, let us go on to examine the topic of good news specifically when it comes to finances. My reasoning is that for many people, their overwhelming situation pertains to money and that by knowing the good news, our faith will grow to meet this need. Assuming that too much money is a "problem" that can likely be solved by finding a reliable financial adviser, we will focus in on the difficulty of not having enough.

Let us avoid the extreme arguments, the first being that God wants us to live a life of poverty, and the other that God "owes" us a life of abundance; and rather concentrate on what the Bible actually has to say about money without filtering through either bias.

Why is this area of finances so difficult for so many? I believe the answer is simple. We all have to provide for ourselves and our families, and money really doesn't grow on trees. It doesn't matter if someone lives in a society that trades labor for goods or one that uses a monetary system to purchase, we all need to supply for the necessities of life.

Perhaps we can find our first agreement with this obvious statement: prosperity is relative to where someone lives on the earth. What might be considered success in one country could be seen as a meager living somewhere else. It is unwise to impose our individual cultural concepts of wealth on each other.

Another position with which most can agree is that a person's individual perspective on life, in general, can affect how he perceives success. One man might be perfectly content with earning just what he needs to pay his bills. A married man will need to make more—add children and the need grows. Someone might be inspired to start a company and make enough money to provide for employees. Another might be motivated to have an abundance to share. Whatever our views on the matter, let's agree that no one way is "right" or "wrong" but more likely has to do with the gifts and callings God has on our lives.

The Lord is Our Provider

Jehovah Jireh, God is My Provider, is perhaps one of the most tender names of God. We find it early on in Scripture when Abraham showed his willingness to give his son to the Lord which was a type of the fact that God gave His only Son for us. Isaac asked His father about where they would get a sacrifice, and Abraham assured him that God would provide. Much has been said about this incident, but without one doubt, Abraham knew that at the end of this story his promised son would be alive, believing that God would even raise him from the dead (Heb. 11:19). Abraham's faith in this situation was amazing indeed.

For us, it reveals the heart of God and who He is—Our Provider.

Genesis 22:13-14
Then Abraham lifted his eyes and looked, and there behind him was a ram caught in a thicket by its horns. So Abraham went and took the ram, and offered it up for a burnt offering instead of his son. ¹⁴And Abraham called the name of the place, The-Lord-Will-Provide; as it is said to this day, "In the Mount of the Lord it shall be provided."

God is our Provider. It is not only what He does for us, but also, who He is to us. His very nature is to provide for us, and He provides for our every need; not only financially, but in every way including sending His own Son to lay down His life for us to take away our sins and place us in righteous fellowship with Him.

Knowing just this marvelous basic fact about God's nature should cause us to cease viewing Him as one who steals, and kills, and destroys instead of the One who gives life and that abundantly. He is for us, not against us. He gives and does not take away. When we go through difficult times, He doesn't sit back and enjoy watching us suffer. He is instead compassionate and caring willing to rescue us from any storm.

He wants us to have peace and joy and satisfaction, not constant internal struggle and sadness and frustration. When trials come, shall we shake our tiny fists at Him and say, "God, what are You trying to do to me?" Shall we not rather remember that He is our Provider, believe in Him, and praise Him that He will take care of us?

Seriously, this is one of the ugliest of practices in which Christians engage. Plans we are making fall through. Who do we blame? God. A job we were counting on is given to someone else. Who is the culprit? God, of course. We get a flat tire. Who is the one working against us? God, again! "What are You trying to teach me, Lord?" we cry as if the only way God can speak to us is through spoiling every plan we make!

No, my dearly beloved brothers and sisters, **God is not our nemesis!** May the Lord set us free from seeing our Father as someone who is determined to make our lives miserable—as someone who can only communicate with us by sending judgments and adversity!

Jesus came to earth taking upon Himself human flesh and lived among us. Though He was Creator of everything, He humbled Himself to the point of dying for us on the cross. Is this the picture of a God who is constantly trying to mess up our finances?

> ### 2 Corinthians 8:9
> *For you know the grace of our Lord Jesus Christ, that though He was rich, yet for your sakes He became poor, that you through His poverty might become rich.*

Don't Worry

Jesus instructed His disciples not to worry about food and clothing and promised to provide for all their needs. He has promised to take care of us. If we are suffering right now—if we don't have food or clothing or shelter, we need only ask, for He who has promised is faithful to keep His promises.

> ### Matthew 6:25-34
> *"Therefore I say to you, **do not worry** about your life, what you will eat or what you will drink; nor about your body, what you will put*

on. Is not life more than food and the body more than clothing? ²⁶Look at the birds of the air, for they neither sow nor reap nor gather into barns; yet your heavenly Father feeds them. **Are you not of more value than they?** ²⁷Which of you by worrying can add one cubit to his stature?

²⁸"So why do you worry about clothing? Consider the lilies of the field, how they grow: they neither toil nor spin; ²⁹and yet I say to you that even Solomon in all his glory was not arrayed like one of these. ³⁰Now if God so clothes the grass of the field, which today is, and tomorrow is thrown into the oven, **will He not much more clothe you**, O you of little faith?

³¹"Therefore do not worry, saying, 'What shall we eat?' or 'What shall we drink?' or 'What shall we wear?' ³²For after all these things the Gentiles seek. **For your heavenly Father knows that you need all these things.** ³³But seek first the kingdom of God and His righteousness, and all these things shall be added to you. ³⁴Therefore do not worry about tomorrow, for tomorrow will worry about its own things. Sufficient for the day is its own trouble.

Some have interpreted verse 33 to mean that in order for this promise to take place, we must put God first and live righteously. Jesus did not say that. We are to seek His kingdom with the purpose of finding it, and we find it and become partakers of it when we receive the King—when we are saved. When we are saved, we become the very righteousness of God.

> **Hebrews 12:28 NASB**
> *Therefore, since we receive a kingdom which cannot be shaken, let us show gratitude, by which we may offer to God an acceptable service with reverence and awe.*
> **2 Corinthians 5:21**
> *For He made Him who knew no sin to be sin for us, that we might become the righteousness of God in Him.*

As our Provider, He has made the way for us to enter His kingdom and receive His righteousness by simply believing in Jesus. Now, as King of His kingdom, He will do as He promised and supply our every need. We don't need to worry or fret about our needs. He knows we have them, and we are of great value to Him. This is excellent news and a reason for rest! We don't need to make a priority list with His name at the top and endlessly seek to live righteously before Him. We have already done what He requires. We have sought and received His kingdom and His righteousness, now "all these things" will be added to us.

A Word about Tithing

In my first book, there is an entire chapter on this topic of tithing which I encourage you to study if you have never been given this glorious news: New Covenant believers are not under a mandate to tithe. This means we are not blessed because we tithe, and we are certainly not cursed if we do not.

When Jesus died, He redeemed us from the curse of the law when He became a curse for us by being crucified on a tree. So even though God through Malachi told the children of Israel that they were "cursed with a curse" because they did not obey the law of tithes and offerings, we are only blessed because we have received the blessing of Abraham through faith in Jesus and are not under the law of tithing.

Galatians 3:13-14
Christ has redeemed us from the curse *of the law, having become a curse for us (for it is written, "Cursed is everyone who hangs on a tree"), ¹⁴that the blessing of Abraham might come upon the Gentiles in Christ Jesus, that we might receive the promise of the Spirit through faith.*

David and I formerly believed that we were required to give ten percent of everything we received and we were quite meticulous to do so for many years. Additionally, since we'd been taught to give more than the tithe, we did this too. We believed that if we did this God would "open the windows of heaven and pour out a blessing" that we would not be able to contain.

We never stopped to question why it was that we were always barely making it. Yes, our very basic needs were being met, but it seemed this promise of overwhelming blessings never manifested.

It wasn't until we came to understand that tithing was not a requirement of New Covenant believers that our finances started taking a turn for the better, and we know multiple friends who have experienced this exact same thing.

Grace Giving

If tithing is not the pattern for those of us under grace, then what is? Paul, the one to whom Jesus personally gave the gospel of grace and who never once told believers that they were required to tithe explains this best.

2 Corinthians 9:7
So let each one give as he purposes in his heart, not grudgingly or of necessity; for God loves a cheerful giver.

Grace giving is motivated by love not law. We give from faith and not out of fear. We don't give to get blessings, for we are already blessed with everything pertaining to life and godliness. Nor do we give because if we don't God will hold back blessings from us. We give because we are blessed and know that God has promised to continue to bless us abundantly so that we can continue to give abundantly.

An Abundance for Every Good Work

Jesus said, "It is more blessed to give than receive." If you've been on the end of needing to receive, you will thoroughly agree. It is a blessing when God provides our needs, but it is also a humbling experience to need to receive. It is far more joyous when God gives us an abundance so that we can be the ones on the giving end.

2 Corinthians 9:8
And God is able to make all grace abound toward you, that you, always having all sufficiency in all things, may have an abundance for every good work.

We give willingly and cheerfully knowing that this pleases God and that He will make sure that all (every) grace superabounds (which is what "abounds" means here) toward us so that we can always have all sufficiency (contentedness) in all things, so that we may have a superabundance for every good work (benefit).

This should encourage us. As we read through 2 Corinthians 8 and 9, we see the whole picture. God causes His grace to abound toward us so that not only are our needs met as He promised, but that we also have an abundance to share for every good work. **This is true prosperity—having an abundance to share.**

We don't give in order to get, but we can rest assured that to the degree we are generous to that same degree God will be generous with us.

> ### 2 Corinthians 9:6
> *But this I say: He who sows sparingly will also reap sparingly, and he who sows bountifully will also reap bountifully.*

I Can Do All Things

We Christians like to quote this verse: "I can do all things through Christ who strengthens me", but do most of us understand the context? What was Paul talking about when he wrote down those words?

> ### Philippians 4:10-13
> *But I rejoiced in the Lord greatly that now at last your care for me has flourished again; though you surely did care, but you lacked opportunity. ¹¹Not that I speak in regard to need, for I have learned in whatever state I am, to be content: ¹² I know how to be abased, and I know how to abound. Everywhere and in all things I have learned both to be full and to be hungry, both to abound and to suffer need. ¹³I can do all things through Christ who strengthens me.*

Paul learned about a special type of contentment. In his ministry, there were times when he had little to eat. Perhaps this was when he was in jail or when he ministered in locations where the people had very little to offer him. There were times when he stayed in the homes of those who were well-off and, therefore, provided for him in abundance, and there were other places when he worked with his own hands to supply his own needs and the needs of those who worked for him. Paul didn't worry about these things. He knew that Jesus promised to take care of him. When he wrote that he could do all things through Christ who strengthened him, he was saying that he could minister in any situation because Jesus strengthened him to do so. He could live in abundance without guilt, and he could live with little without shame. In times of plenty and in times when nothing seems to be going as it should, we can be victorious and live in peace knowing that our Provider will take care of us.

Habakkuk 3:17-19
Though the fig tree may not blossom,
Nor fruit be on the vines;
Though the labor of the olive may fail,
And the fields yield no food;
Though the flock may be cut off from the fold,
And there be no herd in the stalls—
¹⁸Yet I will rejoice in the Lord,
I will joy in the God of my salvation.
¹⁹The Lord God is my strength;
He will make my feet like deer's feet,
And He will make me walk on my high hills.

A Better Covenant with Better Promises

I enjoy studying the blessings of the Old Covenant with the truth in mind that the New Covenant is better and so are its promises. To me, this means that any promise of the Old Covenant is mine also and without obedience to the law.

Many of the blessings of law had to do with our goods and possessions being blessed and increased. Shall not we be blessed this way and even more so under grace?

Deuteronomy 28:2-14

And all these blessings shall come upon you and overtake you, because you obey the voice of the Lord your God[42]:
³"Blessed shall you be in the city, and blessed shall you be in the country.
*⁴"Blessed shall be the **fruit of your body**[43], the **produce of your ground** and the **increase of your herds**, the **increase of your cattle and the offspring of your flocks.***
*⁵"Blessed shall be your **basket** and your kneading bowl.*
⁶"Blessed shall you be when you come in, and blessed shall you be when you go out.
⁷"The Lord will cause your enemies who rise against you to be defeated before your face; they shall come out against you one way and flee before you seven ways.
*⁸"The Lord will command the **blessing on you in your storehouses** and in all to which you set your hand, and He will **bless you in the land** which the Lord your God is giving you.*
*⁹"The Lord will establish you as a holy people to Himself, just as He has sworn to you, if you keep the commandments of the Lord your God and walk in His ways.[44] ¹⁰Then all peoples of the earth shall see that you are called by the name of the Lord, and they shall be afraid of you. ¹¹ And the Lᴏʀᴅ **will grant you plenty of goods**, in the **fruit of your body**, in the **increase of your livestock**, and in the **produce of your ground**, in the land of which the Lord swore to your fathers to give you. ¹² The Lord will open to you **His good treasure**, the*

---

[42] For us, it is because we believe in Him and love each other.

[43] Your children are blessed.

[44] If you believe in Him and love each other.

*heavens, to give the rain to your land in its season, and to **bless all the work of your hand. You shall lend to many nations, but you shall not borrow.*** [13] *And the* LORD *will make you the **head and not the tail**; you shall be **above only, and not be beneath**, if you heed the commandments of the* LORD *your God, which I command you today, and are careful to observe them.* [14]*So you shall not turn aside from any of the words which I command you this day, to the right or the left, to go after other gods to serve them.*

All of these things are ours and even more! To top that off, they are ours by faith!

We Are Not Under Law but Under Grace

I like to read the Psalms now inserting the word "grace" for the word "law" because I know that the Old Covenant believers longed for what we possess. Please don't think that I'm rewriting Scripture. God forbid! I can appreciate the Psalms as they were written, but I always keep in mind the historical and covenantal context. Paul wrote, "Sin will not have dominion over you because you are not under law but under grace," (Rom. 6:14).

Consider Psalm 1, for example, in this light. While the Old Covenant promises were contingent on obeying the Ten Commandments and other statutes, the New Covenant, which is a better covenant based on better promises, is based on believing in Jesus. If prosperity (success) was promised under the Old Covenant due to obeying the law, shall not prosperity be ours who are under grace?

Psalm 1
Blessed is the man
Who walks not in the counsel of the ungodly,

Nor stands in the path of sinners,
Nor sits in the seat of the scornful;
² But his delight is in the law of the LORD
(But His delight is in the grace of God)
And in His law he meditates day and night.
(And in His grace he meditates day and night.)
³ **He shall be like a tree**
Planted by the rivers of water,
That brings forth its fruit in its season,
Whose leaf also shall not wither;
And whatever he does shall prosper.

Entitlement

By the way, no one owes us anything. God has promised to supply, and He may well do that through others, but it is wrong to have the attitude that just because a fellow believer has wealth, we deserve a piece of it. It doesn't matter if he inherited the money or earned it. His money is his, and he is under no obligation to give it to us. Christianity is not a redistribution of wealth. Giving is always voluntary in the kingdom of God. If we need money, we bring our needs before God and expect that He will show us how to earn a living.

2 Thessalonians 3:6-12
*But we command you, brethren, in the name of our Lord Jesus Christ, that you withdraw from every brother who walks disorderly and not according to the tradition which he received from us. ⁷For you yourselves know how you ought to follow us, for we were not disorderly among you; ⁸**nor did we eat anyone's bread free of charge, but worked with labor and toil night and day, that we might not be a burden to any of you,** ⁹not because we do not have authority, but to make ourselves an example of how you*

should follow us. ¹⁰For even when we were with you, we commanded you this: **If anyone will not work, neither shall he eat.** *¹¹For we hear that there are some who walk among you in a disorderly manner, not working at all, but are busybodies. ¹²Now those who are such we command and exhort through our Lord Jesus Christ that they work in quietness and eat their own bread.*

Facts of Life

Christians have a tendency to over-spiritualize circumstances in life, especially with the false view that God is manipulating them to squeeze us into a character change, teach us some spiritual lesson, or punish us for who-knows-what. This is especially true when it comes to financial success. We tend to conclude that if all is going well, God must love us. If things turn south, God is against us.

While it is true that sometimes we make unwise choices when it comes to money, and this results in financial loss, we can learn from these situations, dust ourselves off, learn from our mistakes, and get right up and keep going. It is ridiculous to blame God for the natural consequences of our own wrong business choices. God is so good, however, that He lovingly instructs us by His grace and helps us recover.

The truth is, God is for us 100% at all times. Sure, we will make mistakes and maybe have a bad attitude now and then, but He is still for us and not against us. Let's be reasonable. Weather happens. When it does, economies suffer. Natural disasters are costly, and they can bring whole businesses to a standstill, and there can be great economic loss. If we think that God is sending floods and earthquakes to "teach us a lesson" or that He is "raining on our parade" we are taking the weather personally.

Economic bubbles burst. Stock markets crash. People become hesitant to buy and sell due to economic instability, and this causes financial stress. Let's not blame God for these things. He's not out to destroy us. Let us instead believe that God will take the turmoil that is going on around us and work it together for our good.

If our minds are clouded by images of a God who is working against us, it will be difficult for us to believe for miracles, and our abilities to hear Him will be muffled by our fears. When we know the good and benevolent character of God and believe in Him to help us, we can be inspired and receive the grace to do things we've never dreamed, and God can open doors for us which we didn't even know existed.

This very situation happened to us. When we were younger, we were in a ministry that did not meet all of our needs, so my husband went to work part-time for a friend doing landscape maintenance and then later worked in pest control. These were not in my husband's plans for his life. We both wanted to work in the ministry full-time, but the reality was that this particular ministry could not support us.

With our youngest child then a three-year-old and the desire to still be a stay-at-home mom, it was unclear how I could help financially. A friend of mine in a similar financial situation began doing daycare in her home, but I was sure that was something I would never want to do. As I began to pray about how I might contribute to the family income, grace came sweetly to me to do daycare. In a very short time, I was licensed, and with very little advertising, my legal client load was filled. On a very small scale, I'd started my own business. What was supposed to be a horrible job, turned out to be wonderful. Our son had playmates, my clients had a safe and loving place for their children, I had some extra income, and confidence began to grow in me working with other people's children.

The grace to do this job lasted two and a half years at which time the Lord opened doors for me to take classes toward getting my teaching credential while working as an instructional assistant at our children's school. After I earned my credential, for twelve years, there was grace to work as a teacher. It was a financial risk to let go of teaching, but it was shortly after that when God opened doors of ministry for us, and eventually, the cherished dream of being a Christian author was fulfilled.

Perhaps you have a desire to work in a certain field. There might be several jobs and education that finally bring you to that place. Each one of them will contribute to your future success. When we understand that we are led by the Spirit, that God is for us not against us, and that even if we take a "wrong" turn, He will use that for our good, we are more confident to move forward and are better able to hear the Spirit within us leading. Have faith in Him to take care of you and bring you where He wants you to be.

I Will Never Leave You or Forsake You

We've all heard this verse before, and what a wonderful promise it is—that God will never leave us or forsake us, no, not ever. What many believers don't know is that this promise is set in the context of money!

> ### Hebrews 13:5-6
> *Let your conduct be **without covetousness**;*
> *be content with such things as you have. For*
> *He Himself has said, "I will never leave you*
> *nor forsake you." ⁶So we may boldly say:*
> *"The Lord is my helper;*
> *I will not fear.*
> *What can man do to me?"*

Now that brings a whole new meaning to the verse, especially when there are threats coming in our direction from banks and other creditors. Think about this. Even if our belongings were to be repossessed, God would never abandon us in this area of finances. He will provide for our needs. This is why we can, as Paul did, learn how to be content in every situation—in times of abundance and in times of need. God will not ever abandon us. So we don't need to cover or worry about our needs being met. We can find peace even in the midst of financial turmoil.

Following is a collection of verses about finances which review the contents of this chapter. It is included as an encouragement loaded with good news to anyone who may be frustrated with money matters. Enjoy it as is or write your own prayer of praise. Saying these things doesn't make them so. They are so, and that is why we speak them. As we rehearse these truths, we hear them, and faith in God will come for our finances.

FINANCIAL PRAYER OF PRAISE

Father, in Your Name
I cast my care upon You
Knowing that You care for me (1 Pet. 5:6-7).
I refuse to be anxious any longer
about my finances.
Instead,
I make my request before You
with supplication and thanksgiving (Phil. 4:6-7).
You Yourself
have promised me
that when it comes to finances
You will not in any way
Fail me nor give me up
Nor leave me without support
You will not
You will not
You will not
In any degree
Leave me helpless
Nor forsake nor let me down
Or relax Your hold on me
Assuredly not! (Heb. 13:5 AMP).
You take care of the birds,

and You will make sure that we have food to eat.
You array the grass of the field,
and You will clothe me (Mt. 6:25-32).
I trust You Lord.
I sought and received Your kingdom and have
received Your righteousness,
So now, all of my needs
Will be provided (Mt. 6:33-34).
I thank You that Your Spirit is leading me.
I cry out to You because You are my Father (Rom.
8:14-15),
I trust that as my Father, You will not judge or punish me
by bringing poverty and failure into my life.
Instead, You will lead me by Your Spirit
and teach me by Your grace.
I speak to this mountain of financial need in my life,
I command you in the name of Jesus
to be removed and cast into the sea
and the cause of it (Mk.11:23).
I believe that You are the Lord My Provider (Gen. 22:14).
I believe that because You are my Shepherd,
I will not lack (Psa. 23:1).
I believe that everything I do will prosper
Because I have trusted in Your grace (Psa. 1:3).
I thank You for all You have done
And all You will do.
Thank-You for giving me
the ability to make wealth (Deut. 28:18).
I confess that I can do all things
Through You who strengthens me (Phil 4:13).
Thank-You, Father for the joy of giving.
I purpose to cheerfully and willingly give abundantly,
Not because I need to
Or because I have to,
But because it brings You joy (2 Cor. 9:7-8).
Lord, I trust that You will give to me
All sufficiency in all things, so that

I may have an abundance
For every good work (2 Cor. 9:7-8).
I will sow bountifully, and
I will reap bountifully (2 Cor.9:6).
I will be enriched in everything for all liberality
So that I may bring thanksgiving to You
And bring glory to Your name (2 Cor.9:9-15).
Jesus, I confess that this New Covenant is better
and it is based on better promises.
Everything You promised Your people
Under the Old Covenant is mine
only better (Heb. 8:6).
I am blessed wherever I go.
The fruit of my body is blessed.
My work is blessed (Deut. 28:2-14).
I ask that instead of needing to borrow,
I will be able to lend.
Thank-You, Lord, that You have given to me
All things richly to enjoy (1 Tim. 6:17).
Thank-You for Your indescribable gift!
You are able
to do exceedingly abundantly
Above all that I ask or think,
According to Your power that works in me (Eph. 3:20).
To You, Oh Lord, be glory and majesty
Dominion and power
Both now and forever. (Jude 25)
Amen, so be it!

Compiled by C. D. and D. H. Hildebrand
2007 and 2015

Day 39

HEALING GRACE

I've often wondered why the topic of divine healing wasn't addressed at length in at least one of Paul's letters to the churches, and the only answer that makes any sense to me at all is that it simply was not controversial at that time. Miracles routinely happened, and healing was commonplace (Acts 3-4, 4:29-30, 5:12-16, 8:6-7, 8:13, 9:34, 9:36-42,14:8-12, 15:12, 16:18-19, 19:11-12, 20:9-12, 28:3-6, 28:8, 28:9). However, since then, the church has added and subtracted from this truth just as we have on so many other topics.

How wonderful it would be simply to share the good news about healing (or any other grace for that matter) without needing to address the multiple layers of contradictory teachings that have become the body of what so many collectively believe. Imparting this good news only, seems preferable, but after finishing, there would remain so many ifs, ands, and buts, that the whole of the truth about divine healing would be nullified, and my readers would remain confused on the matter. Good news brings faith and freedom, but just as surely as law cancels out grace, teachings bent on discounting the truth of the grace of God cancel out faith in it. My hand being forced, I shall share the truth as purely from Scripture as I can, while also addressing the traditions that have been added over the centuries which strip this glorious good news of its power in our lives.

If you find yourself preparing your list of objections as if going to battle, or you are cheering me on thinking you know what I am going to say next, may I ask you to please put your current understanding of the topic aside? I'm not asking you not to use your brain or forsake analyzing what is being presented here, only that you allow your heart to listen and to hear.

Consider this, many of us, at first, rejected the good news of the gospel of God's grace later to learn that we had it all wrong. What a joy it was to discover that we are completely forgiven, righteous, and holy before God apart from works. Please consider the possibility that on this topic also, what you were taught or the conclusions to which you came whether pro or con might also be incorrect. If you would, pray like this, "Father, I want to know the truth. If I'm missing something on this topic, please speak to my heart. If I believe things that are not true, show me. If this is not the truth, show me." If after you have heard me, you still disagree, I see no reason to separate into camps, but rather let us agree to disagree knowing that one day we "shall know even as we are known".

This topic becomes confusing because humans are biased and because, as I mentioned before, we tend to form our doctrines around our experiences instead of letting Scripture speak for itself. At one extreme, we have people saying that healing is "guaranteed" to all believers and that if one isn't healed, it's because he lacks faith. On the other side, we have those who absolutely do not believe that divine healing is for believers today, some even declaring that anyone who teaches that it is for today is teaching "doctrines of demons". Both views are ridiculous. That being said, allow me to present the case for the grace of divine healing keeping in mind that when we hear of the good news of His grace toward us, faith will come.

The God Who Heals You

In Exodus 15 we find the children of Israel rejoicing over the miracle of God opening the Red Sea so they could escape the Egyptians who sought to destroy them. From this glorious victory, Moses led the people into the Wilderness of Shur where they were three days without water. When they finally found water in Marah, it was not safe to drink. When Moses cried out to the Lord, God showed him a tree, and after he cast it into the bitter water, the water became drinkable. We can only imagine the joy of this scene. These are the verses that follow.

> **Exodus 15:25-26**
> *There He made a statute and an ordinance for them, and there He tested them, ²⁶and said, "If you diligently heed the voice of the Lord your God and do what is right in His sight, give ear to His commandments and keep all His statutes, I will put none of the diseases on you which I have brought on the Egyptians.* **For I am the Lord who heals you.***"*

Our God calls Himself, Jehovah Rapha, the Lord who heals us. Some have said this was referring only to the waters that were healed and that the truth for us today is that God can heal the difficult situations we encounter, and yes, He can, but notice in verse 26 the Lord makes specific reference to diseases.

Each of God's names reveals His character. Jehovah Rapha tells us that God does not bring sickness upon us, but rather healing. Nowhere does God call Himself "the God who makes you ill".

This concept of healing was well-known even before the cross as here expressed by the Psalmist David. It was viewed as a benefit of God.

Psalm 103:1-5
Bless the Lord, O my soul;
And all that is within me, bless His holy name!
²Bless the Lord, O my soul,
And forget not all His benefits:
³Who forgives all your iniquities,
Who heals all your diseases,
⁴Who redeems your life from destruction,
Who crowns you with lovingkindness and tender mercies,
⁵Who satisfies your mouth with good things,
So that your youth is renewed like the eagle's.

Young's Literal Translation expresses verse three this way,

"Who is forgiving all thine iniquities,
Who is healing all thy diseases."

Even under the Old Covenant, healing of disease was seen as a benefit from God to His people. If this was a benefit for Old Covenant believers, shall it not also be a benefit for us? He is still the God who heals us, and He does not change.

Malachi 3:6
For I am the Lord, I change not.

If You've Seen Me

Understanding the names of God helps us come to recognize His good and benevolent character and loving intentions toward us. These truths about God were revealed through a variety of situations His people faced. God's desire was that the people would know Him, but because their minds were not redeemed they could not see Him perfectly.

All of this changed when God sent His Son to the earth. When we see the life of Jesus, when we hear His words, when we observe his actions, we see the Father in a more excellent way. It is imperative that we understand that Jesus is the exact representation of God the Father.

Colossians 1:15-18

He is the image of the invisible God, the first-born over all creation. ¹⁶For by Him all things were created that are in heaven and that are on earth, visible and invisible, whether thrones or dominions or principalities or powers. All things were created through Him and for Him. ¹⁷And He is before all things, and in Him all things consist. ¹⁸And He is the head of the body, the church, who is the beginning, the firstborn from the dead, that in all things He may have the preeminence.

The Amplified version expresses verse fifteen this way:

He is the exact living image [the essential manifestation] of the unseen God [the visible representation of the invisible].

The above passage is one of the strongest representations of the deity of Jesus. He is God. All things were created through Him and for Him. While on earth, He was not only man but God as is expressed in His name, Emmanuel, God with us. When we observe Him, we are observing God Himself.

For centuries, mankind longed to know God. Little did they know that He was walking among them. After the resurrection, those who heard Him speak and who lived with Him certainly became aware of this amazing fact. Without knowing it, they had physically walked with God. After the resurrection, they became one spirit with Him. Imagine what this was like for them. They had the memories of His physical presence along with the certainty of His continued abiding presence.

John 1:14, 16-18

And the Word became flesh and dwelt among us, and we beheld His glory, the glory as of the only begotten of the Father, full of grace and truth. [16]And of His fullness we have all received, and grace for grace. [17]For the law was given through Moses, but grace and truth came through Jesus Christ. [18]No one has seen God at any time. The only begotten Son, who is in the bosom of the Father, He has declared Him.

Jesus clearly proclaimed these glorious truths in this passage.

John 14:1-11

"Let not your heart be troubled; you believe in God, believe also in Me. [2]In My Father's house are many mansions; if it were not so, I would have told you. I go to prepare a place for you. [3]And if I go and prepare a place for you, I will come again and receive you to Myself; that where I am, there you may be also. [4]And where I go you know, and the way you know."

[5]Thomas said to Him, "Lord, we do not know where You are going, and how can we know the way?"

[6]Jesus said to him, "I am the way, the truth, and the life. No one comes to the Father except through Me.

*[7]"If you had known Me, you would have known My Father also; and from now on **you know Him and have seen Him**."*

[8]Philip said to Him, "Lord, show us the Father, and it is sufficient for us."

⁹Jesus said to him, "Have I been with you so long, and yet you have not known Me, Philip? **He who has seen Me has seen the Father***; so how can you say, 'Show us the Father'?* *¹⁰Do you not believe that I am in the Father, and the Father in Me?* **The words that I speak to you I do not speak on My own authority; but the Father who dwells in Me does the works.** **¹¹Believe Me that I am in the Father and the Father in Me, or else believe Me for the sake of the works themselves.**

To see Jesus, to hear His teachings and see the works He did, is to see God the Father, for Jesus is the visible image of the invisible God. Jesus' words were not His alone; they were the Father's. His words and deeds demonstrate the will of God. When He rebuked the hypocrites, we see God's attitude toward false religion. When He had compassion on sinners, we see His desire to reconcile. When He healed the sick and cast out demons, we see the will of God to liberate and heal. When we read the gospels, we see God. We understand God's will. We hear His heart. This good news of who He was while on earth brings faith to our hearts because as He has always been, He will forever be.

Hebrews 13:8
Jesus Christ is the same yesterday, today, and forever.

I Am Willing

If we want to know what God's will is about healing us, let us look at Jesus while He lived on earth. There are no examples at all of Him ever saying that He was unwilling to heal anyone. This one fact about the life of Christ gives us hope. Jesus was demonstrating the willingness of God to heal us.

Matthew 8:2-3

And behold, a leper came and worshiped Him, saying, "Lord, if You are willing, You can make me clean."
³Then Jesus put out His hand and touched him, saying, "I am willing; be cleansed." Immediately his leprosy was cleansed.

When Jesus said, "I am willing," He was speaking of God's willingness to heal, not just His willingness to heal this one person.

Who Heals All Our Diseases

Another amazing demonstration of God's willingness to heal is that Jesus healed all of those who asked believing. This did not include a person here and another there, but multitudes.

Matthew 12:9-15

*Now when He had departed from there, He went into their synagogue. ¹⁰And behold, there was **a man who had a withered hand**. And they asked Him, saying, "Is it lawful to heal on the Sabbath?"—that they might accuse Him. ¹¹Then He said to them, "What man is there among you who has one sheep, and if it falls into a pit on the Sabbath, will not lay hold of it and lift it out? ¹²Of how much more value then is a man than a sheep? Therefore it is lawful to do good on the Sabbath." ¹³Then He said to the man, "Stretch out your hand." And he stretched it out, and it was restored as whole as the other. ¹⁴Then the Pharisees went out and plotted against Him, how they might destroy Him. ¹⁵But when Jesus knew it, He*

withdrew from there. **And great multitudes followed Him, and He healed them all.**
Luke 4:40
When the sun was setting, **all those who had any that were sick with various diseases brought them to Him;** *and He laid His hands on* **every one of them and healed them.**
Luke 6:17-19
And He came down with them and stood on a level place with a crowd of His disciples and **a great multitude of people** *from all Judea and Jerusalem, and from the seacoast of Tyre and Sidon, who came* **to hear Him and be healed of their diseases,** [18]*as well as those who were tormented with unclean spirits.* **And they were healed.** [19]*And the* **whole multitude sought to touch Him,** *for power went out from Him and* **healed them all.**

Sickness is Not God's Punishment

One fact must be made clear. Not once did Jesus ever place His hands on anyone to make them sick. As some today think God uses sickness to keep us humble or teach us a lesson, then why is there no example of this, not even one, in all of the records of His life? We can rest confidently that this is simply a false tradition. **God does not send sickness on His children to teach them. He speaks to us by His Holy Spirit and teaches us by His grace.** This is good to know because if we are sick or when sickness tries to come on us we can confidently conclude it is not from God and resist it. When we seek healing, we know He is willing for us to be well and not sick.

This is not to say that if one is sick, he is out of God's will as if being sick displeases God. We can confidently know that we don't need to submit to illness, and this good news can set us free to believe for healing.

By Whose Wounds You Were Healed

While we call healing a promise of God, it is also a provision. I delight in the fact that when Isaiah prophesied that the Messiah *would* be a healer, he used the present tense as if it was already done even though Jesus had not been wounded.

> ### Isaiah 53:4-6
> *Surely He has borne our griefs*
> *And carried our sorrows;*
> *Yet we esteemed Him stricken,*
> *Smitten by God, and afflicted.*
> *⁵ But He was wounded for our transgressions,*
> *He was bruised for our iniquities;*
> *The chastisement for our peace was upon Him,*
> *And by His stripes we **are** healed.*
> *⁶All we like sheep have gone astray;*
> *We have turned, every one, to his own way;*
> *And the Lord has laid on Him the iniquity of us all.*

While Jesus walked the earth one of His main ministries was to heal the sick and set free those who were oppressed by the devil. According to Matthew, under the inspiration of the Holy Spirit, this was a fulfillment of Isaiah's prophesy about Him healing our sicknesses.

> ### Matthew 8:16-17
> *When evening had come, **they brought to Him many who were demon-possessed. And He cast out the spirits with a word, and healed all who were sick**, ¹⁷that it might be fulfilled which was spoken by Isaiah the prophet, saying:*
> *"He Himself took our infirmities*
> *And bore our sicknesses."*

Then Peter looking back on the fulfillment of Isaiah's prophecy uses not the present tense, but the past—clearly saying that the prophecy had been fulfilled. Notice the reference to us being as sheep who had gone astray which clearly reflects Isaiah 53:6.

> **1 Peter 2:24-25**
> *Who Himself bore our sins in His own body on the tree, that we, having died to sins, might live for righteousness—by whose stripes you **were** healed. ²⁵For you were like sheep going astray, but have now returned to the Shepherd and Overseer of your souls.*

The word "healed" means "to cure, heal, make whole", so some have argued that this statement is not about physical healing but only about the fact that when we come to Jesus, we are made whole. Certainly it is true that Jesus makes us whole in every way, but why exclude the physical body in this verse? Of the 28 times this word is used in the New Testament, 25 of those instances are clearly referring to physical healing. The other three can be seen as some other type of wholeness. It is irresponsible to claim that 1 Peter 2:24 is *only* referring to the wellness of the spirit and soul and not the body especially when we consider that **Peter makes clear reference to Isaiah 53:6, and Matthew said that the fact He healed the sick and cast out demons was a fulfilment of that prophesy.**

The fact that 1 Peter 2:24 is in the past tense should cause hope to spring from within our hearts, for it clearly declares that this is already provided and that just as salvation is already available for all, and we need only receive it, so healing has already been given to us, and it is ours to receive. It is not sinful to ask to be healed, of course, but we can do so not begging for it to be so, but knowing it is already provided.

For those bent on nullifying this glorious truth, please don't put words in my mouth. I'm not cold-heartedly accusing people who are suffering or those who have died of disease as being culpable. I'm declaring that healing for our spirit, soul, and body has already been provided for us in the same way salvation is available to all. To be saved, we believe it and confess it. The same is true with healing.

Christina's Faith

Our daughter, Christina, had an inguinal hernia at about age five. I didn't notice it until she began to take gymnastics. When she would jump, we could see it pop out. So, we showed this to the doctor. He said it wasn't life-threatening, and we could watch it for a while. Over time, it got bigger about the size of a small walnut. The doctor said that the next step would be surgery. I was not pleased with this option.

So, I told Christina, "When you see it pop out, say, 'By His stripes I am healed.'" Thankfully, she didn't have layers of negative ideas to get in her way of believing. She simply had faith that Jesus was her Healer.

On her next check-up, the doctor said to her, "Jump. Jump again." Then he looked at me and said, "Didn't she have a hernia right here?" I looked, and sure enough, it was gone. I said, "Yes," and then explained to him what happened. He said, "Well, I don't know what you did, but whatever it was, it worked." Christina heard the good news that Jesus was her Healer and based on the fact that by His wounds we are healed, she received healing.

Gifts of Healing

I don't pretend to understand everything about what the Bible calls "gifts of healing". We know from Scripture that they are given by the Holy Spirit "as He wills". It could be that He gives such a gift to someone, and they continue to operate in it, and it may also be that at times, as is needed, He gives a gift of healing to someone for a specific person.

I believe it exists because Paul taught that it does, and I have both witnessed it in operation and been healed as a result of it. My grandfather had a gift of healing. I'd heard about it all my life, and as a young child, I attended one of his ministry meetings and remember someone getting out of a wheelchair. These memories served me well when, as a teenager, I was dedicating myself to trying not to believe in God. I just could not deny what I had seen.

One day as my husband and I were visiting my grandparents, I had a really bad headache. My grandmother gave me aspirin, but as we continued our visit with them, it hadn't helped at all. As we were leaving, my grandmother asked me if I'd like my grandfather to pray for me, and I said yes. He placed his hand on my head and prayed, but I don't remember a word he said because the second he touched me all of the intense pain in my head went away. I remember that as he continued to pray, I sat there stunned. After he stopped praying, I turned my neck this way and that to see if I could get the headache to return, but it was completely gone! I believe this was an operation of a gift of healing.

Another time, we were attending a teaching conference. At the end of the session, they invited people up for prayer. Instead of the main speaker praying for people, they had a team lined up front. The minister asked that if anyone had pain in their back to come forward. I remembered that my husband had been experiencing pain in his back for quite some time. A chiropractor told him that his discs were compressed. So, I encouraged my husband to go up for prayer. Since he wasn't having any pain at the moment, he hesitated. I nearly pushed him out of his chair to go up there, and he finally did. When he returned to his seat, I asked him about it. He said, "I believe I am healed," but since he didn't have any pain, he couldn't physically tell.

For many days, he had no back pain, but one day after he went out jogging, his back hurt him again. He felt discouraged because he had great hopes that he would be better. He made an appointment with a different chiropractor who took new X-rays. He brought them out to show David saying, "Look here. You have the back of a 30-year-old. (David was about 50 then.) David looked at the films, and sure enough, each disc was in perfect condition. At first, he was a little disappointed. Being focused on the pain he was experiencing, he was upset that the chiropractor couldn't help him, but then it hit him! He'd been healed.

We don't know in this instance if it was because David believed or because someone who prayed for him had a gift of healing. We do know it was an amazing miracle and to God be all the glory for this great thing that He did.

In Jesus' Name

It is beautiful how pure the faith of children is. In their eyes, if God says it, it is true. They don't have the disadvantage of hearing for years that maybe God's Word isn't always true, or that it might not be true for everyone. Here is the story of our dear friend, Don Harris.

"In 1983, I was dealing with a constant cough. It had been going on for nearly two months. My chest was hurting, and breathing was getting difficult. Due to our financial situation at the time, seeing a physician was not an option.

"My daughter, Vicki, who was nearly four, was already tucked into bed and had heard me coughing. When I came into her room to hug her and pray with her as we normally did, something unexpected happened.

As I was leaning over to hug her, she grabbed my shoulder with one hand and placed her other on my chest just as I was about to start coughing again. Before I could get the cough out, she said, "Be healed in Jesus' name," and instantly the cough stopped. The pain in my chest also was gone.

"I was amazed. To my daughter, it was just matter-of-fact. You pray. Jesus heals. Since then (for 35 years) I have not suffered from coughing or pain in my chest. I get a cold occasionally, but there is never any coughing with it."

Was this a gift of healing or the simple faith of a child? Whichever it was, to God be the glory for His precious gifts to us.

Call for the Elders of the Church

James 5:14
Is anyone among you sick? Let him call for the elders of the church, and let them pray over him, anointing him with oil in the name of the Lord.

Perhaps the idea of the grace of divine healing is new to you. You might need time to study about it and hear this good news before having the courage to believe. Perhaps as you learn, you could avail yourself of this verse. Are you sick? Then call for the elders of the church, and let them pray over you, anointing you with oil in the name of the Lord. There is no shame in receiving from God via the faith of another. If the elders of your church don't believe in this practice, visit a church that does.

Ifs, Ands, and Buts

Over the years, I have heard many arguments against the grace of divine healing. One of them that I find particularly weak is that of proving that believers in the early church got sick. I don't know of anyone who believes in divine healing who claims that they didn't get sick. So, the premise is odd to begin with. Still, I'll address it.

This argument usually includes pointing out that Paul advised Timothy to "take a little wine" for his frequent problems with his stomach. This doesn't negate divine healing; rather it demonstrates that natural remedies can also be used by God for our healing.

Those who object to the belief that the grace of divine healing is for us today will also bring attention to the fact that Epaphroditus was sick and almost died.

> ### Philippians 2:25-30
> *Yet I considered it necessary to send to you Epaphroditus, my brother, fellow worker, and fellow soldier, but your messenger and the one who ministered to my need; ²⁶ since he was longing for you all, and was distressed because you had heard that he was sick. ²⁷ For indeed he was sick almost unto death; but God had mercy on him, and not only on him but on me also, lest I should have sorrow upon sorrow. ²⁸ Therefore I sent him the more eagerly, that when you see him again you may rejoice, and I may be less sorrowful. ²⁹ Receive him therefore in the Lord with all gladness, and hold such men in esteem; ³⁰ because for the work of Christ he came close to death, not regarding his life, to supply what was lacking in your service toward me.*

Yes, Epaphroditus was sick—very sick. Did God make him sick? No. Why was he sick? Like many of us sometimes, he nearly worked himself to death. He was so intent on accomplishing the task of providing for Paul what the Philippians had not been able to provide, that he weakened his body and got sick—but did God heal him? Yes! Many things can be learned from this story, but surely this story supports the truth of healing rather than negating it.

The other argument, which is one of the most ill-extrapolated, is that of saying that Paul's thorn in the flesh was an illness in his eyes and that when Paul asked the Lord three times to remove this sickness, God refused, telling Paul that His "strength is made perfect in weakness".

First of all, when Paul shared his experience of the Lord refusing to remove his thorn in the flesh, there is not one hint that he is referring to his eyes. Clearly from context, Paul is talking about the frequent troubles and persecutions that he experienced (2 Cor. 12:7-10).

Consider also the parallel of Paul's account with that of Jesus in the Garden of Gethsemane when Jesus asked God three times, if possible, to "remove this cup" from Him. We all know that He wasn't talking about being sick. He knew he was going to be scourged and suffer crucifixion. Paul in like manner asked the Lord to take away his sufferings three times, and it wasn't sickness. As we've said, we are promised persecution as believers (2 Tim. 3:12). While God will deliver us out of our troubles, we will still have them.

Did Paul have an on-going disease in his eyes? Let us examine the facts. First, let's look at the verse often used to "prove" that he did.

Galatians 4:12-16

*Brethren, I urge you to become like me, for I became like you. You have not injured me at all. [13]You know that because of physical infirmity I preached the gospel to you at the first. [14]And my trial which was in my flesh you did not despise or reject, but you received me as an angel of God, even as Christ Jesus. [15]What then was the blessing you enjoyed? For I bear you witness that, if possible, **you would have plucked out your own eyes and given them to me.** [16]Have I therefore*

*become your enemy because I tell you
the truth?*

In verse thirteen, Paul states that the reason he came to them was because he had physical weakness. So, it is fair to conclude that even the great apostle Paul suffered pain and was in need of healing. Do we have any clues as to if there was a **reason** for the weakness he mentions? Consider this passage.

Acts 14:19-20
*Then Jews from Antioch and Iconium came
there; and having persuaded the multitudes,
they stoned Paul and dragged him out of the
city, **supposing him to be dead.** [20] However,
when the disciples gathered around him, he
rose up and went into the city. And the next
day he departed with Barnabas to Derbe.*

There is no pretty picture to be painted here of what Paul experienced. The purpose of stoning is to kill the one being stoned. Often the person to be stoned would be pushed off a sufficient height to render it impossible for him to escape or protect himself. No one stone was to kill the victim, but it was an execution carried out by the community. Stoning could take from ten to twenty minutes.

His persecutors stoned him until they thought he was dead. After this, the disciples gathered around Paul, and amazingly, he rose up and went with them. The next day he went with Barnabas to Derbe.

Where was Derbe? It was a province of Galatia.

*Derbe was a city in the district of Lycaonia in
the Roman province of Galatia in south cen-
tral Asia Minor. It sat on a major route con-
necting Iconium to Laranda and was about
60 miles from Lystra. Paul and Barnabas fled*

to Derbe and Lystra on his first missionary
journey when city officials of Iconium plotted
to stone them (Acts 14:6-21).[45]

When someone has been pushed over a small cliff and battered by stoning to the point of death, what would be the condition of his body? Paul's body was exceedingly weakened. No doubt he had multiple injuries to his head, including to his eyes since it was common for the executioners to force the victim to take his punishment face up. His recovery from this experience was painful and lengthy causing him to remain in Galatia where he preached to them through it all. The Galatians were doubtless concerned about Paul's weakness and would have done anything within their power to help him, including plucking out their own eyes to bring healing to his. Certainly, this is a better explanation of what Paul meant. His infirmity in his eyes was a result of having been stoned, not an illness which God refused to heal.

Did this experience affect Paul's vision permanently? There are hints of this possibility but no clear proof. If Paul did have poor vision, the stoning could certainly have been the cause. Yet, consider the more provable point that Paul's vision was restored to him after this experience. Here are two passages that took place later that make reference to what Paul saw—in other words, that he could still see.

Acts 17:16
Now while Paul waited for them at Athens, his
*spirit was provoked within him when he **saw***
that the city was given over to idols.
Acts 28:15
And from there, when the brethren heard
about us, they came to meet us as far as
*Appii Forum and Three Inns. When Paul **saw***
them, he thanked God and took courage.

---

[45] http://www.bibleplaces.com/derbelystra.htm

Another explanation sometimes given for Paul's supposed eye problem is that of when he lost his vision on the road to Damascus when he first encountered the Lord and became blind. This example is extremely flimsy because the Lord told Ananias to lay hands on him so that he would receive his sight again.

Acts 9:11-16

*So the Lord said to him, "Arise and go to the street called Straight, and inquire at the house of Judas for one called Saul of Tarsus, for behold, he is praying. [12]And in a vision he has seen a man named Ananias coming in and putting his hand on him, **so that he might receive his sight.***"

[13]Then Ananias answered, "Lord, I have heard from many about this man, how much harm he has done to Your saints in Jerusalem. [14]And here he has authority from the chief priests to bind all who call on Your name."

[15]But the Lord said to him, "Go, for he is a chosen vessel of Mine to bear My name before Gentiles, kings, and the children of Israel. [16]For I will show him how many things he must suffer for My name's sake."

Notice that Jesus tells Ananias that Paul would suffer many things for His name's sake. This is clearly speaking of persecution, his actual thorn in the flesh.

Whatever it is we conclude, there is zero connection with Paul's eyes and his account of his thorn in the flesh. They are not mentioned in the same context anywhere in Scripture.

God does not give each one of us some weakness to keep us humble. On the contrary, He provides for our needs, restores our souls, and heals our bodies. What is true is that we all will suffer persecution, and some will suffer more than others.

We have to ask ourselves, why go to such great lengths to prove that early Christians got sick? Of course, they got sick. The good news for us to realize is that God provided and promised that they and we could be healed. Either they could believe for healing themselves, or be near someone who had a gift of healing, or call for the elders of the church to pray for them to be healed. There is no point in emphasizing that believers got sick except to try and negate this glorious grace for us today. How much more powerful is it to recognize that they were healed?

For Those Who Are Suffering

We hear people say, in an attempt to discredit the truth that God is still healing today, "If divine healing is true, then let's go into the hospitals and heal everyone there and close down the hospitals." This makes no sense. Let me counter the question with the same harshness. If we really believe that Jesus will save anyone, why aren't we pronouncing salvation on everyone we meet? Can you see the comparison? Salvation is not something we thrust on people, and neither is healing. Not even Jesus forced healing on people. They came to Him. In fact, there were some instances where it says that He could not heal people. On the other hand, if someone feels God is calling him to go to the local hospital and offer to pray for people, let him go.

> ***Matthew 13:54-58***
> *When He had come to His own country, He taught them in their synagogue, so that they were astonished and said, "Where did this Man get this wisdom and these mighty works? ⁵⁵Is this not the carpenter's son? Is not His mother called Mary? And His brothers James, Joses, Simon, and Judas? ⁵⁶And His sisters, are they not all with us? Where then*

*did this Man get all these things?" ⁵⁷So they
were offended at Him.
But Jesus said to them, "A prophet is not
without honor except in his own country and
in his own house." ⁵⁸**Now He did not do
many mighty works there because of their
unbelief.***

Jesus didn't roam the earth waving a magic wand of salvation and healing! He taught them the good news. Those
who believed were healed. Those who didn't, were not. How
shall people today who don't even believe in God believe in
healing when those who do believe in God don't believe in
this grace? How can faith come to them if we don't preach it,
and how can we preach it if we don't believe?

This strawman situation should not in any way discredit
the provision and promise of healing. It speaks more of
where we are today in the body of Christ. Just as we nearly
extinguished the gospel of the grace of God, so even those
who now understand the gospel of grace still hold to the
practice of nullifying the fact that He now freely gives us all
things. Healings happen in the lives of those who believe, but
how can people believe when they are being taught that the
grace of divine healing "is not for today", that sickness and
weakness are God's way of "teaching us" something, that
He allows us to be sick so that He can keep us humble, that
He uses sickness to punish us, or that God "allows" sickness
to bring about good?

Grace preachers, don't we sometimes feel frustrated that
the church at large is still resisting the grand news that we
are saved by God's grace alone through faith in Christ alone
and that we do not need to add our works to improve on
what we've been given? Do you ever feel like a lone voice
in the sea of unbelief? This is how those who are sharing the
good news of the grace of divine healing also feel. Please
hear. The same Jesus who saves you also heals you! He

was wounded to give us healing. **Shall we refuse and even *ridicule* anything that He suffered to give us?**

There are many things that are difficult to understand when it comes to the topic of the grace of divine healing. Many Christians are deaf or blind. Some were born with disabilities. Others are currently struggling with their health. Many of them do believe, and yet have not yet seen the result. For many, their health is their overwhelming circumstance. What is the encouragement for them?

I believe this to be the wisdom of God, not only for those who are tackling physical challenges but for anyone who is facing a circumstance that is overwhelming: We walk by faith and not by sight. Our situations are on the natural plane, but we can live above our circumstances on the supernatural plane knowing that we are dearly beloved of God and that He is working all things together for our good. He is with us in our struggles. If we don't know or understand why "things" aren't right this minute as we believe they should be, we can still live an abundant life while we either improve our understanding, or God speaks something directly to our hearts.

Worthy to Be Praised[46]

You are worthy,
Worthy to be praised.
You are worthy
Each and every day.
You are wonderful,
Marvelous,
Amazing,
Mighty.

You are worthy
No matter how I feel.
You are worthy.

---

[46] A song by C. D. Hildebrand

Your promises are real.
So, no matter what I feel today,
You're worthy,
Worthy
To be praised.

Only Believe

If you are sick and want to be healed, and are not yet convinced that healing is a grace for you today, or you sense that perhaps your understanding of it might be incomplete, let me encourage you to get out your Bible and a notebook. Begin to read through the entire Bible without one bias or another. Find out what is written on this topic. Ask God to show you the truth. Write down every verse you find that has to do with someone getting healed. I trust that God will speak to you. This is what I set out to do in 2002. In 2004, I wrote a book entitled <u>Healing Verses</u> that I printed out and bound with ribbon for dear friends that I knew were struggling with their health.

In 2007 when we began teaching in a church-based Bible school, I wrote the following which is a summary of that book. I pray that you will find it a blessing. May the Lord speak this good news to our hearts and enlighten our eyes to the truth about this glorious grace of divine healing so that we may receive it.

HEALING CONFESSIONS

I will praise You, Lord, with my whole heart (Ps. 9:1).
I bless Your holy name.
You are the Lord that Heals Me (Ex. 15:26).
It is your very nature to heal me.
It is who You are.
Your Name is above every name (Phil. 2:8-11).
At Your name, every knee must bow.
Sickness must submit to Your holy name.

Jesus, You are My Healer.
Nothing is impossible for You (Lk. 1:37).
You are both able and willing to heal me.
You demonstrated this
while You were on earth by healing all
who came to You believing. (Mt., Mk., Lk. & Jn.).
You did not and You do not
show preferences (Acts 10:34).
You have not
and will not change (Heb. 13:8).
All of Your promises
are "yes" and "amen" (2 Cor.1:20).
Your word is truth. (Jn. 17:17).
I choose to believe in Your word
and not the circumstances
nor the experience of others.
How I will bless Your holy name!
I will remember
all of Your benefits (Ps. 103:2).
You bore my sins
in Your own body on the cross.
I died to sins,
I live for righteousness—
I was healed by Your wounds.
It is already done (1 Pet. 2:24).
You have already provided
both salvation and healing
by Your atoning suffering and death.
The same Spirit of Him
Who raised You from the dead
Lives in me (Rom. 8:11).
Your resurrection proves that
You are victorious over death.
Your sacrifices merit my belief in You.
Oh, Lord, You are worthy to be praised,
and I believe in You
and praise You with my whole heart.

You are My Lord Who Heals Me.
I believe in Your word.
I receive from You
what You have already provided.
You forgive all my sin.
You heal all my diseases.
You redeem my life from destruction (Ps. 103:3-4).
Your thoughts toward me are to give me
a future and a hope (Jer. 29:11).
You will satisfy me
with a long life (Ps. 91:16).
You do not steal, kill and destroy.
You give me abundant life (Jn. 10:10).
You have delivered me
from the fear of death.
You have rendered the enemy
powerless (Heb. 2:14-15).
I submit to You.
As a steadfast one, I resist the enemy in the faith.
He must flee from me in Jesus' name (Jms. 4:7).
In Jesus' name I reject
an evil heart of unbelief (Heb. 3:12).
I choose to believe in You and Your word.
No weapon formed against me
will prosper (Isa. 54:17).
I have this confidence in You that
when I pray anything according to Your will,
You Hear me.
Since I know that You hear me
I know that I have
what I requested of You (1 Jn. 5:14).
Healing is who You are.
Healing is what You demonstrated on earth (Acts 5:16).
Healing is what You provided on the cross.
Healing is Your will (1 Pet. 2:24).
You have given to me the faith I need
to receive from You (Rom. 12:3).

*Therefore, in Your name I speak
to this mountain of sickness in my life.
I command you in the name of Jesus
To be removed and cast into the sea
never to return,
and every cause of it.
I do not doubt in my heart.
I believe that what I am saying is God's will,
that it is granted to me already,
And therefore, I shall have it (Mk. 11:23-24).
Sickness you are bound in Jesus name.
Healing you are released in my body (Mt. 18:18).
I believe in You, therefore, I speak (2 Cor. 4:13).
I am healed in Jesus' name.
Whatever I ask in prayer believing
I will receive (Mt. 21:22).
I am fully convinced
that what God has promised
He will do (Rom. 4:20-22).
I have been forgiven
therefore, I forgive (Eph. 4:32).
God did not spare His own Son.
Now He will, with Him,
freely give me all things (Rom. 8:32).
It is not based on my goodness
but Your grace (Gal. 3:5).
It is not by my power
or my personal holiness.
You have made me
the righteousness of God in Christ Jesus (2 Cor. 5:21).
I am free from condemnation (Rom. 8:1).
I refuse to worry. (Phil. 4:6-7)
I bring my request to You
with thanksgiving.
You will give me the
peace that passes understanding.
You crown me with lovingkindness*

*and tender mercies
So that my youth is renewed
like the eagle's (Ps. 103:4-5).
It is Your will for me to be in health (3 Jn. 2).
I will grow healthier
and stronger day by day.
I will run and not be weary.
I will walk and not faint (Isa. 40:31).
I am strong (Joel 3:10).
You are able
to do exceedingly abundantly
above all that I ask or think,
according to Your power
that works in me (Eph. 3:20).
To You, Oh Lord, be glory and majesty
Dominion and power
Both now and forever (Jude 25).
Amen, so be it!*

Compiled by
C. D. Hildebrand 2007

Day 40

ABOVE ALL WE CAN ASK OR THINK

John 16:33
These things I have spoken to you, that in Me you may have peace. In the world you will have tribulation; but be of good cheer, I have overcome the world.

This verse was spoken to Jesus' closest followers immediately prior to His arrest and crucifixion. He knew how heartbroken they would be after His death. He knew that after the joy they would experience after His resurrection they would be persecuted and rejected by their own. For a normal human being, such rejection is overwhelming, but Jesus promised them that instead of turmoil, they would have peace in Him.

The reason we can be of good cheer and experience this peace is because Jesus has overcome the world. Even though He was God, He lived on earth as a man. He experienced those things that are common to all. He knew both joy and sorrow. Imagine the joy it was for Him to walk among those He'd created—to hold and be held by us, to converse face to face with us, to laugh and to cry with us, to teach us and to heal us, and to demonstrate to us by His words and deeds the will of His Father.

What pleasure it must have given Jesus to see the faces of those who believed in Him, and what grief He surely felt when the ones He came to save, refused to believe.

He was and is mankind's only hope of salvation. We were dead in sin and bullied by darkness. Yet His immense love for us led Him to the cross and kept Him there to suffer and die in our place so that we could be set free.

What condescension, bringing us redemption
That in the dead of night, not one faint hope in sight
God, gracious, tender, laid aside His splendor
Stooping to woo, to win, to save my soul.

O how I love Him, how I adore Him
My breath, my sunshine, my all in all
The great Creator became my Savior
And all God's fullness dwelleth in Him.[47]

None of us will ever fully fathom the intensity of the sacrifice He made for us. He overcame the world so that all of those who believe in Him might also overcome the world.

1 John 5:4-5
*For whatever is born of God overcomes the world. And this is the victory that has overcome the world—**our faith**. [5]Who is he who overcomes the world, but he who **believes** that Jesus is the Son of God?*

By the simple fact that we have put our faith in the One who has overcome the world, we have also overcome. A closer look at the meaning of the word "overcome" reveals that overcoming is not simply enduring, but means "to subdue, to conquer, prevail, to get the victory". While certainly enduring is part of the process of overcoming, our position is that of conquerors even while we are enduring. Though the world may be spinning out of control all around

---

[47] Down from His Glory", William E. Booth-Clibborn, Public Domain

us, we live above it all as victors. Through rejections, persecutions, struggles, and even in death—we win.

1 Corinthians 15:54-55
So when this corruptible has put on incorruption, and this mortal has put on immortality, then shall be brought to pass the saying that is written: "Death is swallowed up in victory."
55 "O Death, where is your sting?
O Hades, where is your victory?"

Perhaps my biggest frustration as an author is that of knowing there is so much more to be said, but being constrained by time and space. Who could ever fully declare the glories of His majesty?

John 21:25
And there are also many other things that Jesus did, which if they were written one by one, I suppose that even the world itself could not contain the books that would be written. Amen.

There is so much more left for us to discover, understand, and enjoy. His abiding presence, His unending love, His unlimited power in us and through us—who has the words to proclaim this? May the Lord open our eyes so that we may know and experience everything that He died and rose to give us!

Ephesians 1:15-23
Therefore I also, after I heard of your faith in the Lord Jesus and your love for all the saints, 16do not cease to give thanks for you, making mention of you in my prayers: 17that the God of our Lord Jesus Christ, the Father of glory, may give to you

- *the spirit of wisdom and revelation in the knowledge of Him,*
- *[18]the eyes of your understanding being enlightened;*
- *that you may know what is the hope of His calling,*
- *what are the riches of the glory of His inheritance in the saints,*
- *[19]and what is the exceeding greatness of His power toward us who believe,*

according to the working of His mighty power [20]which He worked in Christ when He raised Him from the dead and seated Him at His right hand in the heavenly places, [21]far above all principality and power and might and dominion, and every name that is named, not only in this age but also in that which is to come. [22]And He put all things under His feet, and gave Him to be head over all things to the church, [23]which is His body, the fullness of Him who fills all in all.

Believing in Him brings Him joy, and it gives us victory. As we learn of the hope of His calling, begin to benefit from the riches of the glory of His inheritance, and experience the greatness of His power toward us who believe in Him, how can we possibly not overcome anything and everything that seeks to overtake us? How can we not be filled and overflowing with the joy and peace of believing in Him (Rom 15:13)? This demonstration of His love toward us will continue throughout the ages to come.

Ephesians 2:4-7

But God, who is rich in mercy, because of His great love with which He loved us, [5]even when we were dead in trespasses, made us alive together with Christ (by grace you have been saved), ⁶and raised us up together, and made us sit together in the heavenly places in Christ Jesus, ⁷that in the ages to come He might show the exceeding riches of His grace in His kindness toward us in Christ Jesus.

How my heart has longed to share with you the victory that is ours in Christ because of His amazing grace toward us and His power within us. He is rich in mercy. His love for us is great. He has made us alive, raised us up, and seated us in heavenly places with Himself. We have overcome because we have faith in Him.

The exceeding riches of His grace in His kindness toward us who believe in Him will be proclaimed in all the ages to come. We who are the object of His grace, who have put our trust in Him, are His glory and joy. What He has done in us through the gift of His Son will glorify His name forevermore.

Ephesians 3:20-21
Now to Him who is able to do exceedingly abundantly above all that we ask or think, according to the power that works in us, ²¹to Him be glory in the church by Christ Jesus to all generations, forever and ever.

Let these words sink into your heart. God is able to do exceedingly—abundantly—above—all—that we ask or think. We are still to ask, but God is able to do even more by the power that works in us.

I pray that this journey has encouraged and inspired you to believe that God will do in you, for you, and through you wonderful things that you cannot yet imagine or dream.

So Much More[48]

Lord, I place my life before You
As a living sacrifice
Not knowing what the future has in store,
But there's one thing You've taught me
As I've traveled through this life
Your plans for me are always so much more.

More than I ask
More than I need
More than my mind can ever think
Far above anything I can dream
So much love
Abounding grace
Endless power in my life
Your plans for me
Are always so much more.

Now, Lord, I come before You
With confidence and joy
Knowing that Your promises are true
Amazed at all You're doing
And all that You have done
And all the things that You still have in store.

Plans of hope
Plans of peace
Plans to prosper all I do
Far beyond anything I can dream
So much love
Abounding grace
Endless power in my life
Your plans for me are always so much more

---

[48] By. C. D. Hildebrand, 2009, as we embarked on our new ministry, Studies in Grace and Faith

So much more
So much more
More than I could ever ask
Or even dream
So much more
So much more
Your plans for me are always so much more.

More than I ask
More than I need
More than my mind could ever think
Far beyond anything I could dream
So much love
Abounding grace
Endless power in my life
Your plans for me are always so much more
Because Your love for me is always so much more.
Your plans for me are always so much more.

Grace and peace be with you all with love, and may the Lord richly bless you exceedingly abundantly above all that you can ask or think.

Epilogue

L ast night, as I sat in the dark so that I could see the stars in the late night sky through the window of my office, I asked the Lord if there was anything else He wanted me to add to my book.

Almost instantly, the thought came to me, "Remind them that I love them," and I began weeping tears of joy.

Dear Friends, God *loves* you. He really does. Oh, if we could only understand this one thrilling and profound truth, all fear and doubt would cease! "In every high and stormy gale"[49] Jesus *loves* you.

Please carefully consider the glorious certainty of how perfectly you are *adored* by your God. *Let* Him love you. You don't have to *feel* anything; simply *believe*.

> And we have known and believed the
> love that God has for us.
> God is love,
> and he who abides in love
> abides in God, and God in him.
> **1 John 4:16**

---

[49] Author: Edward Mote, c. 1834, Composer: John Stainer, 1873, Public Domain

About the Author

*M*other to three, and grandmother to ten, Cathy Hildebrand has lived in California all of her life where she has served in a variety of roles within the church working side-by-side with her husband of over 40 years. After being a stay-at-home mom, she worked as a public and private school teacher for twelve years. In 2007, Cathy chose to retire early from teaching to pursue her love of writing and become involved again in ministry at which time she and her husband renewed their ordination with the Assemblies of God. She and David were extensively involved in co-founding a church-based Bible institute where they both began to teach the gospel of God's grace.

In 2009, God asked Cathy if she was "willing to preach the gospel to the saved?" Understanding what He meant by this, but not knowing exactly what this would entail, she happily accepted this calling which her husband, David, received as one for them both.

Currently, when not being Mom and Grandma or writing a book, she works with him in sharing the good news with God's people of His great love for them and super-abounding grace toward them in a ministry called Studies in Grace and Faith. Their ever-increasing library of teachings and extensive teaching notes for SGF are available for free download at www.graceandfaithministries.org.

Further Discussion

*I*f you'd like to discuss topics covered in this book with Cathy or others who are reading her books, feel free to "Like" her Facebook Page at https://www.facebook.com/cdhildebrandgrace.

Grace and Faith Ministries Website

*I*f you'd like to learn more about the gospel of God's amazing grace, visit our website at www.graceandfaithministries.org. All of our teachings and study notes are available free of charge with new titles in progress.

C. D. Hildebrand's First Book

Are We Preaching "Another" Gospel?
A 31-Day Journey toward Rediscovering the Gospel of the Grace of God

From the Back of the Book

From the author's perspective the answer to Are We Preaching "Another" Gospel? is a resounding, "Yes." "It isn't that we don't understand the basic tenants of Christianity," she writes, "but that we have added to them."

We used to joyfully proclaim, "Christianity isn't a religion. It's a relationship with Jesus Christ," but if this is so, then why are so many Christians today "miserable"? Why do they have a sense that God is far off or lack confidence that He loves them? What happened to the joy they knew "the hour they first believed"? Why does their "relationship" with Jesus actually seem more like a "religion"—a very difficult, demanding, and unsatisfying religion? Why are so many believers, even though they love Jesus with all of their hearts, giving up on "church" or simply attending out of duty or tradition?

The answers to these questions found in the content of this book are challenging—not that they are difficult to understand—but that our long-held traditions and false beliefs which keep getting passed on from generation to generation stand in our way of perceiving the truth. Jesus said that knowing the truth would set us free, but if our teaching nullifies that truth, bondage follows. So it is reasonable for us, the church, to consider whether or not what we teach is the "grace of Christ" that sets believers free or whether we are preaching "another" gospel which is tying God's people in hundreds of painful and complicated knots.

So, let the journey begin toward rediscovering the "gospel of the grace of God" (Acts 20:24)! Be prepared to be stretched, challenged, and then set free into the glorious good news of your relationship with God.

CPSIA information can be obtained
at www.ICGtesting.com
Printed in the USA
LVOW10s0142260617

539313LV00032B/1083/P